THE SAGA OF
...HE EVIL
8

ORIGINAL STORY: Carlo Zen

ART: Chika Tojo

CHARACTER DESIGN: Shinobu Shinotsuki

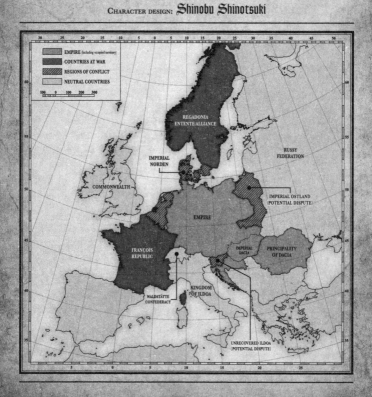

EMPIRE (Including occupied territory)
COUNTRIES AT WAR
REGIONS OF CONFLICT
NEUTRAL COUNTRIES
100 0 100 200 300
REGADONIA ENTENTE ALLIANCE
RUSSY FEDERATION
IMPERIAL NORDEN
COMMONWEALTH
IMPERIAL OSTLAND (POTENTIAL DISPUTE)
EMPIRE
FRANÇOIS REPUBLIC
IMPERIAL DACIA
PRINCIPALITY OF DACIA
KINGDOM OF ILDOA
WALDSTÄTTE CONFEDERACY
UNRECOVERED ILDOA (POTENTIAL DISPUTE)

Die Zeiten

DIE KRIEGSGESCHICHTE EINES KLEINEN MÄDCHEN No.008

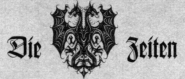

The battle log so far...

Our protagonist, a coolheaded salaryman in contemporary Japan, dies after being pushed off a train platform by a resentful man he fired.

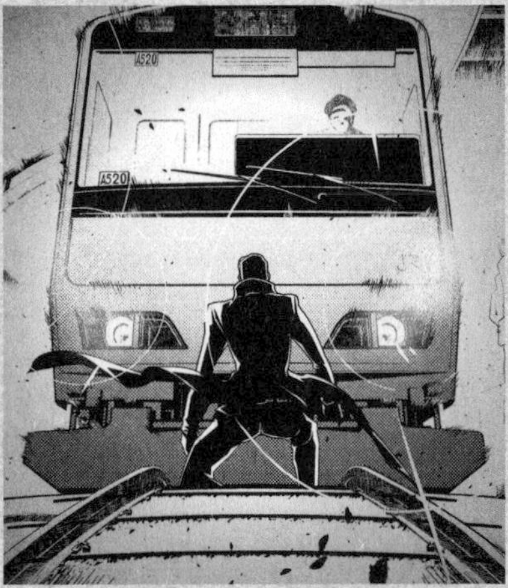

In the world beyond death, he encounters Being X, who claims to be the Creator. His lack of faith angers the being, and he is reborn in another world where gunfire and magic intermingle in combat. "You will be born into an unscientific world as a woman, come to know war, and be driven to your limits!"

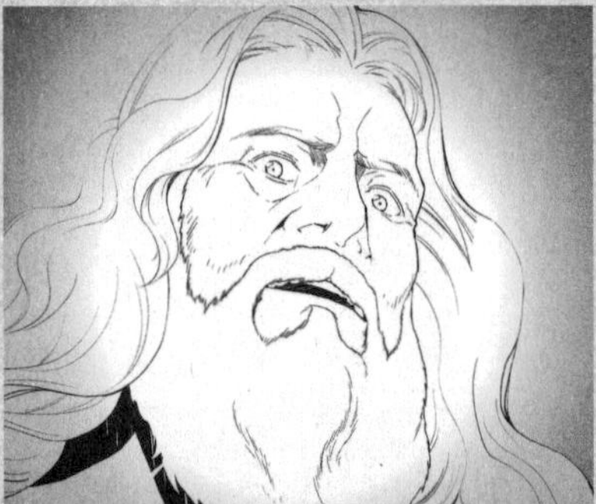

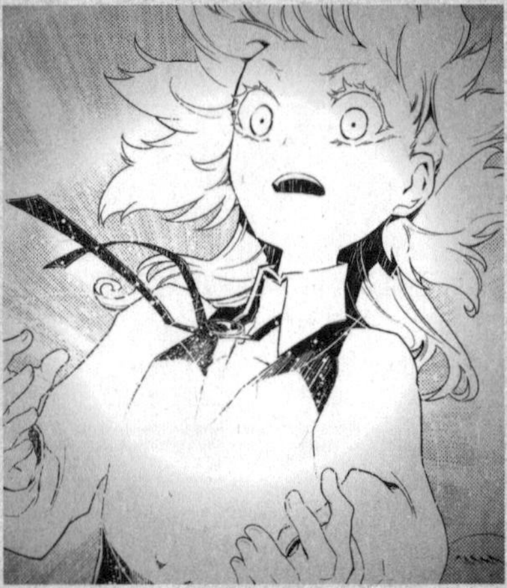

In the other world, he is reincarnated as Tanya Degurechaff. Upon recognition of her magic aptitude, she is sent to the battlefield at the age of nine.

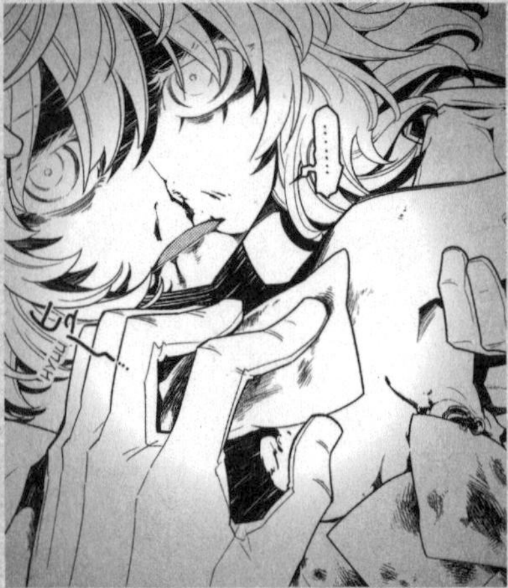
HYUU

Using the knowledge from her previous life, she climbs the ranks, aiming for a safe position in the rear, but her outstanding achievements and bravery make such a good impression on her superiors that she is, on the contrary, repeatedly sent to the front lines...

The plan calls for aerial mages to drop in and subdue coastal guns to allow the main fleet to burst into the Osfjord. Using the fact that they are low on personnel to her advantage, Tanya achieves the right to suggest the operation be aborted. Contrary to her expectations, she ends up earning the respect of the navy.

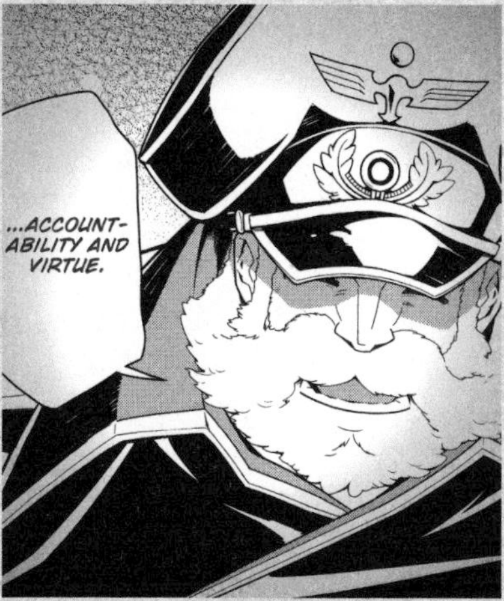
...ACCOUNT-ABILITY AND VIRTUE.

On the day of the operation, Tanya joins in neutralizing the Regadonian guns as part of the vanguard herself. Waiting for her, however, is Colonel Anson Sue, a Named she met on the Rhine lines. The extremely talented commander makes use of his forces' numerical superiority to keep the pressure on Tanya. In response, a tenacious Tanya attempts a reversal, putting her life at risk in the process. What will be her fate...?

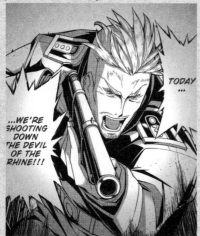

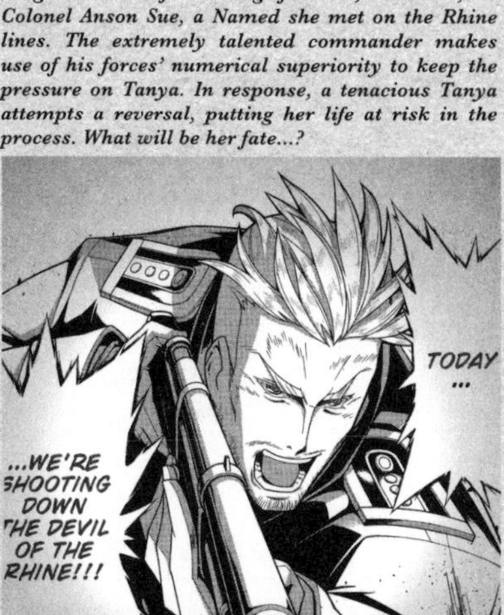
TODAY...
...WE'RE SHOOTING DOWN THE DEVIL OF THE RHINE!!!

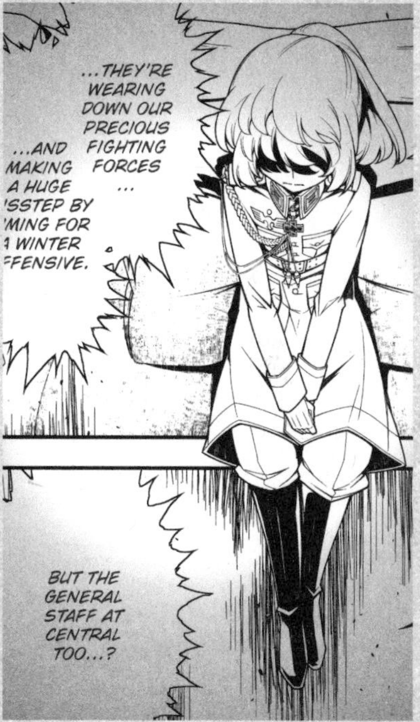
...THEY'RE WEARING DOWN OUR PRECIOUS FIGHTING FORCES...
...AND MAKING A HUGE ISSTEP BY MING FOR A WINTER FFENSIVE.
BUT THE GENERAL STAFF AT CENTRAL TOO...?

Forced into a two-front war and deadlocked, the Imperial Army decides to take out the Regadonia Entente Alliance in one fell swoop with a winter offensive. Tanya desperately opposes the move, deeming it reckless, until Rudersdorf explains to her that the Northern Army Group's operation will be a distraction for the main sneak attack carried out by aerial mages. After hearing his words, she finally understands what the General Staff is aiming to do.

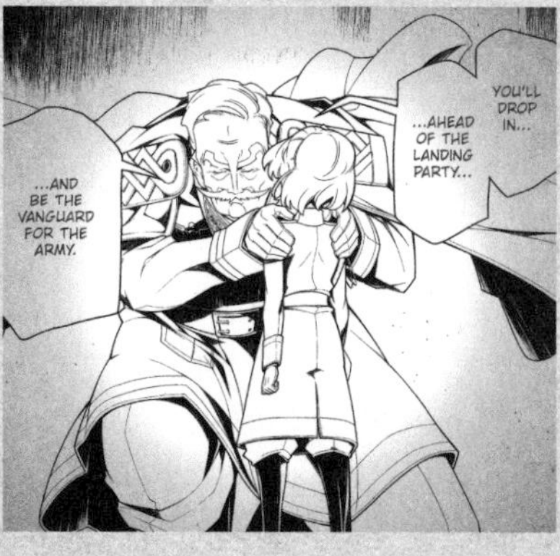
YOU'LL DROP IN...
...AHEAD OF THE LANDING PARTY...
...AND BE THE VANGUARD FOR THE ARMY.

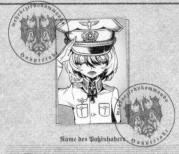

THE SAGA OF TANYA THE EVIL

Character Introductions

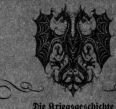

Die Kriegsgeschichte
eines Kleinen Mädchen

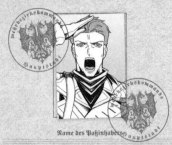

Name des Paßinhabers

Tanya von Degurechaff

(Rufname, Familienname)

Dienstgrad	Dienststellung
MAJOR	AERIAL MAGIC OFFICER

An extremely rational little girl who was a salaryman in her previous life. Joins the army to escape life in the orphanage. Becomes a mage after her talent for magic is recognized. She couldn't care less about national defense and simply wants to live a quiet life safe in the rear. Unfortunately, misunderstanding after misunderstanding causes others to think she is a patriot full of fighting spirit.

(Angaben zur Person)

Name des Paßinhabers

Johann-Mattäus Weiss

(Rufname, Familienname)

Dienstgrad	Dienststellung
FIRST LIEUTENANT	AERIAL MAGIC OFFICER

A mage in the Imperial Army and a member of Major Degurechaff's 203rd Aerial Mage Battalion. He's an earnest, outstanding soldier, but because he doesn't have much combat experience, most of his knowledge comes from textbooks. Having made it through the hellish training, it's clear his skills and fighting spirit are impeccable. That plus his talent for unit management means the army has high expectations of him.

(Angaben zur Person)

Name des Paßinhabers

Viktoriya Ivanovna Serebryakov

(Rufname, Familienname)

Dienstgrad	Dienststellung
SECOND LIEUTENANT	AERIAL MAGIC OFFICER

A mage in the Imperial Army. After being practically forced to enlist in the cadet corps due to her magic abilities, she is stationed in a unit on the front lines. Having proven herself capable in combat, she is recommended for the officer track. She sees Major Degurechaff as a kind, peace-loving individual and respects and supports her as her outstanding adjutant.

(Angaben zur Person)

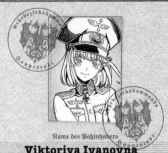

Name des Paßinhabers

Anson Sue

(Rufname, Familienname)

Dienstgrad	Dienststellung
COLONEL	REGADONIA ENTENTE ALLIANCE AERIAL MAGIC OFFICER

A veteran who has been fighting in the war since the beginning and possesses Named-level skills. When the war between the Entente Alliance and the Empire broke out, he was the one who drove Tanya, then an artillery observer, to self-destruct. As the war situation worsened, he was promoted to colonel and is in charge of defending the city Os, a key location in the rear.

(Angaben zur Person)

Name des Paßinhabers

Hans von Zettour

(Rufname, Familienname)

Dienstgrad	Dienststellung
MAJOR GENERAL	DEPUTY DIRECTOR OF THE SERVICE CORPS IN THE GENERAL STAFF

Employing his clear thinking and wealth of knowledge, he works on logistics and plans operations with his friend and colleague Major General Rudersdorf, the deputy director of Operations. He has a very high opinion of Major Degurechaff and does what he can to take her wishes into account. He's so far learned that in war college, evaluators had concerns that he was "too scholarly and thus not suited to becoming a general."

(Angaben zur Person)

Name des Paßinhabers

Being X

(Rufname, Familienname)

Dienstgrad	Dienststellung
———	———

A lofty being calling himself the Creator who is disappointed by humanity's loss of faith. Having concluded that the protagonist's impiety stems from living a comfortable life in a scientific world as a man with no experience of war, he has him reborn into the opposite circumstances. He's even willing to plunge the world into the chaos of war in order to mend the man's ways.

(Angaben zur Person)

Name des Paßinhabers

Erich von Lergen

(Rufname, Familienname)

Dienstgrad	Dienststellung
LIEUTENANT COLONEL	SENIOR STAFF OFFICER IN THE GENERAL STAFF

A sensible man whose hard work shows. The army expects great things from this General Staff officer; he is currently gaining experience in Personnel. Major Degurechaff makes him nervous because he can sense how abnormal and insane she is, but he's also forced to admit that she is right when it comes to the war, so his personal feelings and duty come into conflict.

(Angaben zur Person)

The Saga of Tanya the Evil
08

Original Story: Carlo Zen   Art: Chika Tojo
Character Design: Shinobu Shinotsuchi

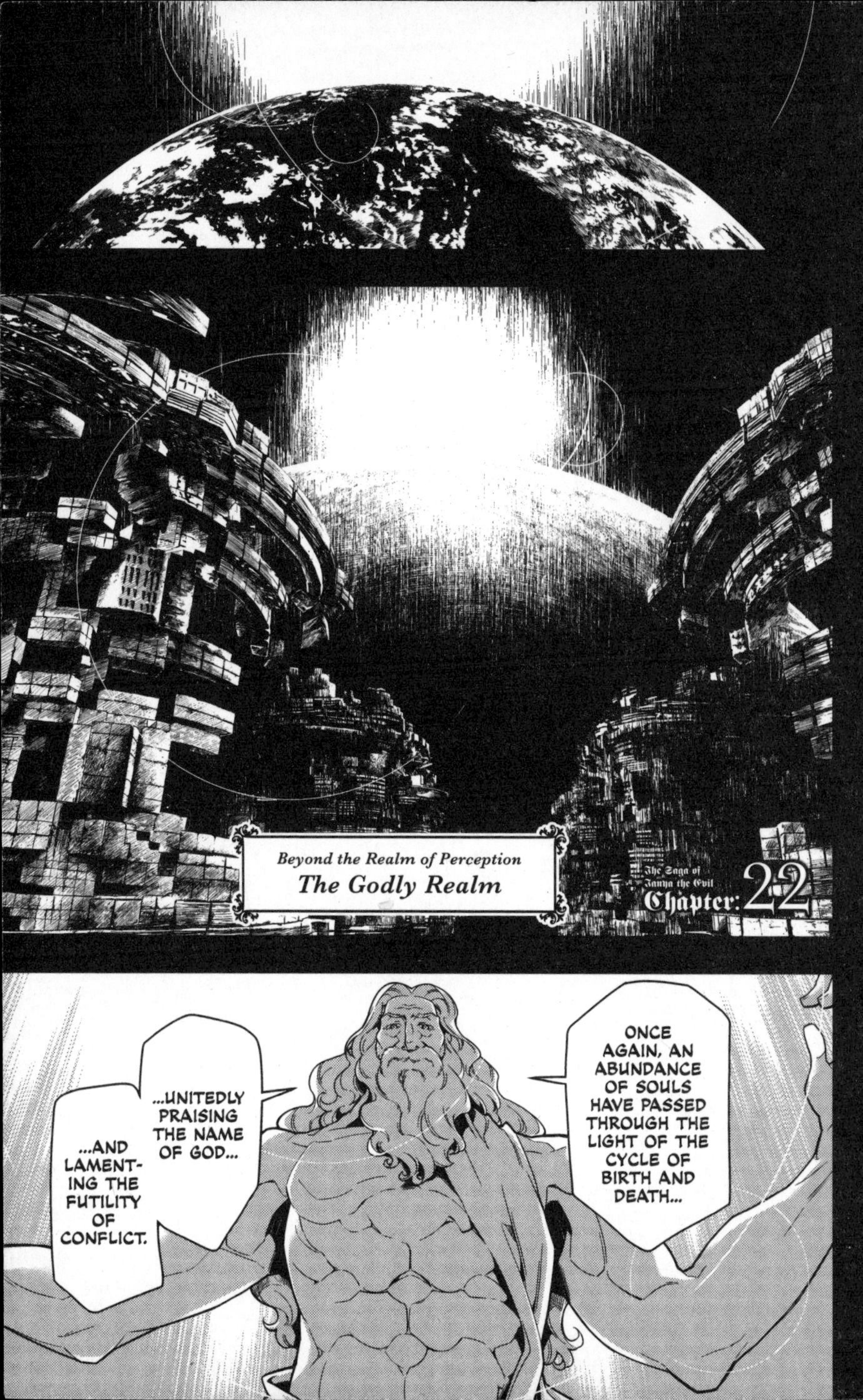
Beyond the Realm of Perception
The Godly Realm
The Saga of Tanya the Evil
Chapter: 22
ONCE AGAIN, AN ABUNDANCE OF SOULS HAVE PASSED THROUGH THE LIGHT OF THE CYCLE OF BIRTH AND DEATH...
...UNITEDLY PRAISING THE NAME OF GOD...
...AND LAMENTING THE FUTILITY OF CONFLICT.

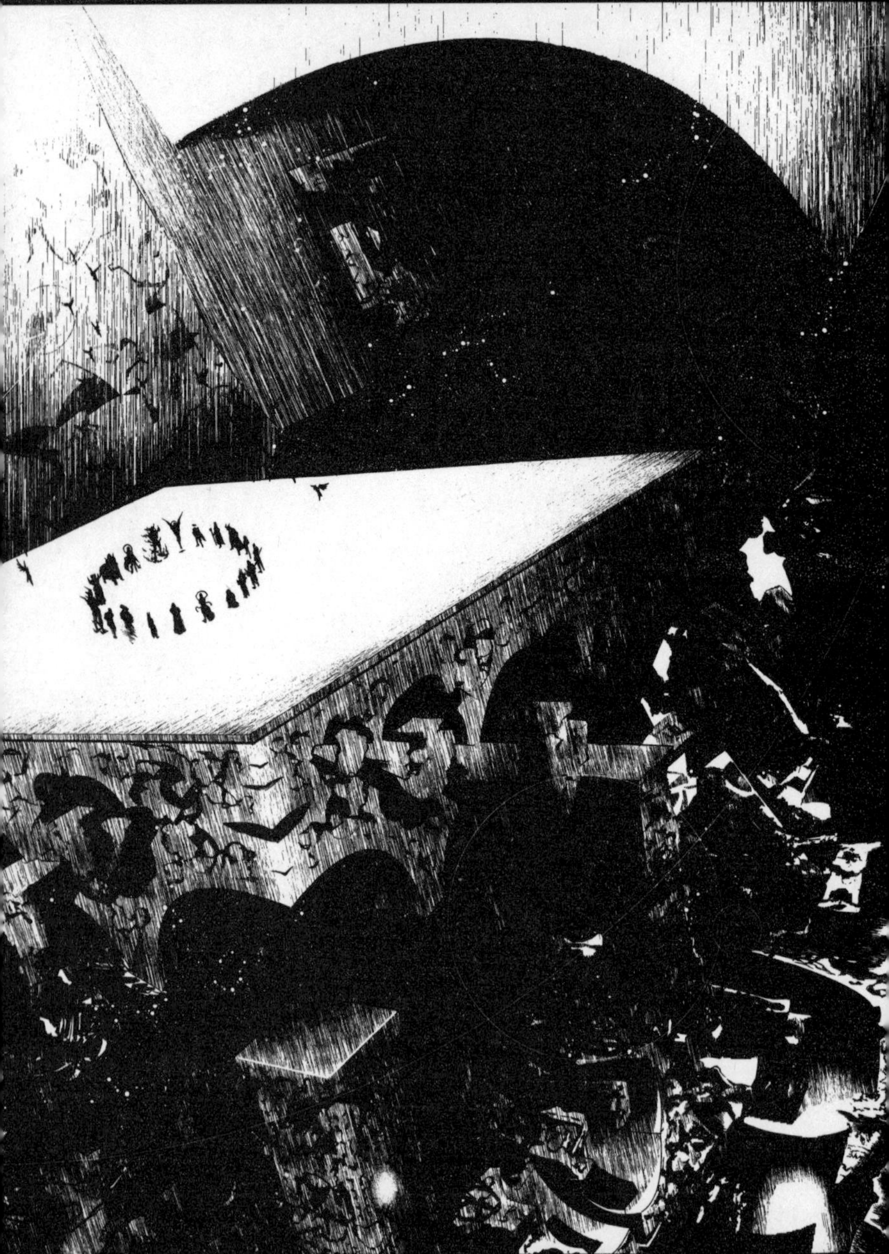

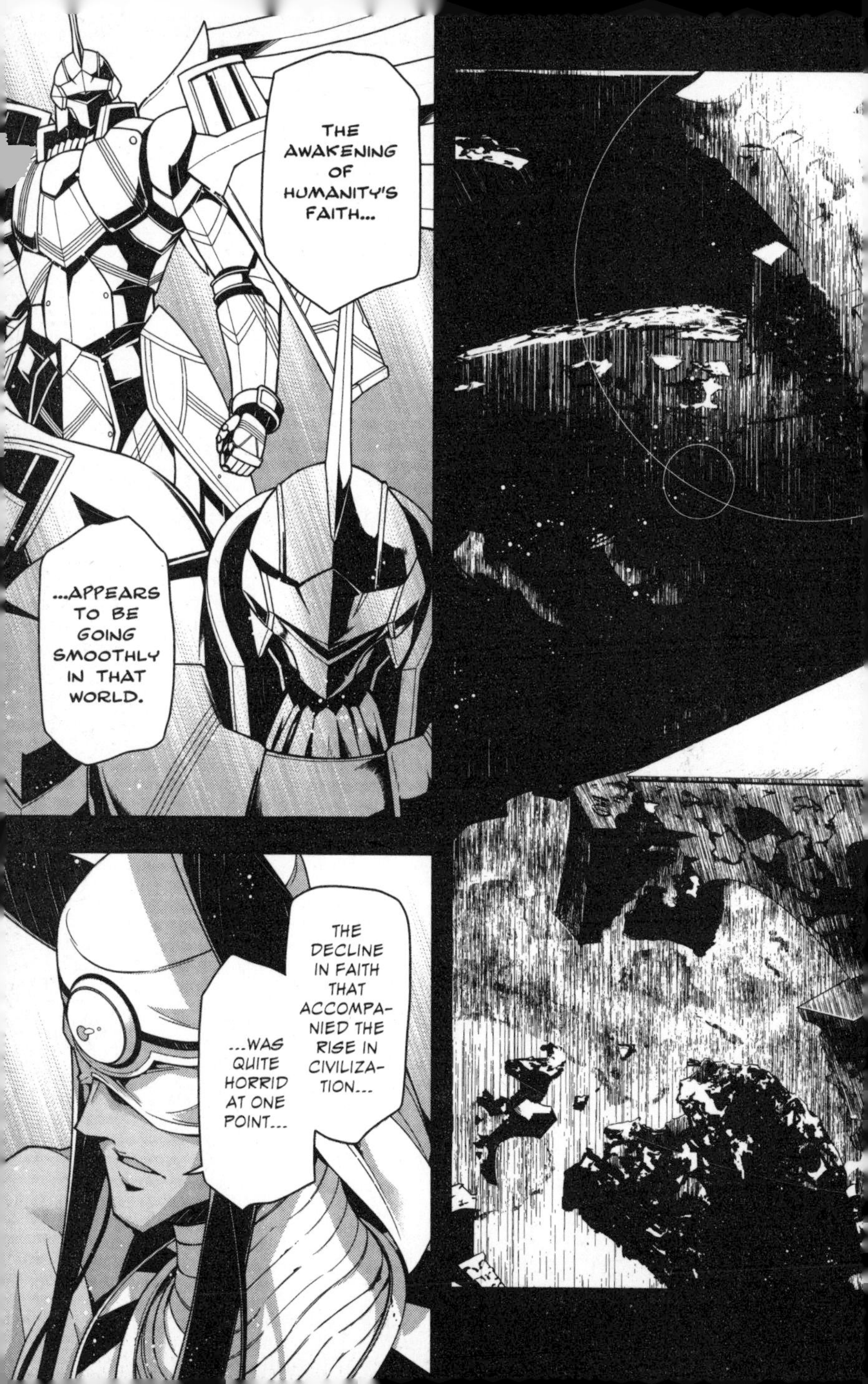
THE AWAKENING OF HUMANITY'S FAITH...
...APPEARS TO BE GOING SMOOTHLY IN THAT WORLD.
THE DECLINE IN FAITH THAT ACCOMPANIED THE RISE IN CIVILIZATION...
...WAS QUITE HORRID AT ONE POINT...

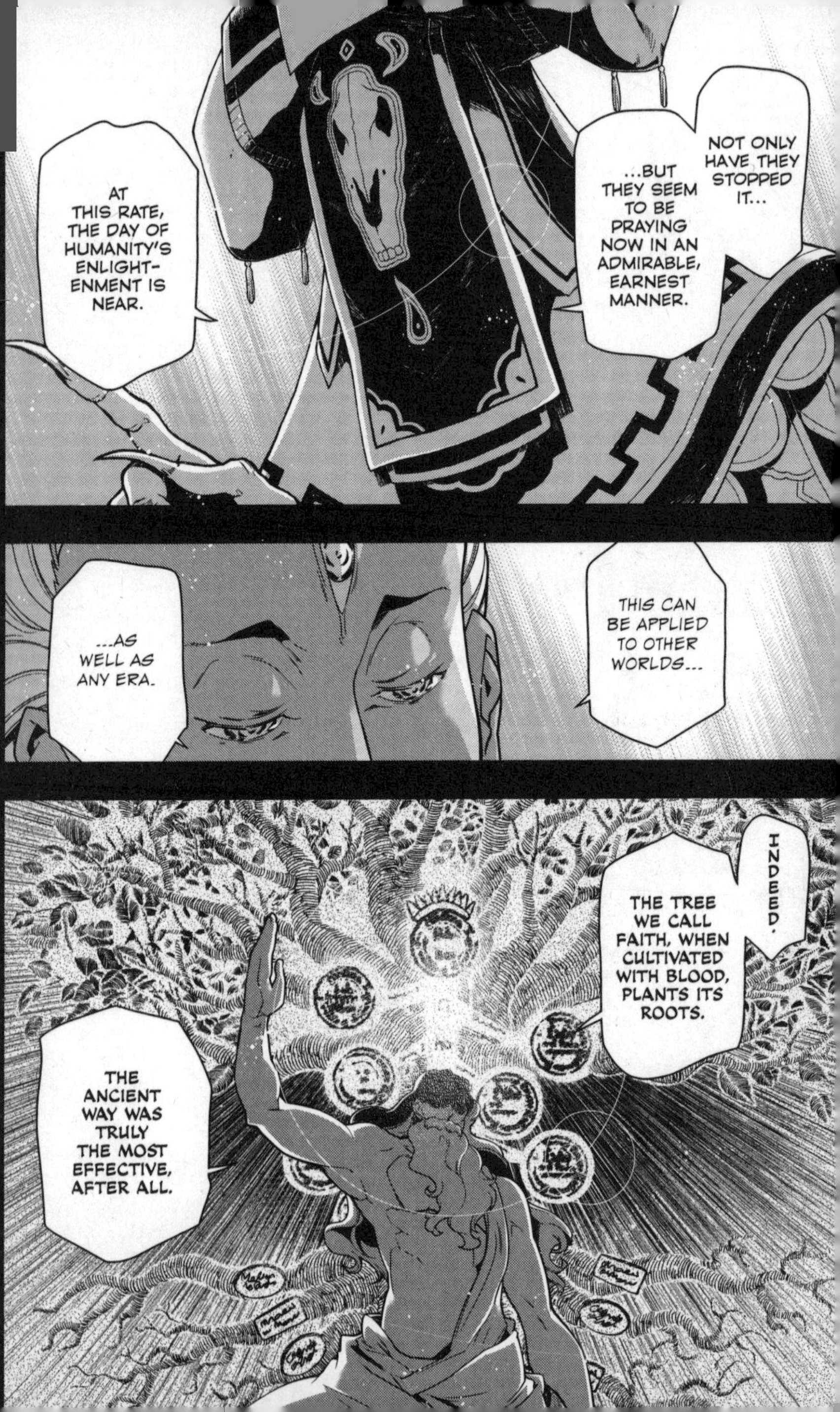
NOT ONLY HAVE THEY STOPPED IT...
...BUT THEY SEEM TO BE PRAYING NOW IN AN ADMIRABLE, EARNEST MANNER.
AT THIS RATE, THE DAY OF HUMANITY'S ENLIGHTENMENT IS NEAR.
THIS CAN BE APPLIED TO OTHER WORLDS...
...AS WELL AS ANY ERA.
INDEED.
THE TREE WE CALL FAITH, WHEN CULTIVATED WITH BLOOD, PLANTS ITS ROOTS.
THE ANCIENT WAY WAS TRULY THE MOST EFFECTIVE, AFTER ALL.

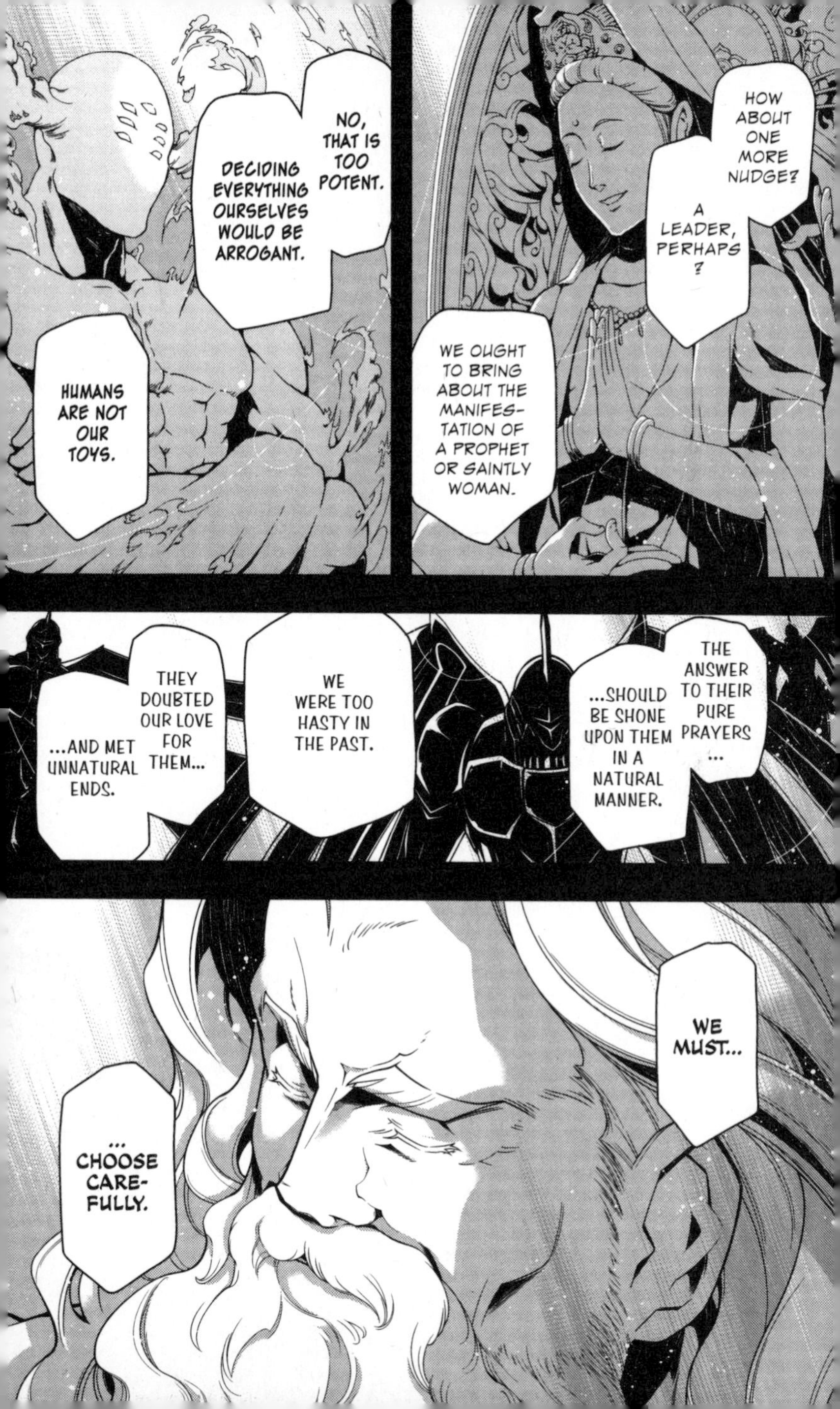
HOW ABOUT ONE MORE NUDGE?
A LEADER, PERHAPS?
WE OUGHT TO BRING ABOUT THE MANIFESTATION OF A PROPHET OR SAINTLY WOMAN.
NO, THAT IS TOO POTENT.
DECIDING EVERYTHING OURSELVES WOULD BE ARROGANT.
HUMANS ARE NOT OUR TOYS.
THE ANSWER TO THEIR PURE PRAYERS...
...SHOULD BE SHONE UPON THEM IN A NATURAL MANNER.
WE WERE TOO HASTY IN THE PAST.
THEY DOUBTED OUR LOVE FOR THEM...
...AND MET UNNATURAL ENDS.
WE MUST...
...CHOOSE CAREFULLY.

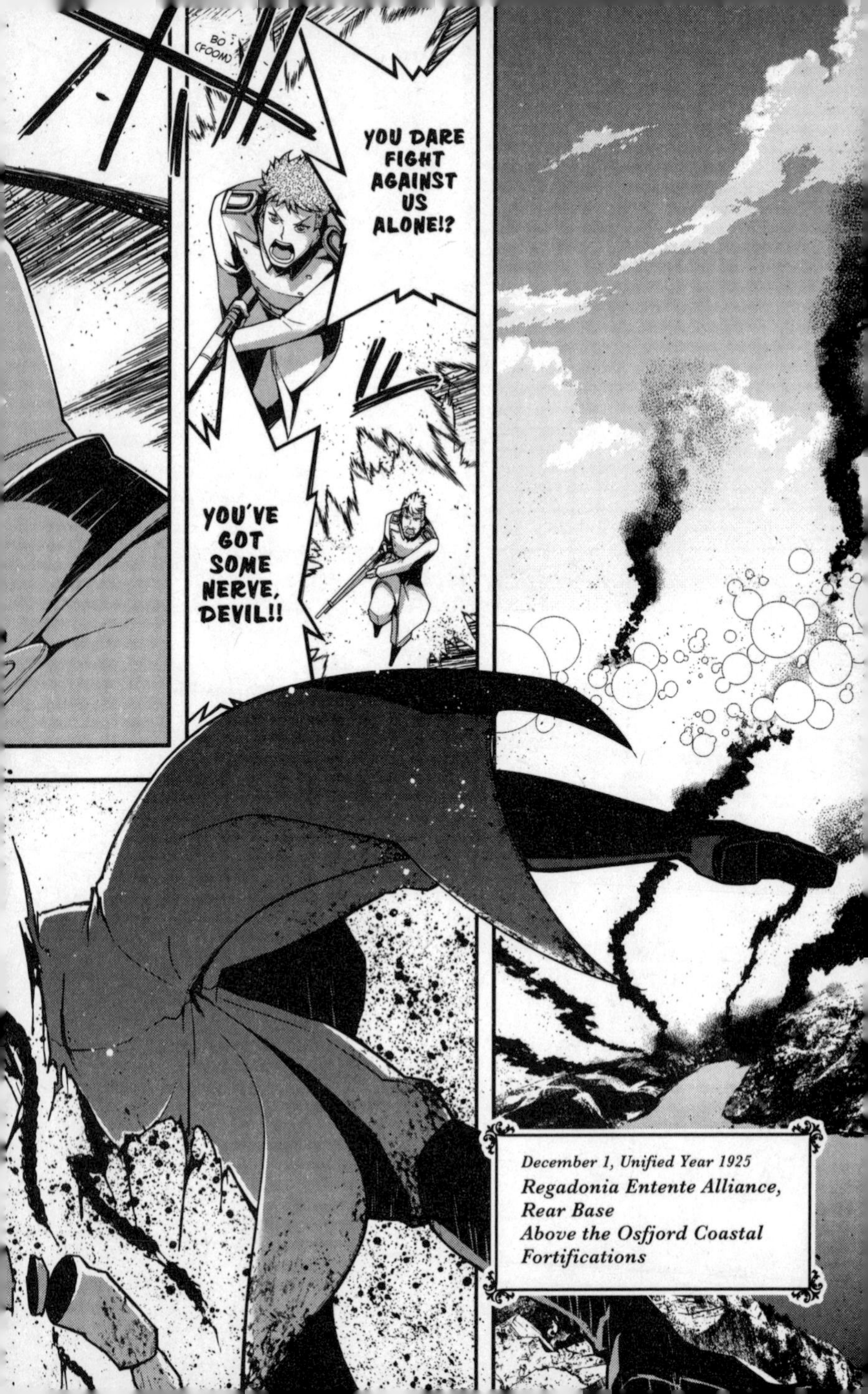
December 1, Unified Year 1925
Regadonia Entente Alliance, Rear Base
Above the Osfjord Coastal Fortifications
BO (FOOM)
YOU DARE FIGHT AGAINST US ALONE!?
YOU'VE GOT SOME NERVE, DEVIL!!

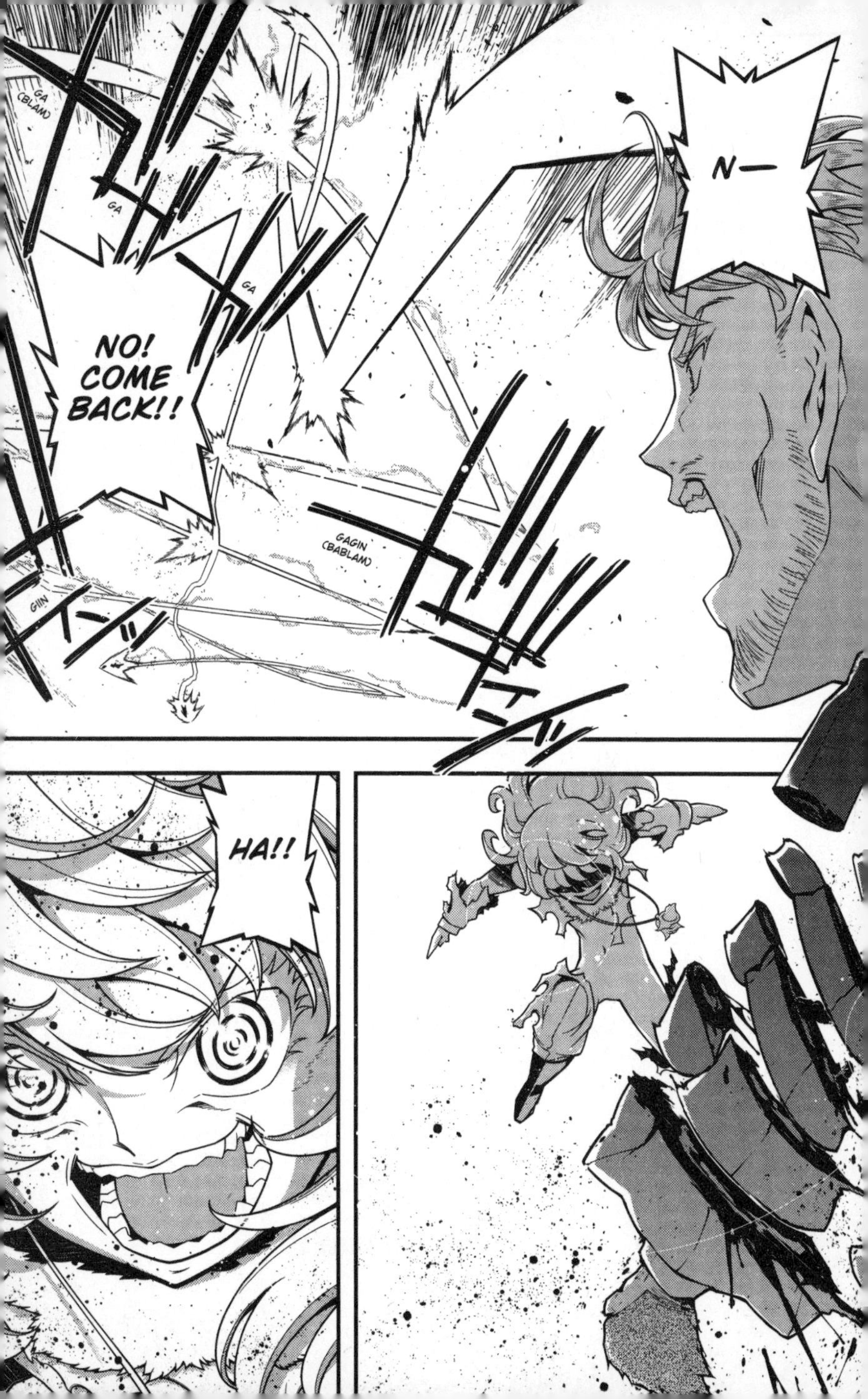
N—
NO! COME BACK!!
GA (BLAM)
GA
GA
GAGIN (BABLAM)
GIIN
HA!!

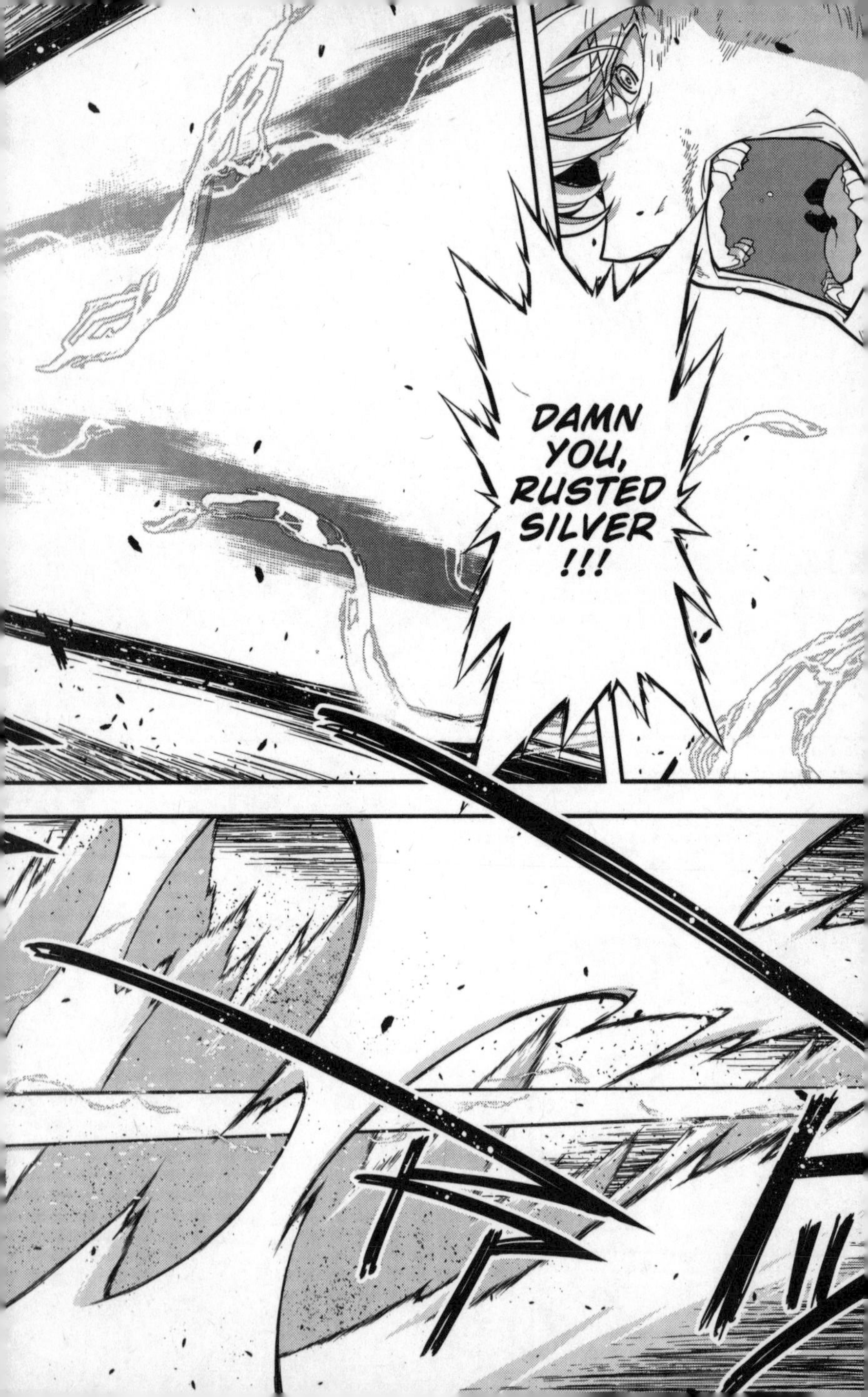
DAMN YOU, RUSTED SILVER!!!

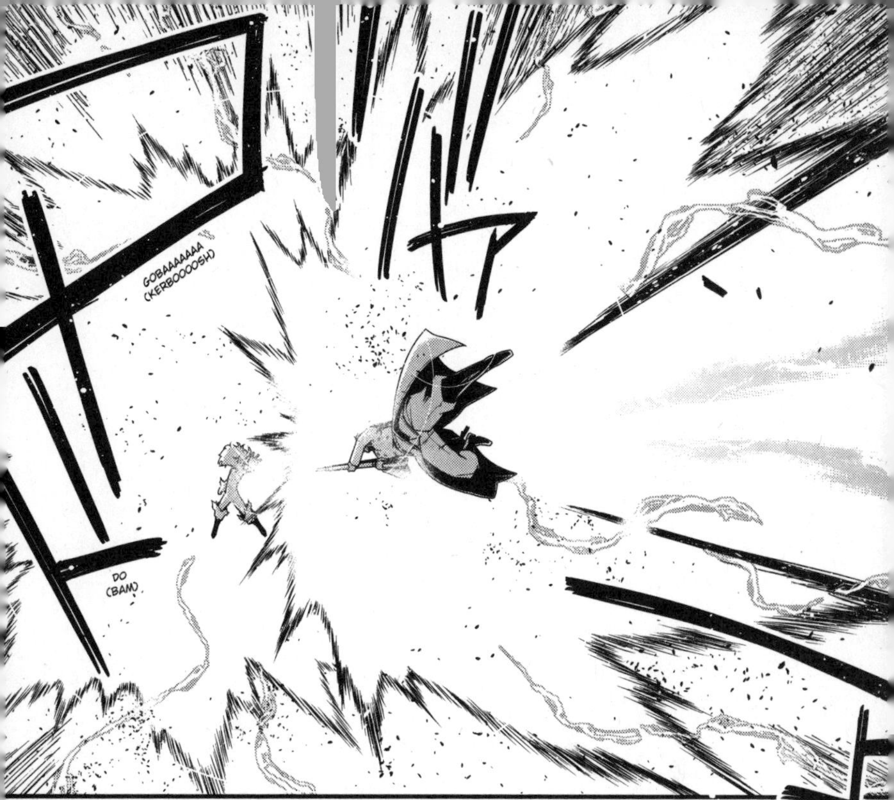
GOBAAAAAAA
(KERBOOOOSH)
DO
(BAM)
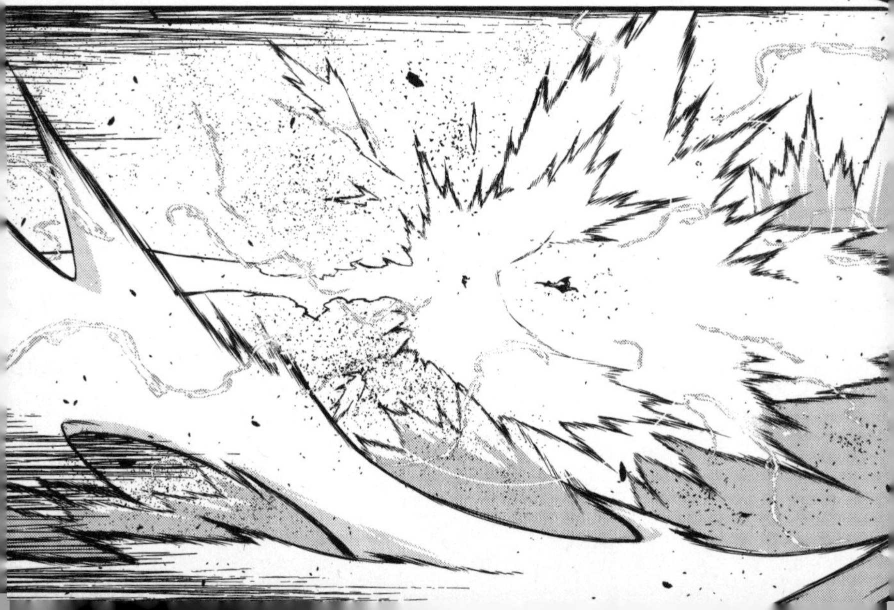

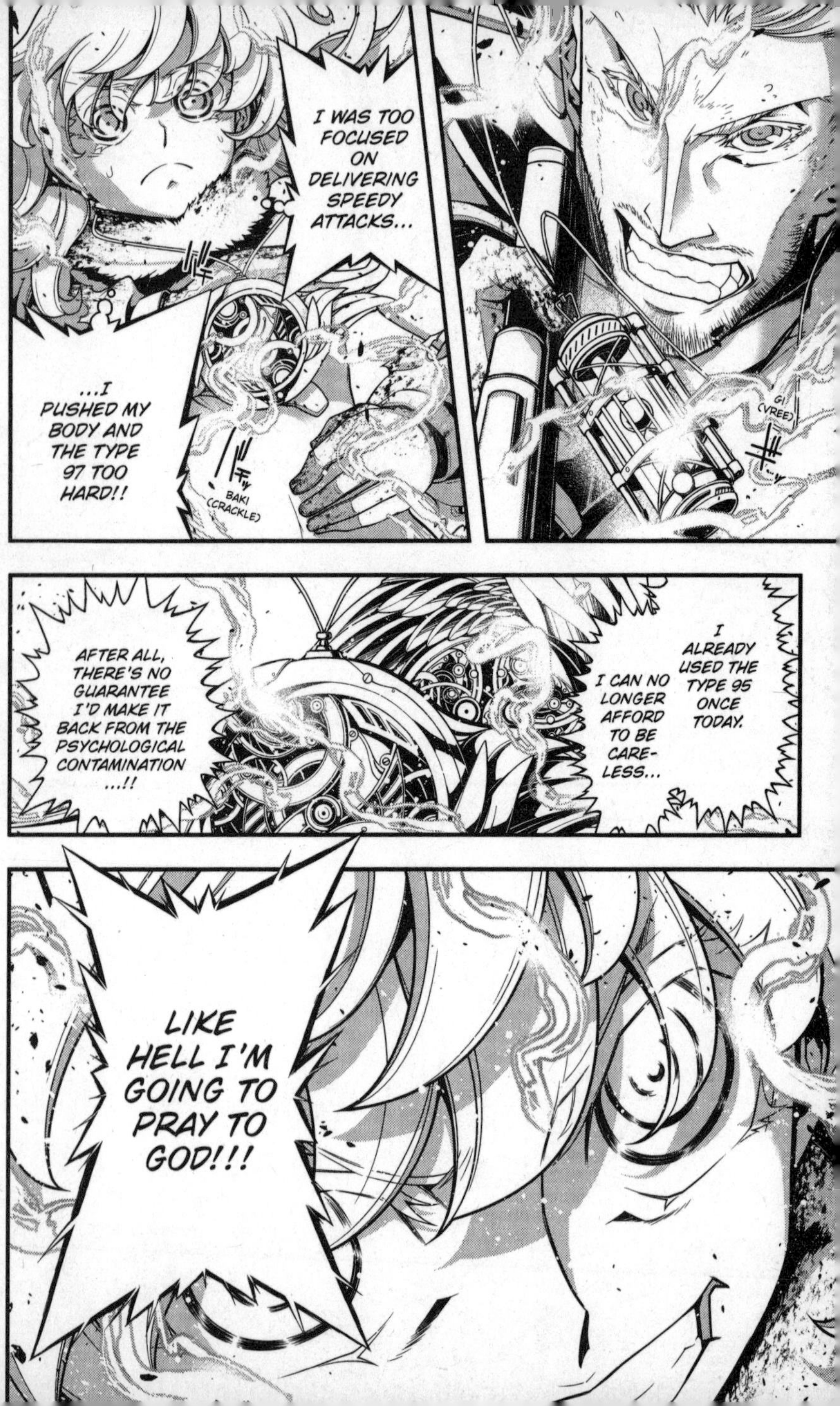
GI (VREE)
I WAS TOO FOCUSED ON DELIVERING SPEEDY ATTACKS...
...I PUSHED MY BODY AND THE TYPE 97 TOO HARD!!
BAKI (CRACKLE)
I ALREADY USED THE TYPE 95 ONCE TODAY.
I CAN NO LONGER AFFORD TO BE CARE-LESS...
AFTER ALL, THERE'S NO GUARANTEE I'D MAKE IT BACK FROM THE PSYCHOLOGICAL CONTAMINATION ...!!
LIKE HELL I'M GOING TO PRAY TO GOD!!!

Chapter 22

Norden IX

The Saga of Tanya the Evil

Chapter: 22

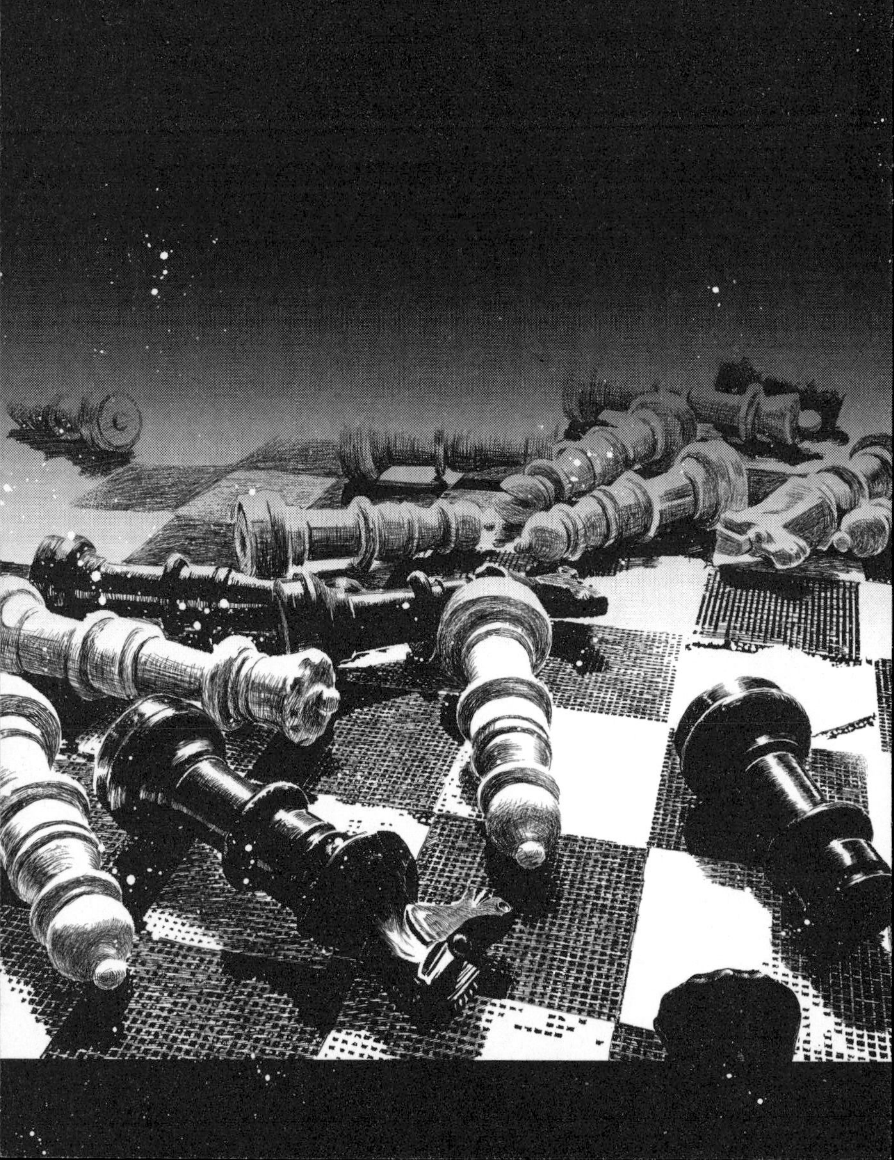

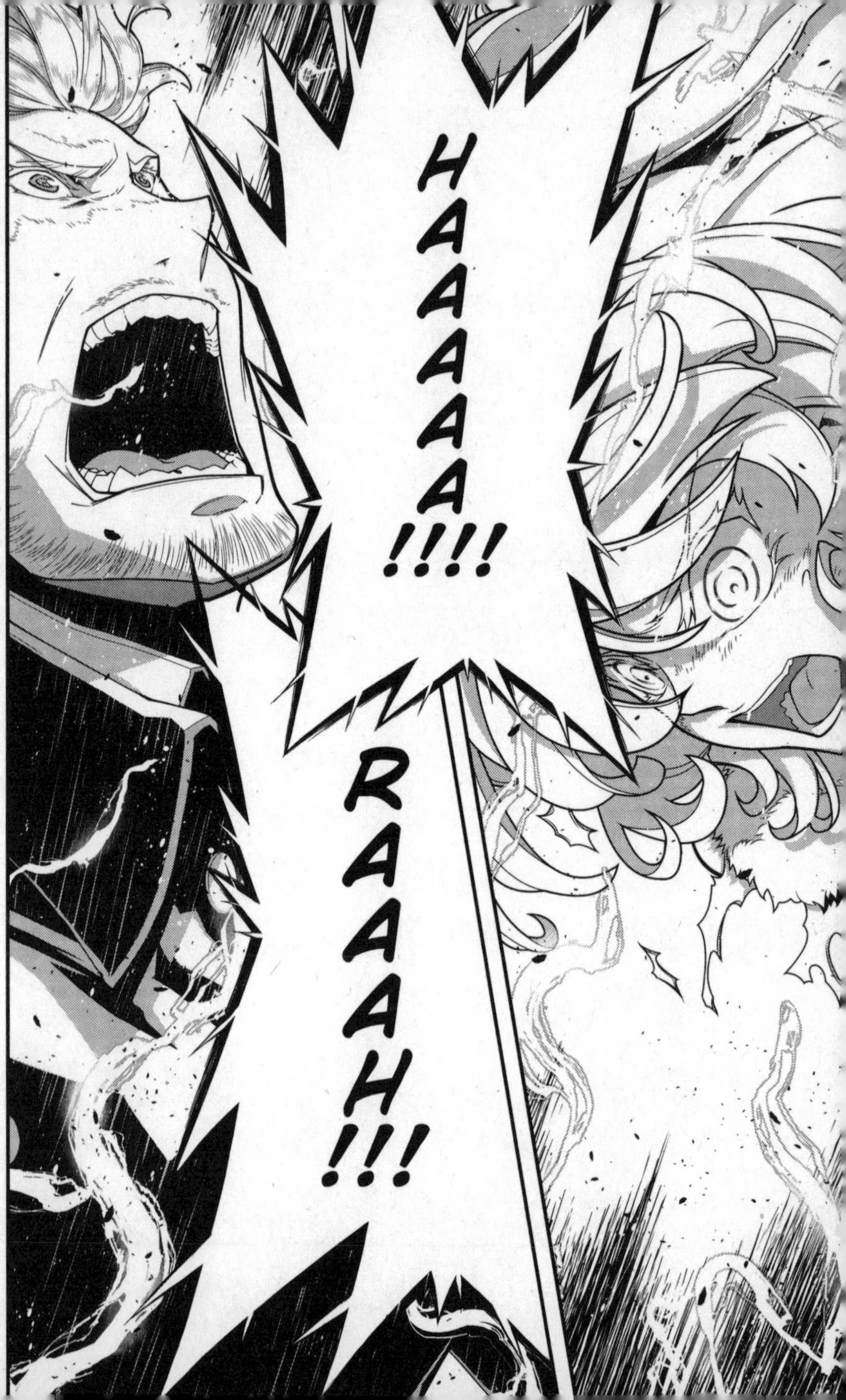
HAAAAA!!!!
RAAAAH!!!

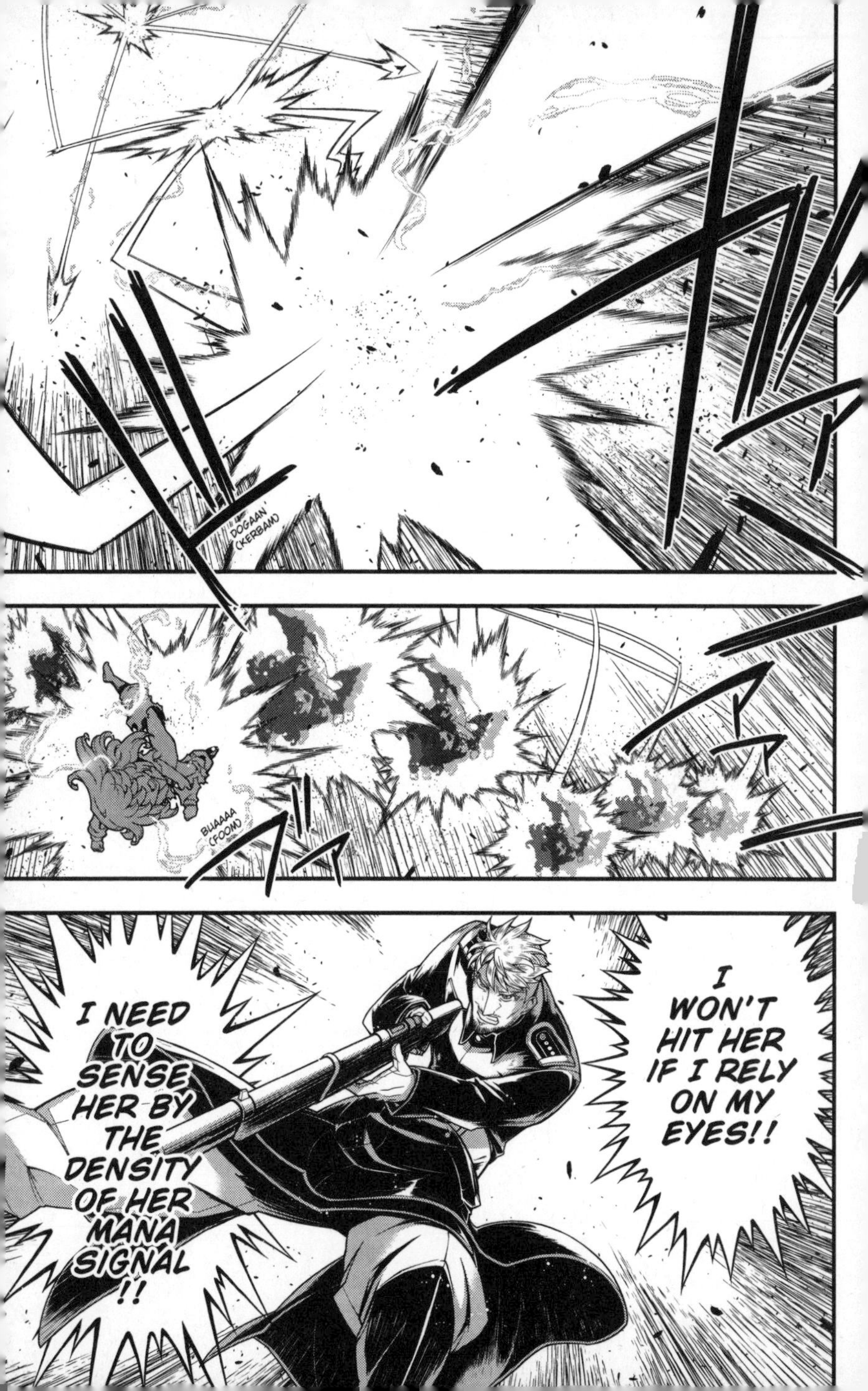
DOGAAN (KERBAM)
BUAAAA (FOOM)
I WON'T HIT HER IF I RELY ON MY EYES!!
I NEED TO SENSE HER BY THE DENSITY OF HER MANA SIGNAL!!

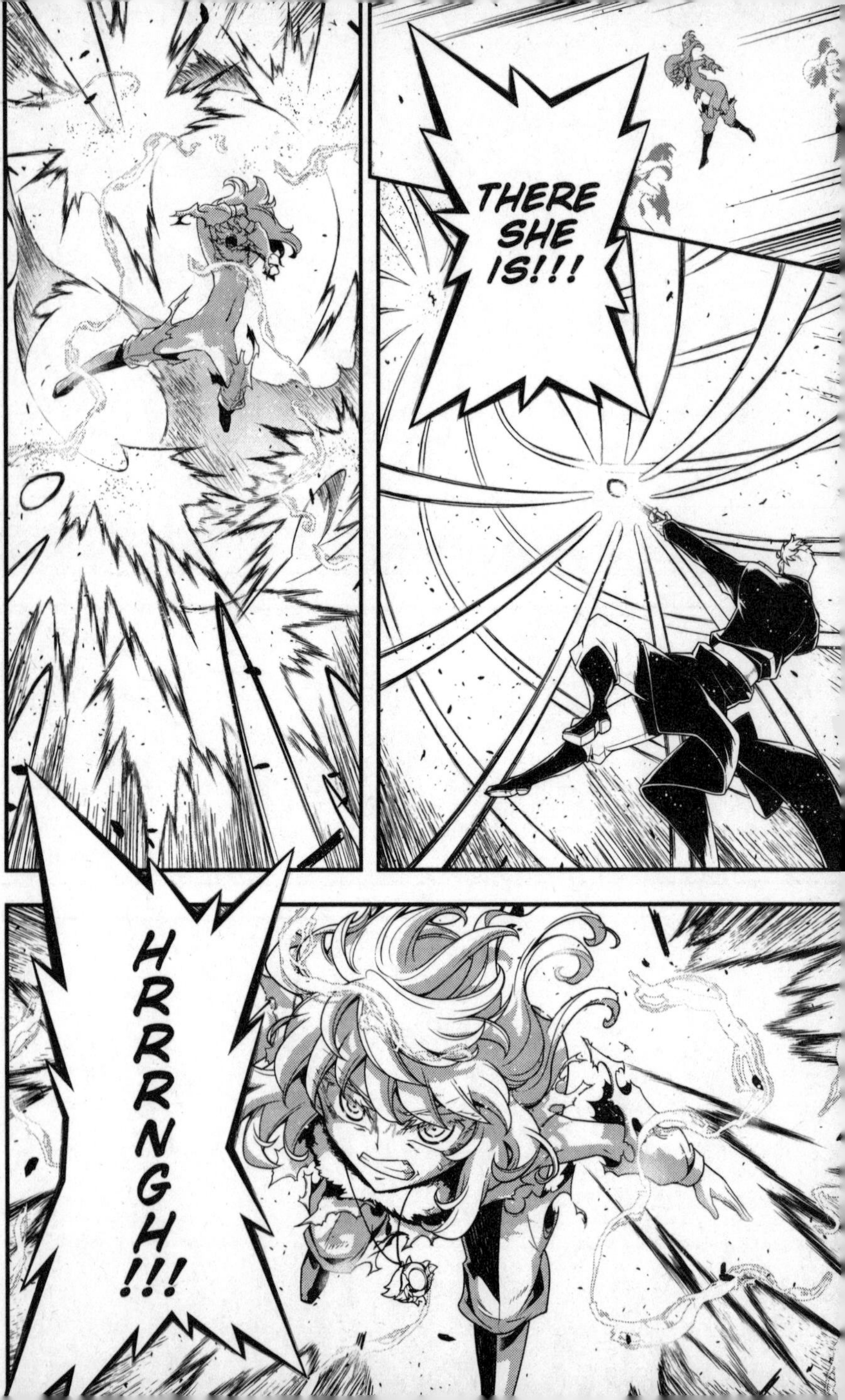
THERE SHE IS!!!
HRRRNGH!!!

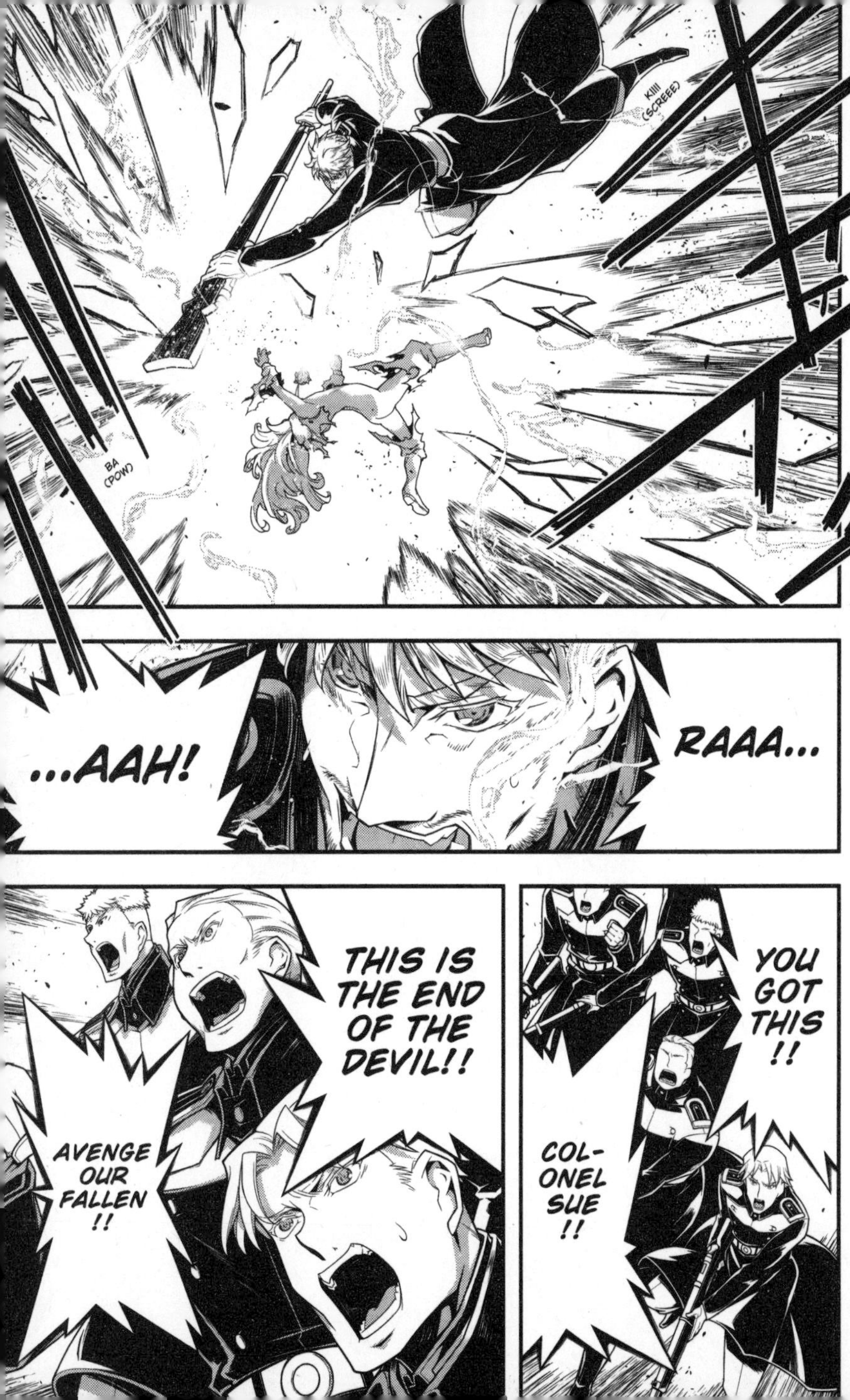
KIIII
(SCREEE)
BA
(POW)
RAAA...
...AAH!
YOU GOT THIS!!
COL-ONEL SUE!!
THIS IS THE END OF THE DEVIL!!
AVENGE OUR FALLEN!!

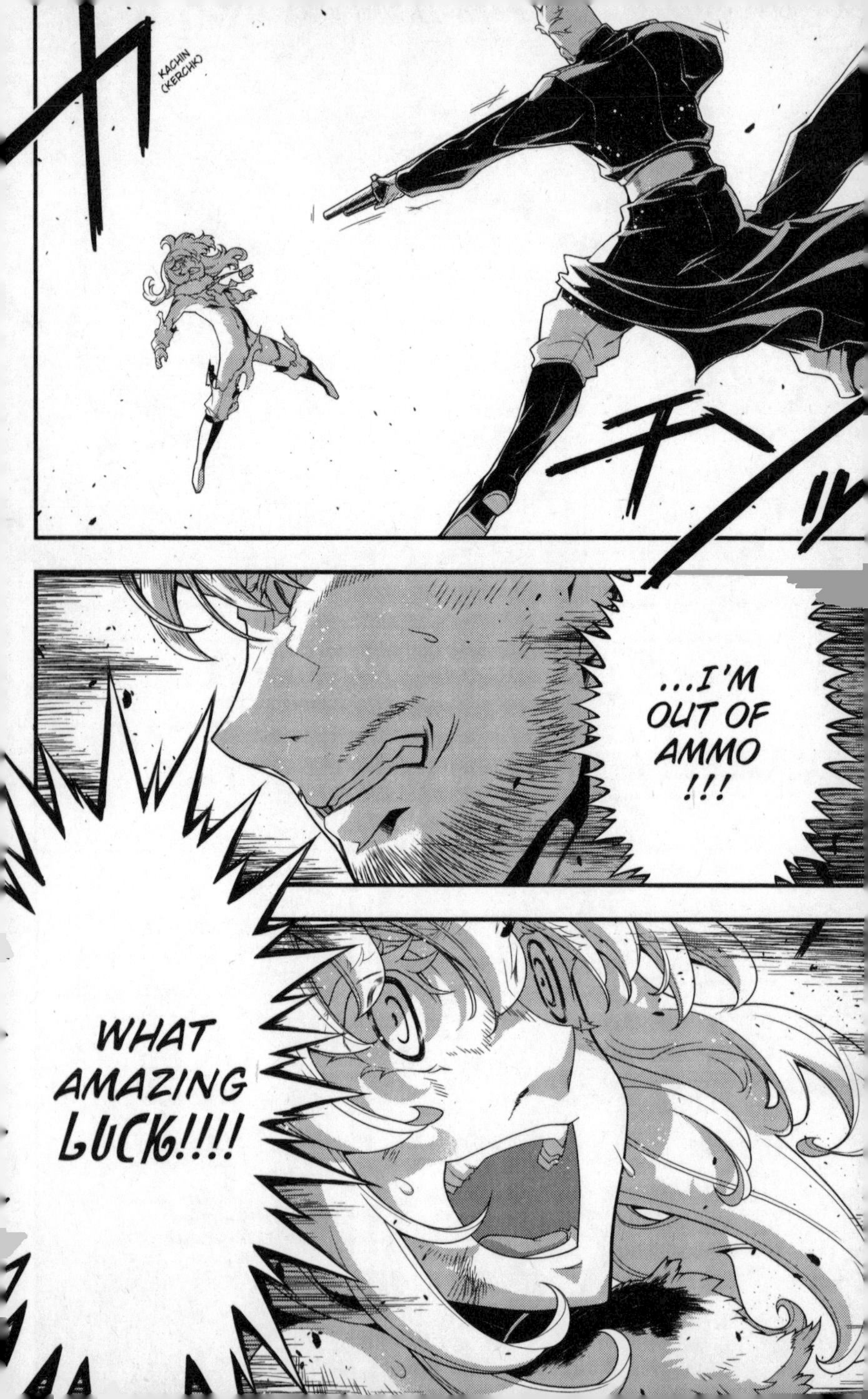
KACHIN
(KERCHK)
...I'M OUT OF AMMO!!!
WHAT AMAZING LUCK!!!!

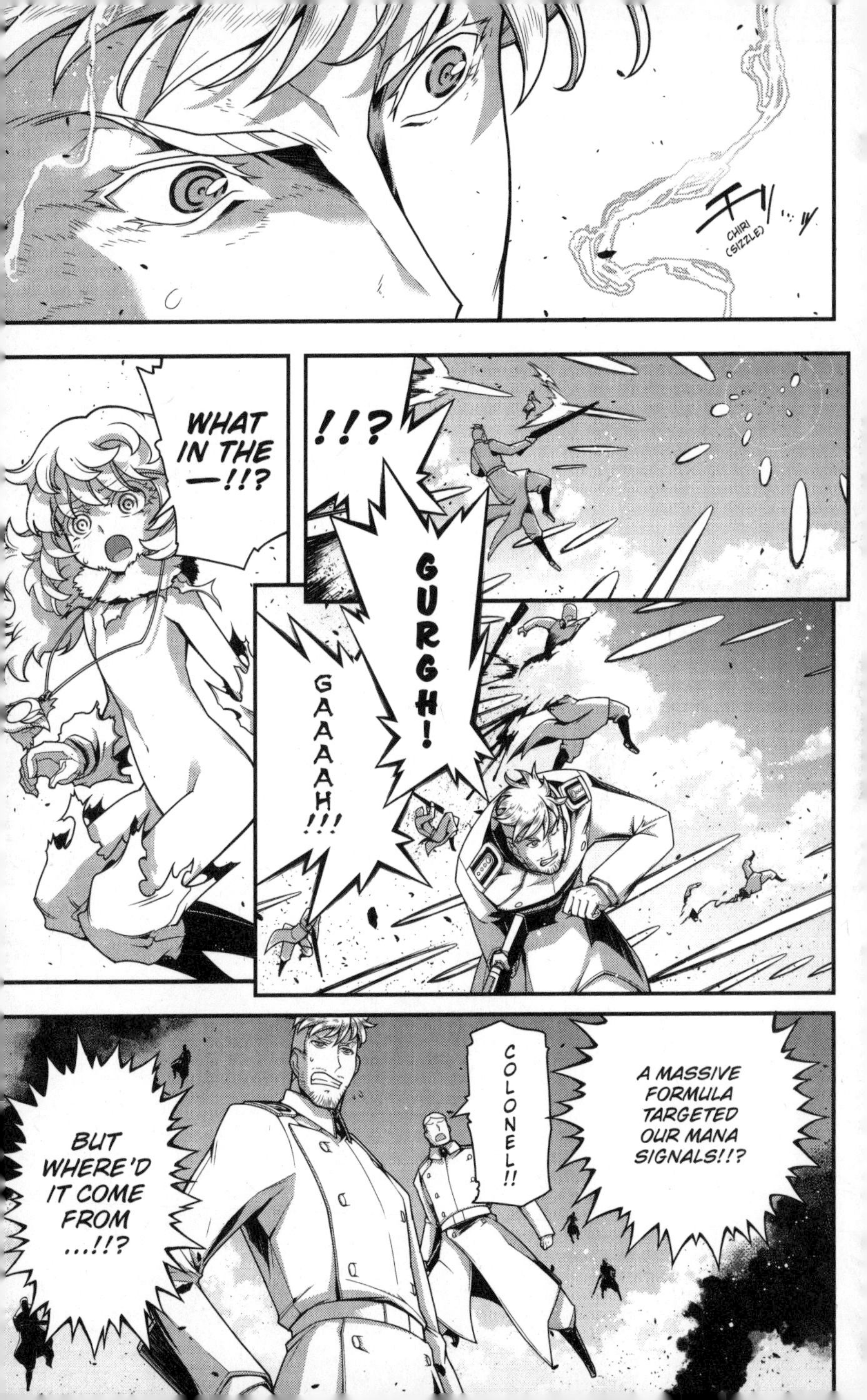
CHIRI (SIZZLE)
!!?
GURGH!
GAAAAH!!!
WHAT IN THE—!!?
A MASSIVE FORMULA TARGETED OUR MANA SIGNALS!!?
COLONEL!!
BUT WHERE'D IT COME FROM...!!?

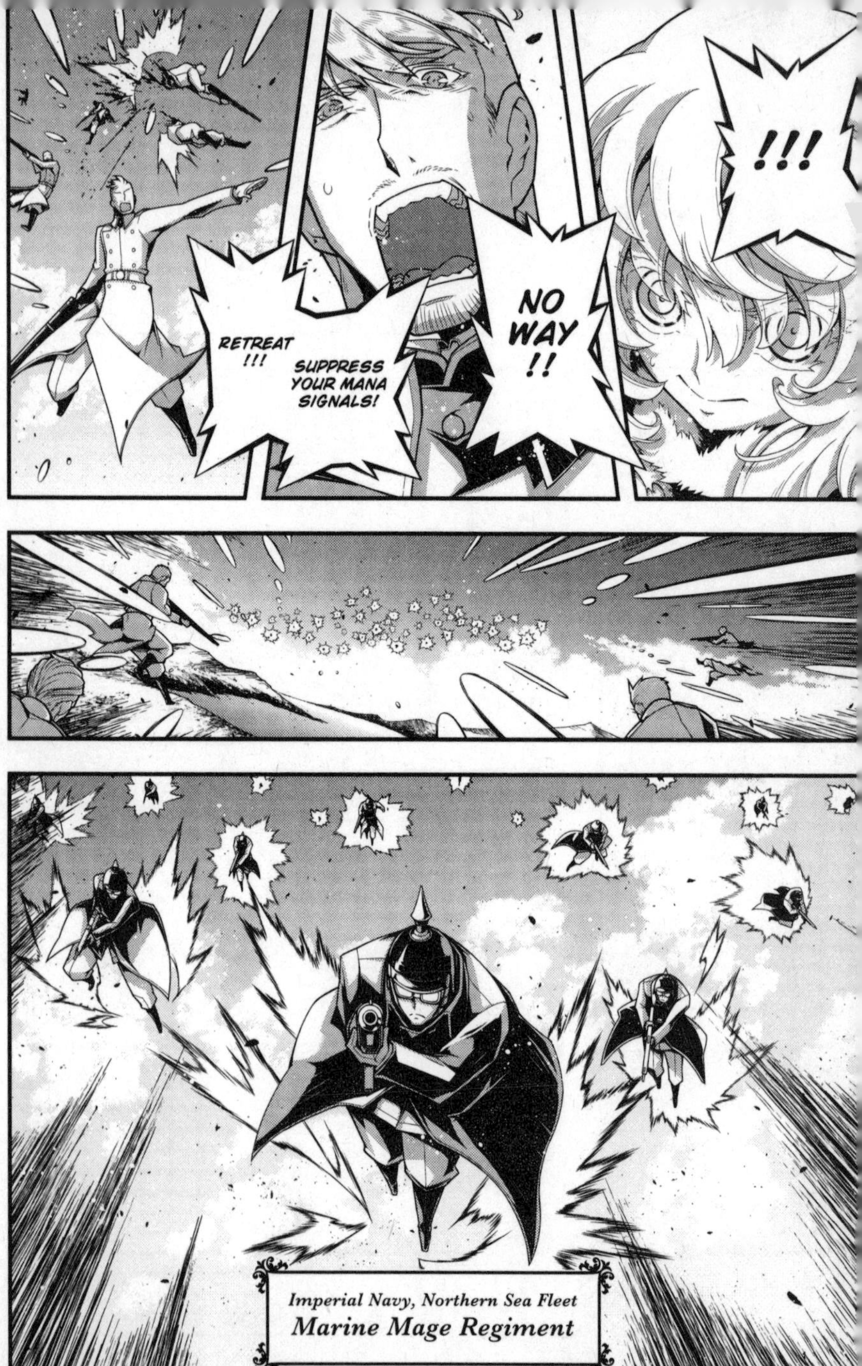
!!!
NO WAY!!
SUPPRESS YOUR MANA SIGNALS!
RETREAT!!!
Imperial Navy, Northern Sea Fleet
Marine Mage Regiment

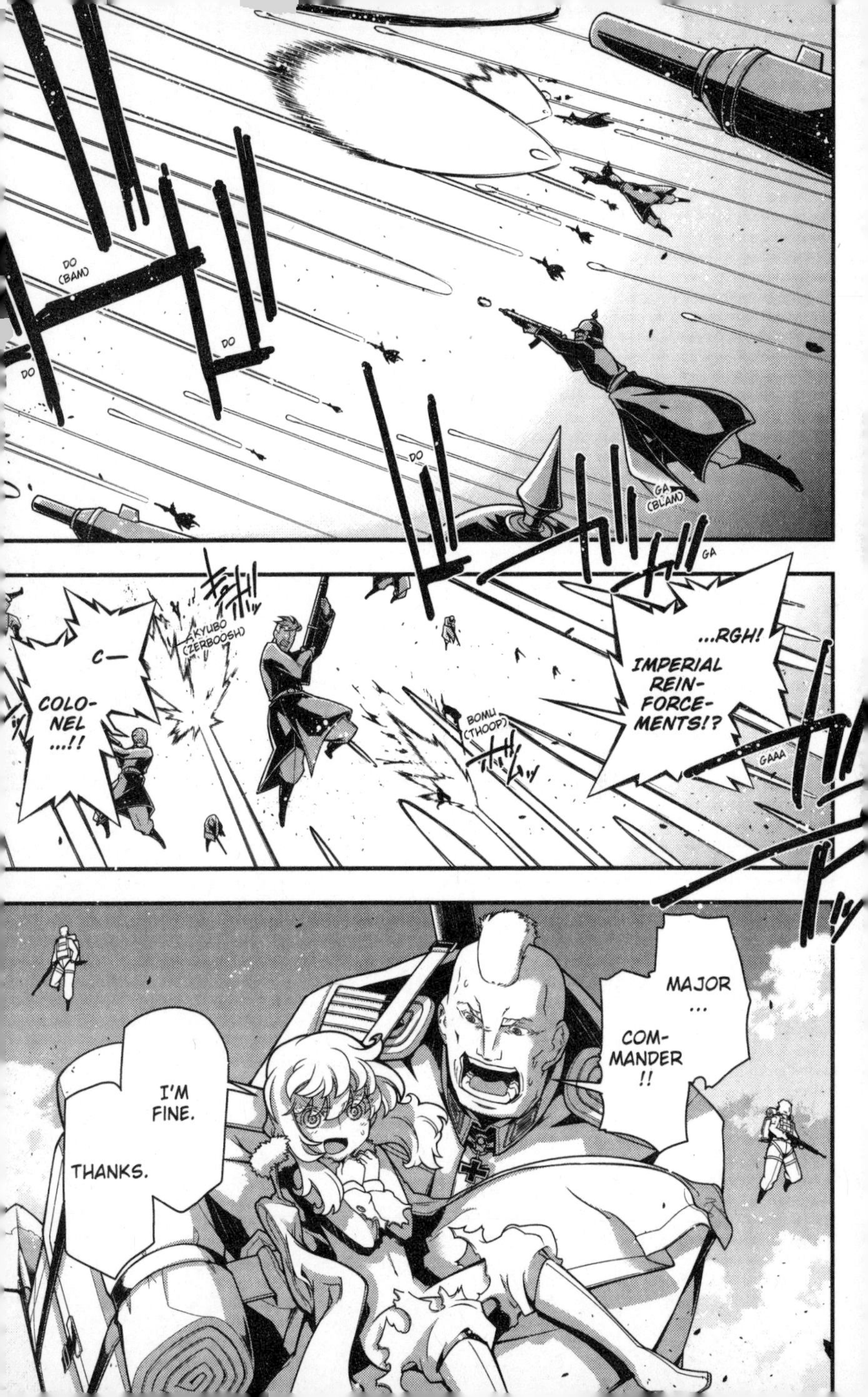

GA (BLAM)
GA
DO
DO
DO (BAM)
DO
...RGH! IMPERIAL REIN-FORCE-MENTS!?
GAAA
BOMU (THOOP)
KYUBO (ZERBOOSH)
C— COLO-NEL ...!!
MAJOR ... COM-MANDER !!
I'M FINE.
THANKS.

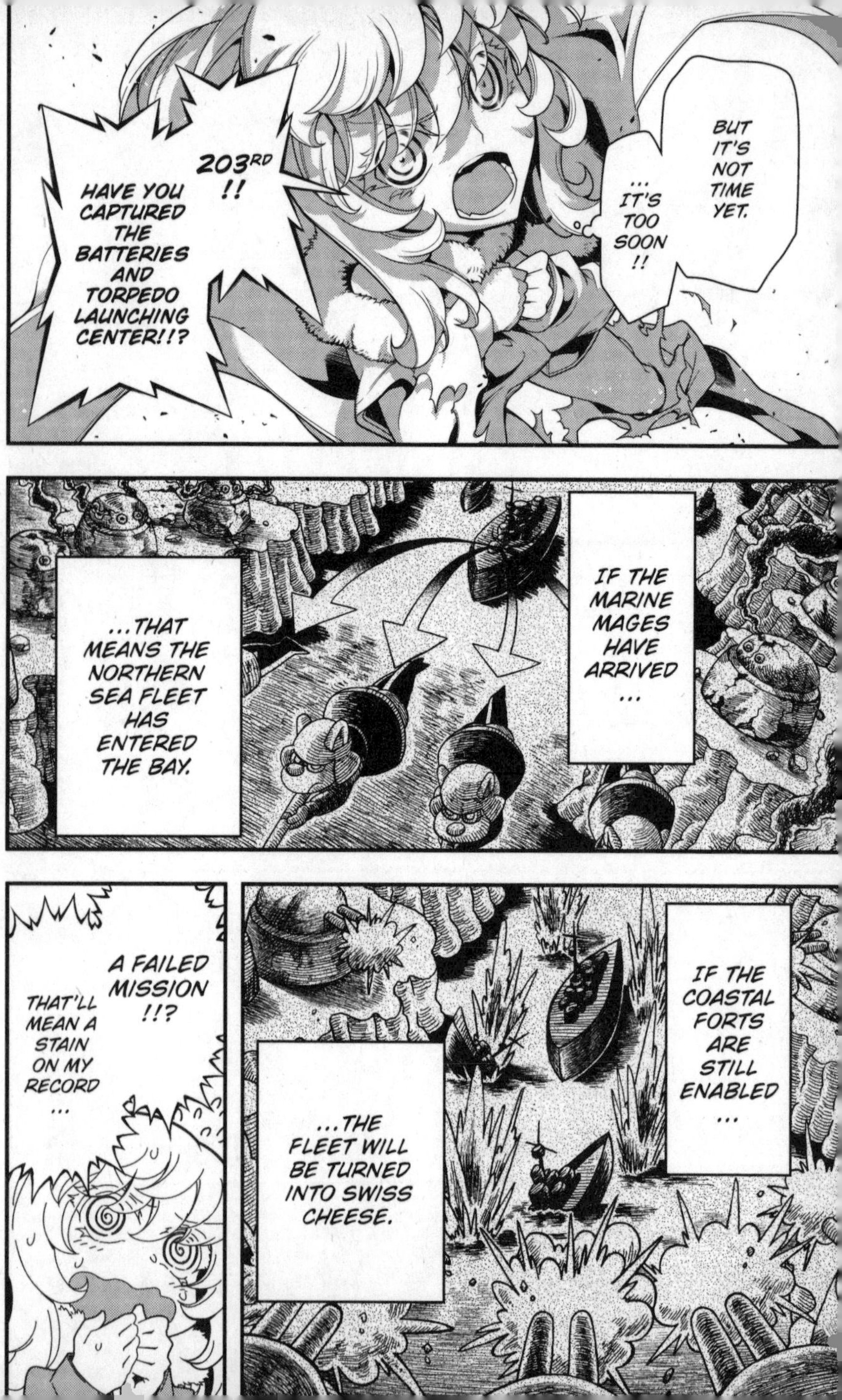
BUT IT'S NOT TIME YET.
... IT'S TOO SOON !!
203RD !!
HAVE YOU CAPTURED THE BATTERIES AND TORPEDO LAUNCHING CENTER!!?
IF THE MARINE MAGES HAVE ARRIVED ...
...THAT MEANS THE NORTHERN SEA FLEET HAS ENTERED THE BAY.
IF THE COASTAL FORTS ARE STILL ENABLED ...
...THE FLEET WILL BE TURNED INTO SWISS CHEESE.
A FAILED MISSION !!?
THAT'LL MEAN A STAIN ON MY RECORD ...

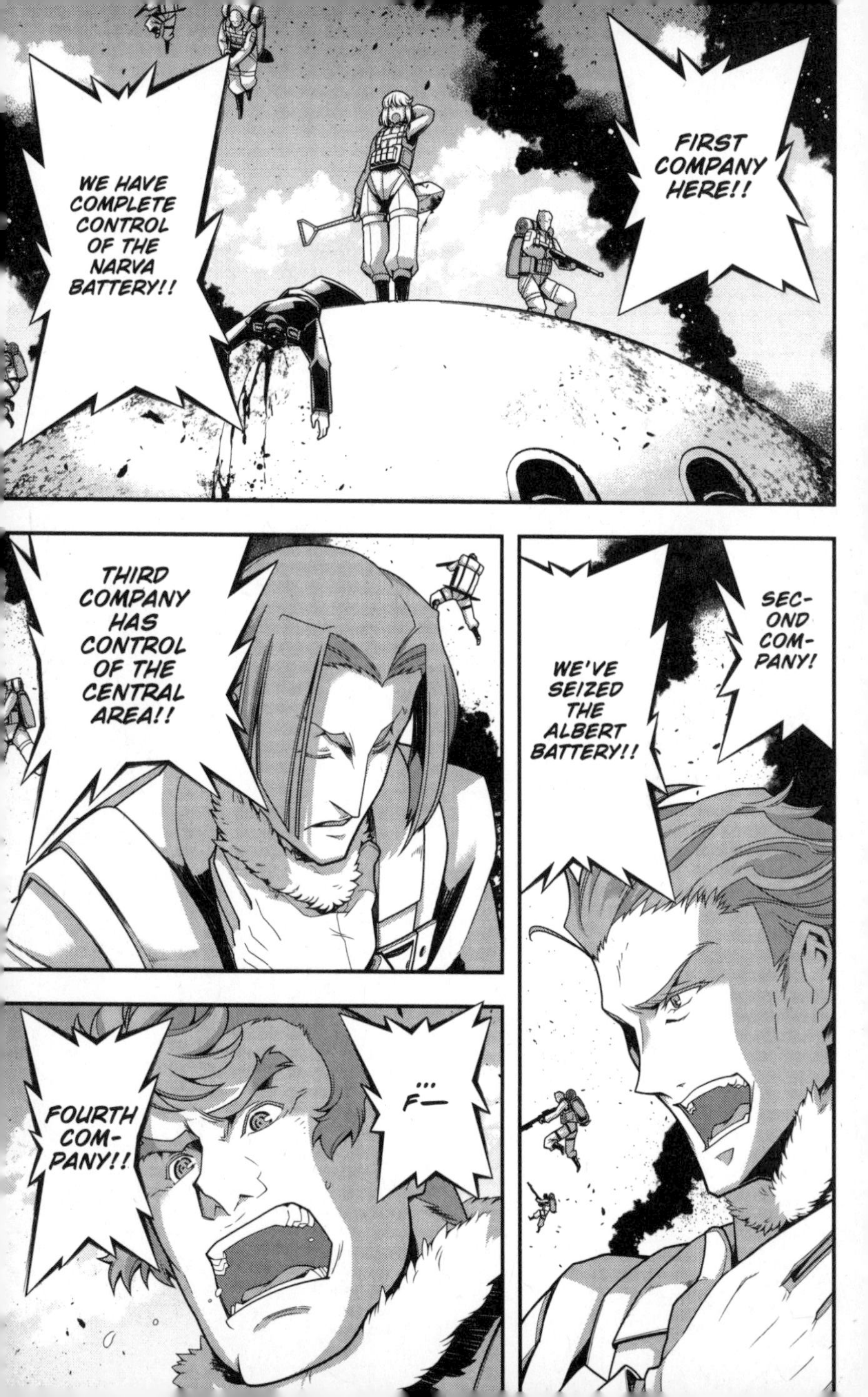
FIRST COMPANY HERE!!
WE HAVE COMPLETE CONTROL OF THE NARVA BATTERY!!
SEC-OND COM-PANY!
WE'VE SEIZED THE ALBERT BATTERY!!
THIRD COMPANY HAS CONTROL OF THE CENTRAL AREA!!
... F—
FOURTH COM-PANY!!

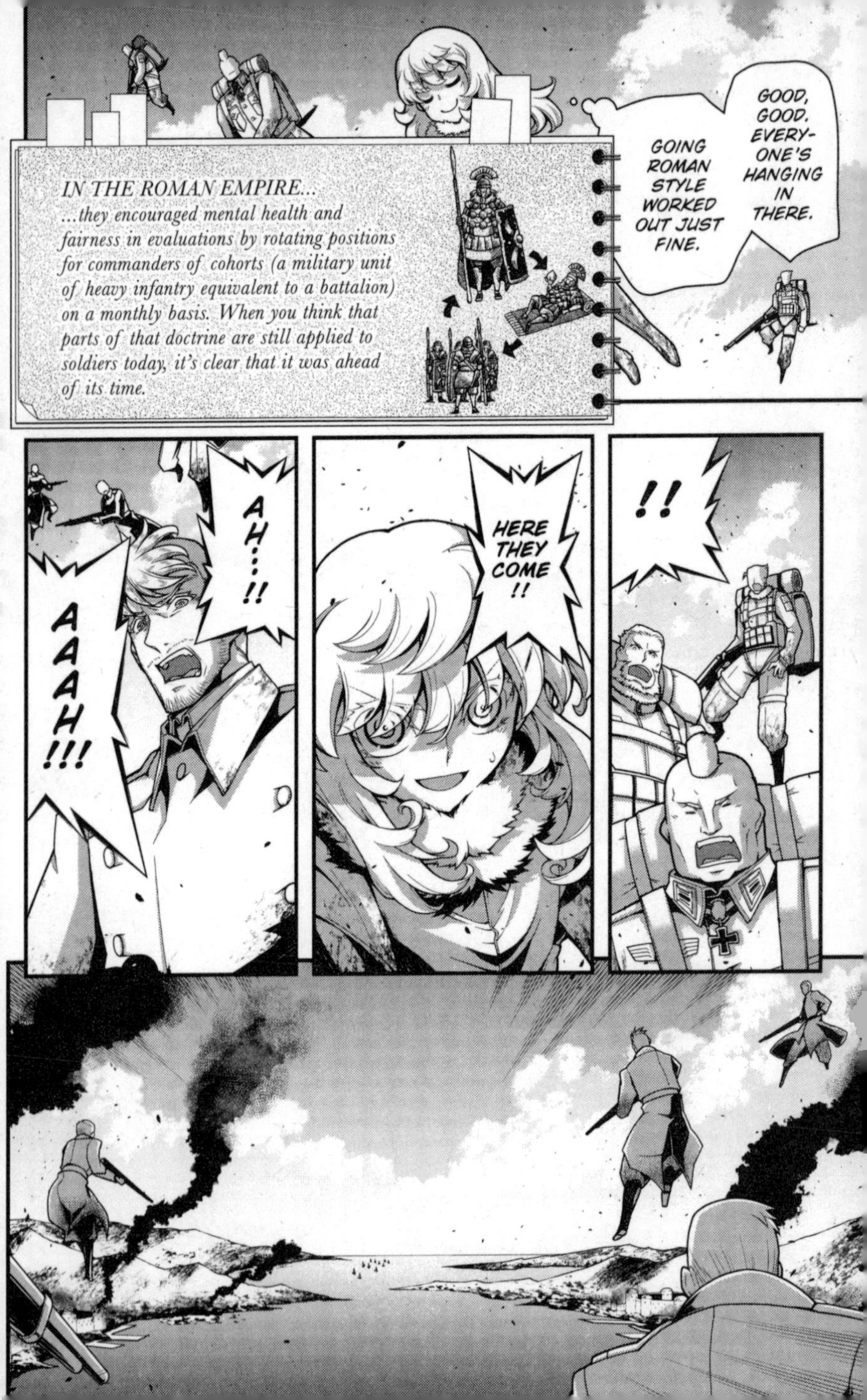
GOOD, GOOD. EVERY-ONE'S HANGING IN THERE.
GOING ROMAN STYLE WORKED OUT JUST FINE.
IN THE ROMAN EMPIRE...
...they encouraged mental health and fairness in evaluations by rotating positions for commanders of cohorts (a military unit of heavy infantry equivalent to a battalion) on a monthly basis. When you think that parts of that doctrine are still applied to soldiers today, it's clear that it was ahead of its time.
!!
HERE THEY COME!!
AH...!!
AAAAH!!!

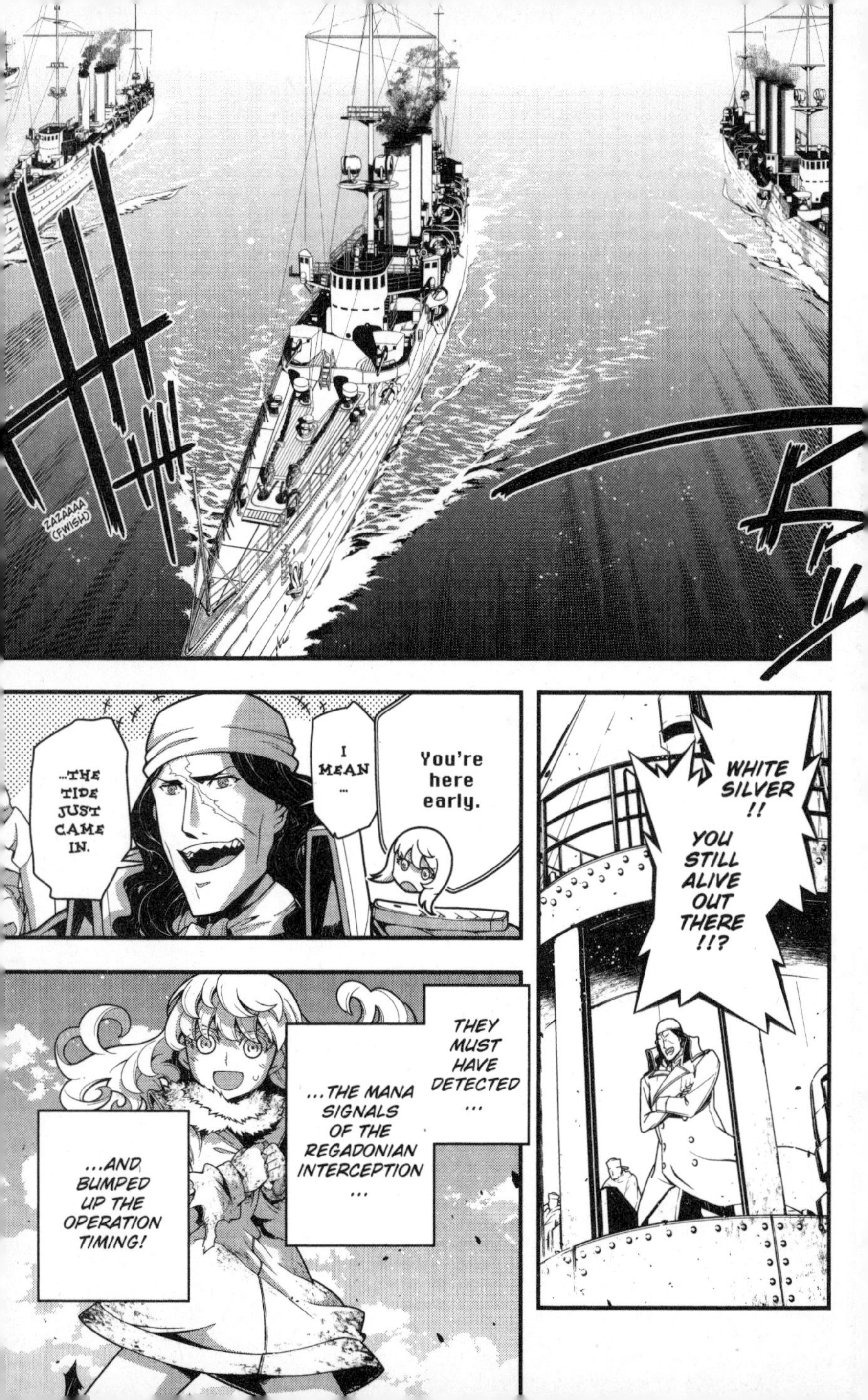
ZAZAAAA (FWISH)
WHITE SILVER!!
YOU STILL ALIVE OUT THERE!!?
You're here early.
I MEAN...
...THE TIDE JUST CAME IN.
THEY MUST HAVE DETECTED...
...THE MANA SIGNALS OF THE REGADONIAN INTERCEPTION...
...AND BUMPED UP THE OPERATION TIMING!

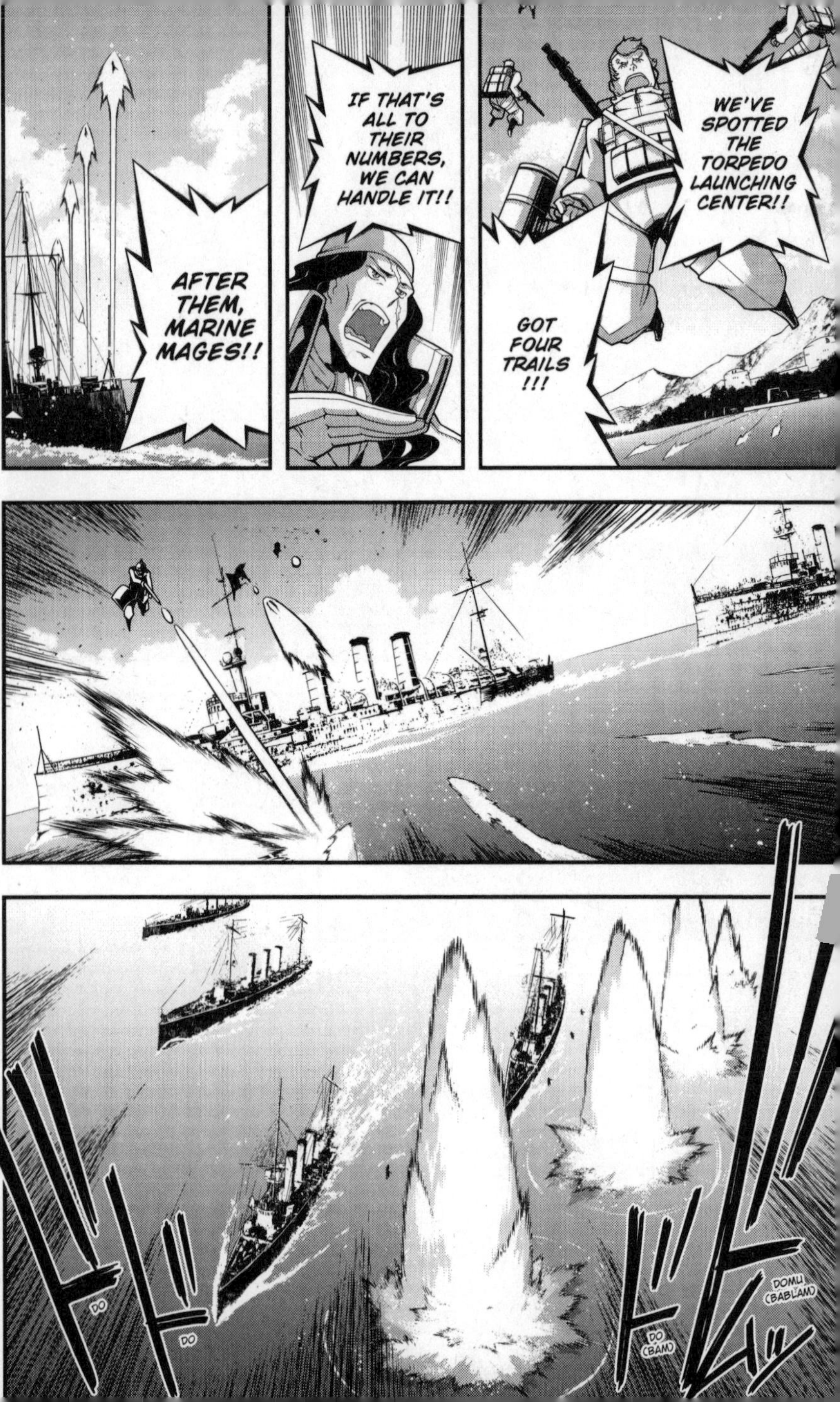
WE'VE SPOTTED THE TORPEDO LAUNCHING CENTER!!
GOT FOUR TRAILS!!!
IF THAT'S ALL TO THEIR NUMBERS, WE CAN HANDLE IT!!
AFTER THEM, MARINE MAGES!!
DOMU (BABLAM)
DO (BAM)
DO
DO

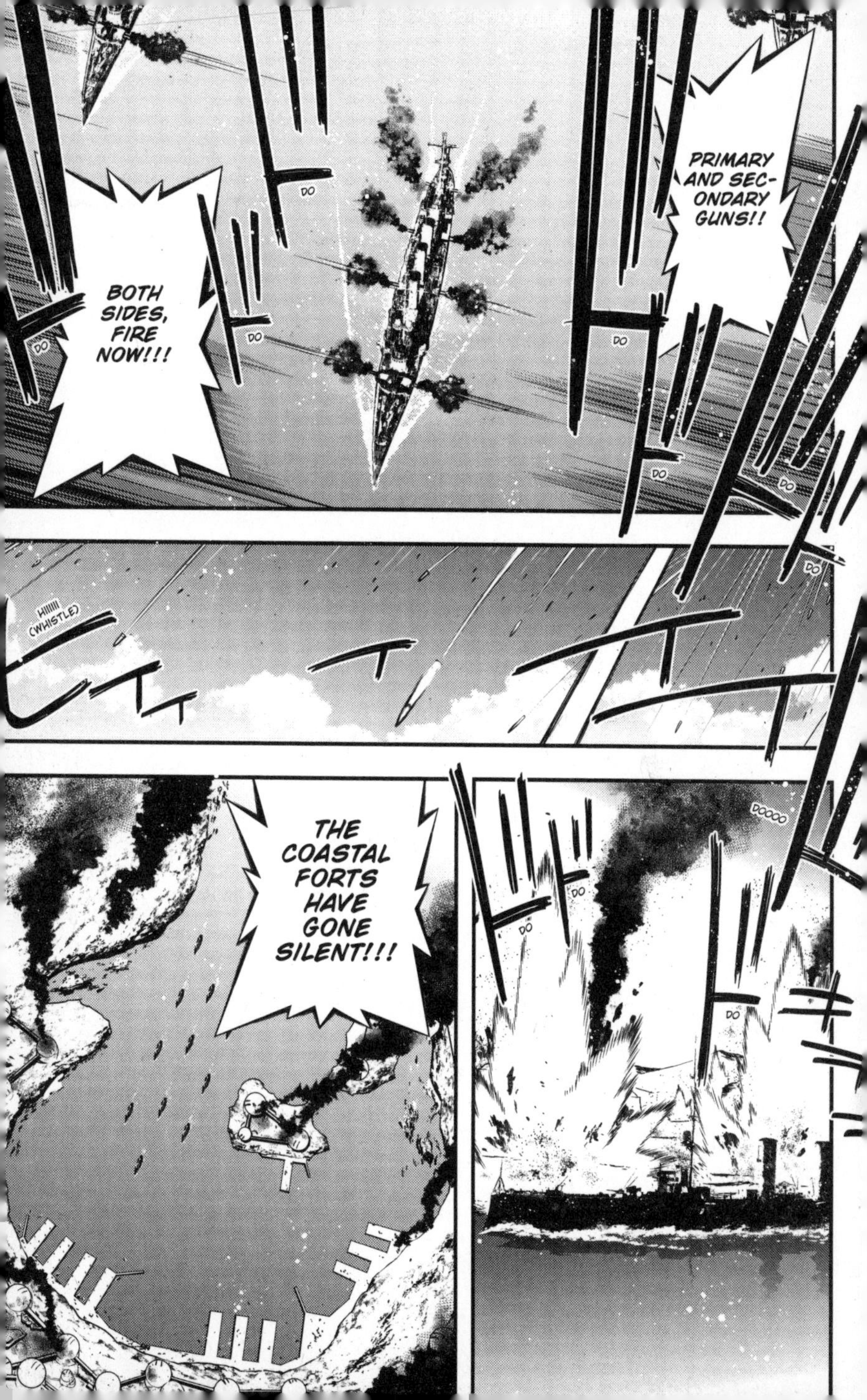
PRIMARY AND SECONDARY GUNS!!
DO
DO
DO
BOTH SIDES, FIRE NOW!!!
DO
DO
DO
DO
HIIIII (WHISTLE)
DOOOO
DO
DO
DO
THE COASTAL FORTS HAVE GONE SILENT!!!

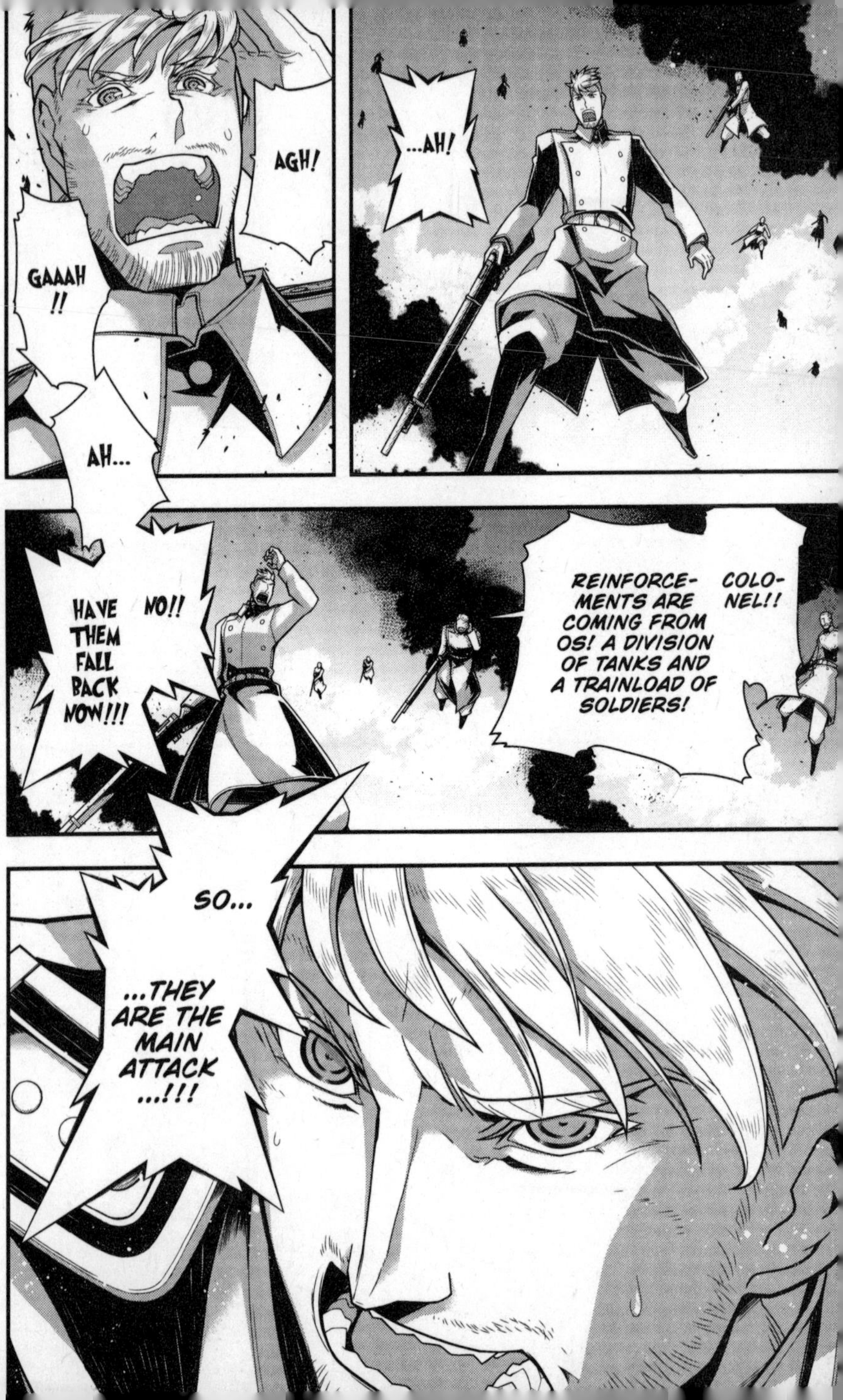
...AH!
AGH!
GAAAH!!
AH...
COLONEL!!
REINFORCEMENTS ARE COMING FROM OS! A DIVISION OF TANKS AND A TRAINLOAD OF SOLDIERS!
NO!! HAVE THEM FALL BACK NOW!!!
SO...
...THEY ARE THE MAIN ATTACK ...!!!

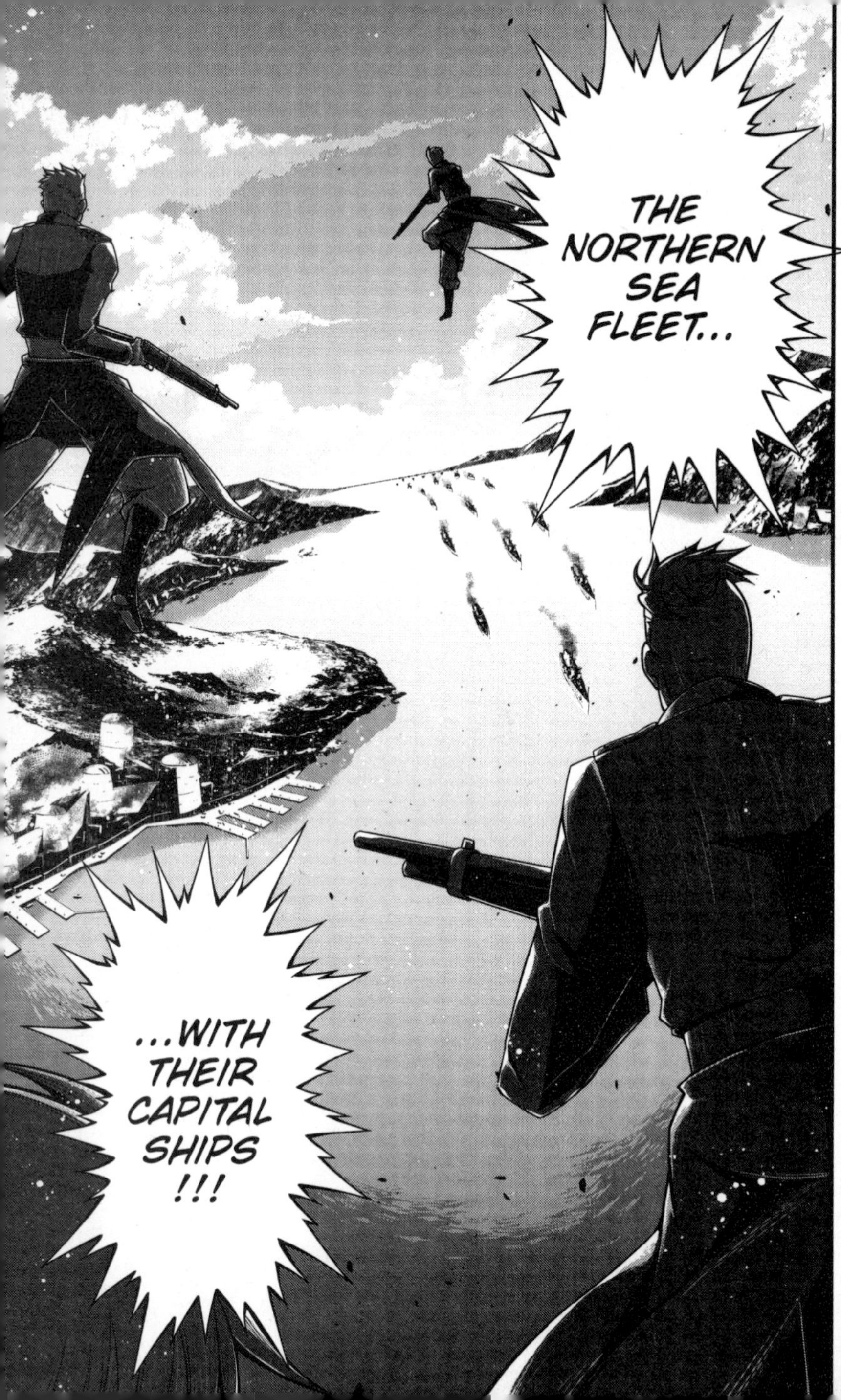
THE NORTHERN SEA FLEET...
...WITH THEIR CAPITAL SHIPS !!!

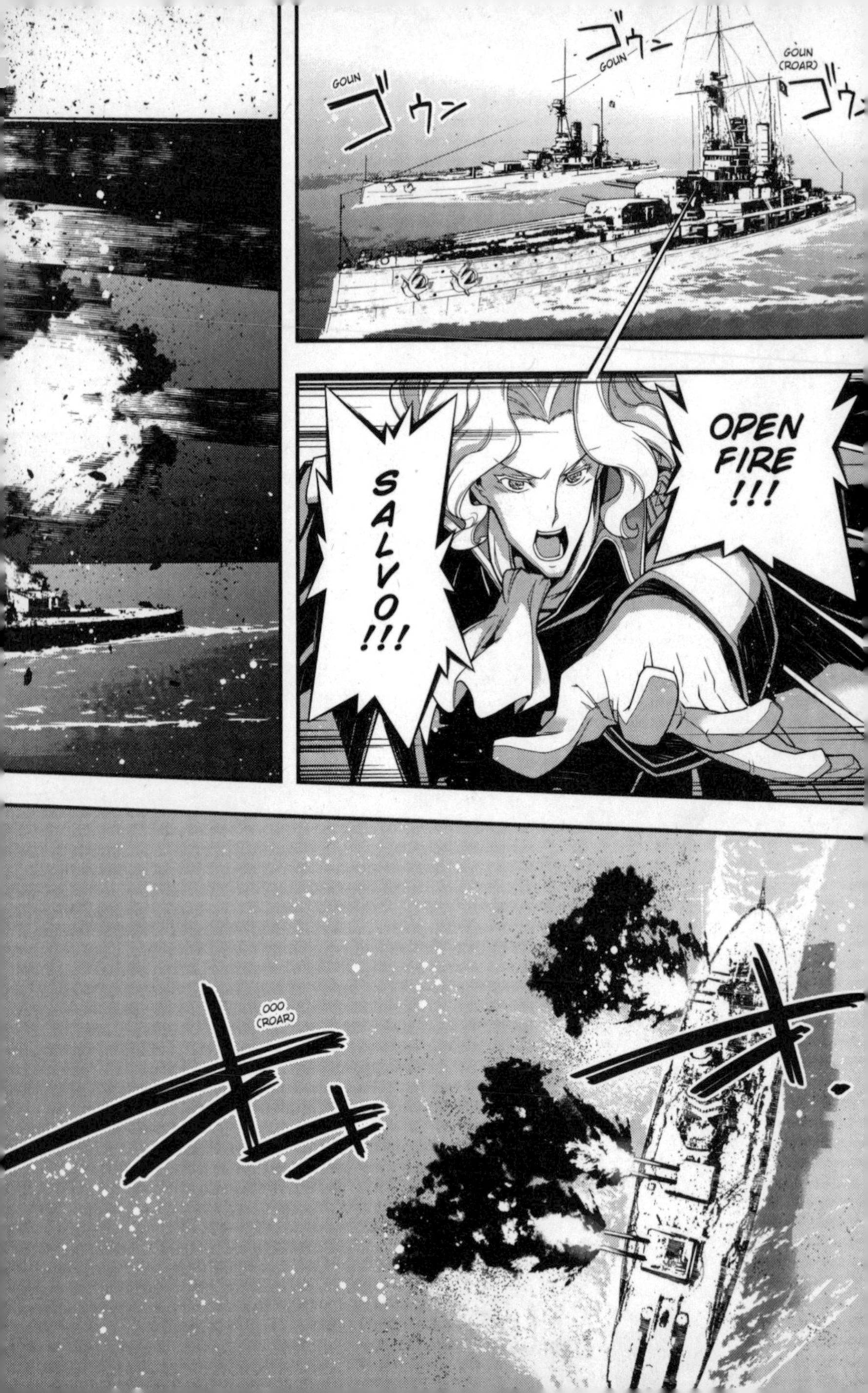
GOUN (ROAR)
GOUN
GOUN
OPEN FIRE!!!
SALVO!!!
OOO (ROAR)

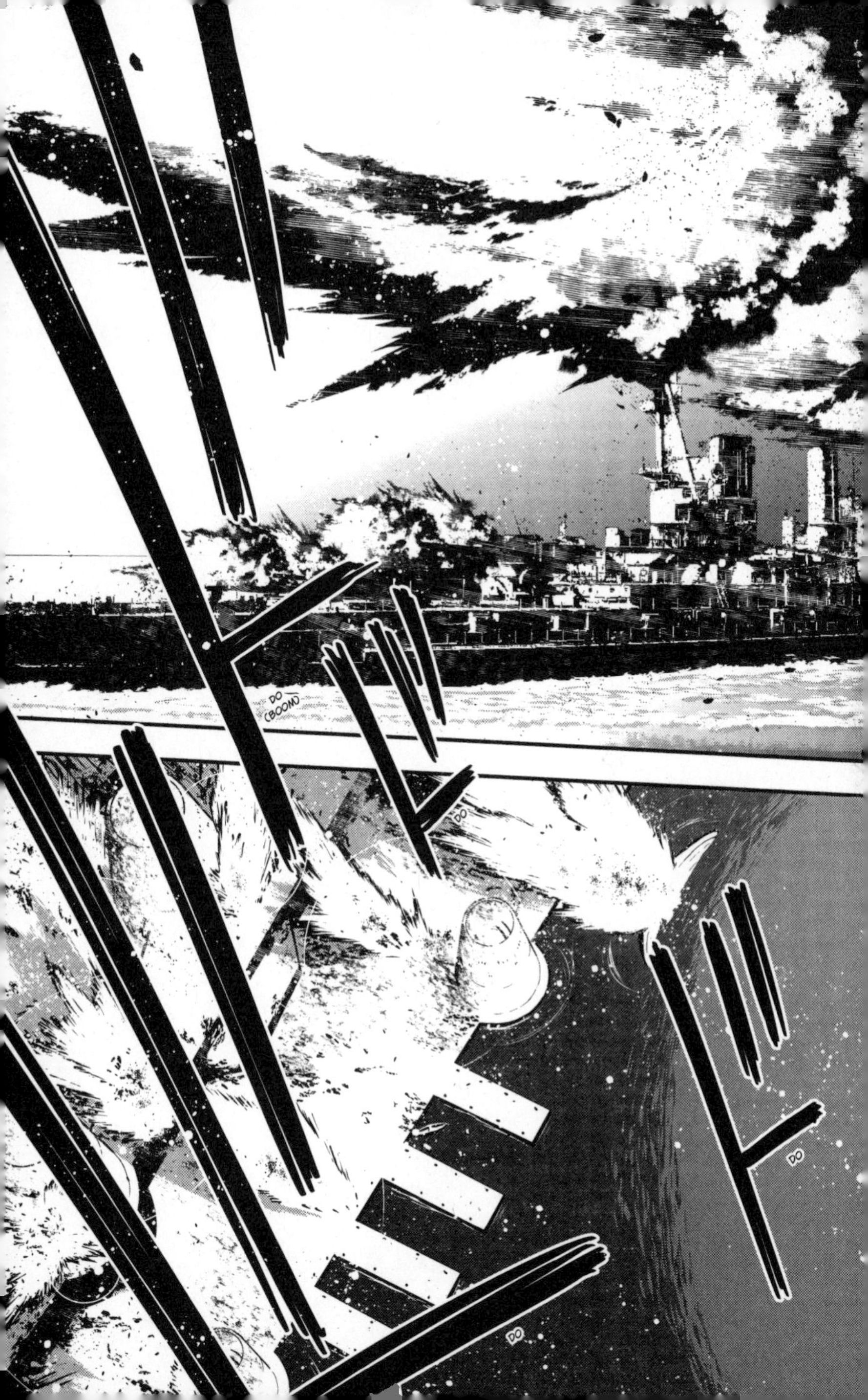
DO
(BOOM)
DO
DO
DO

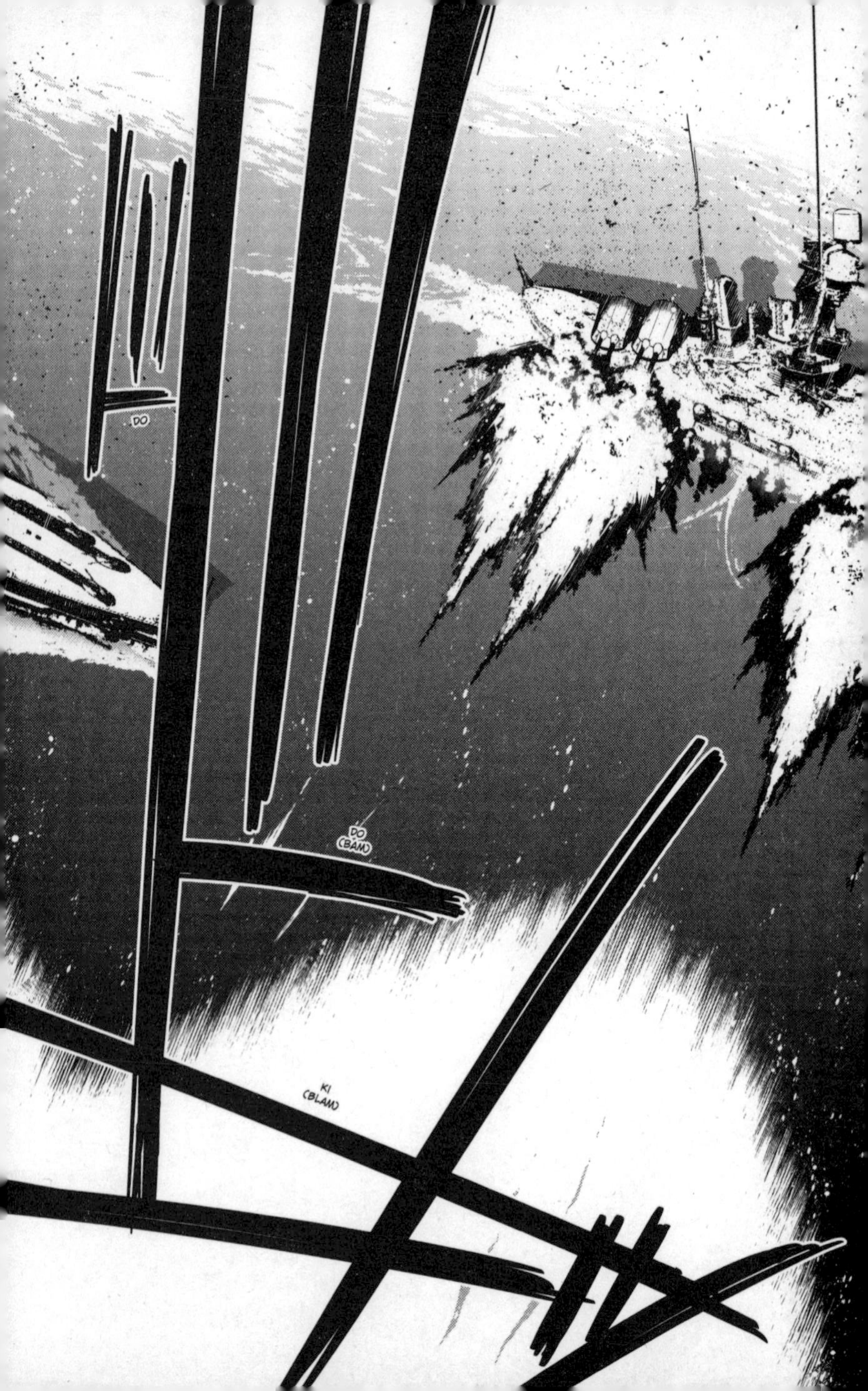
DO
DO
(BAM)
KI
(BLAM)

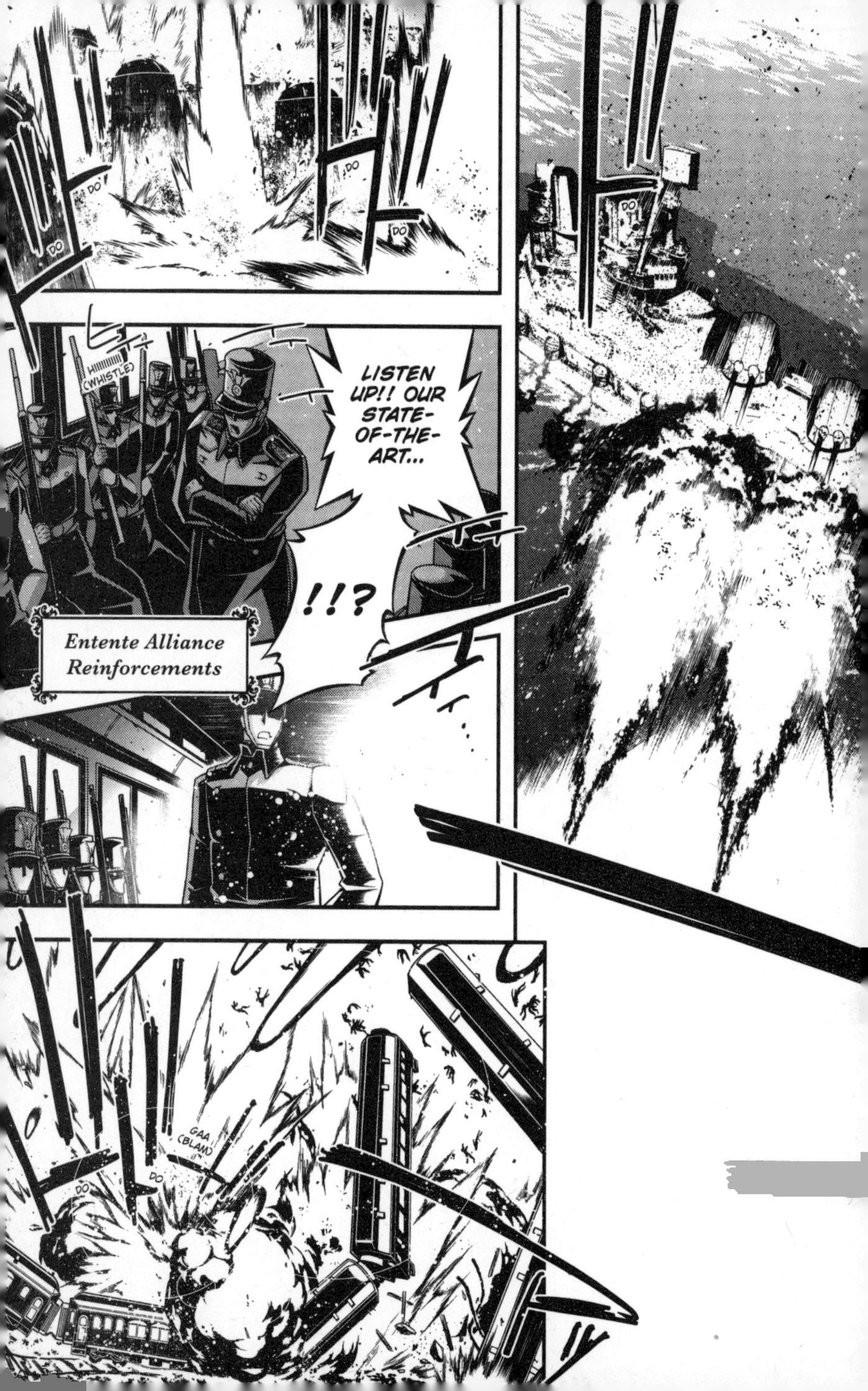
DO
DO
DO
DO
DO
LISTEN UP!! OUR STATE-OF-THE-ART...
HIIIII (WHISTLE)
!!?
Entente Alliance Reinforcements
GAA (BLAM)
DO
DO

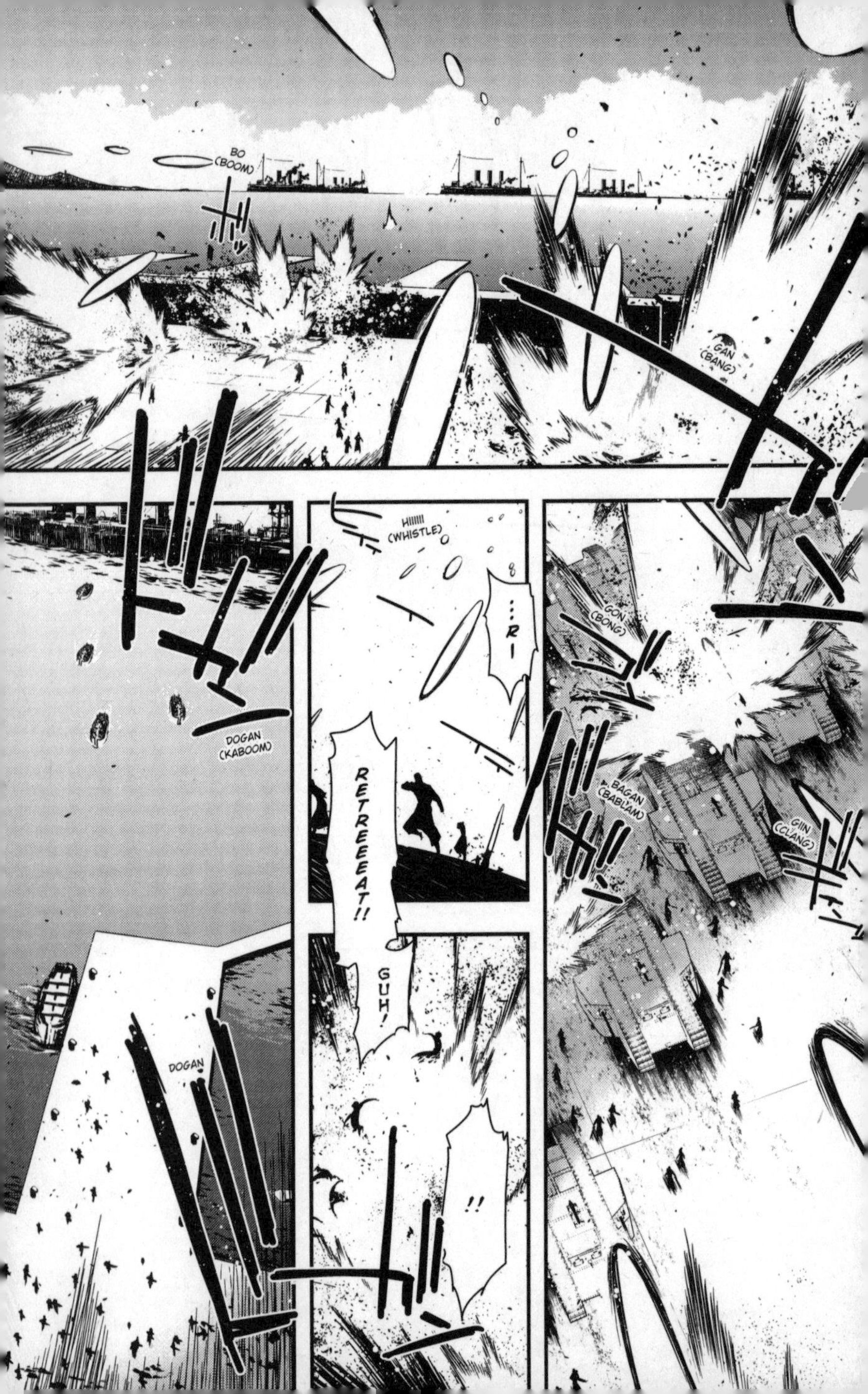
GAN (BANG)
BO (BOOM)
GON (BONG)
BAGAN (BABLAM)
GIIN (CLANG)
HIIIII (WHISTLE)
...RI
RETREEEAT!!
GUH!
!!
DOGAN (KABOOM)
DOGAN

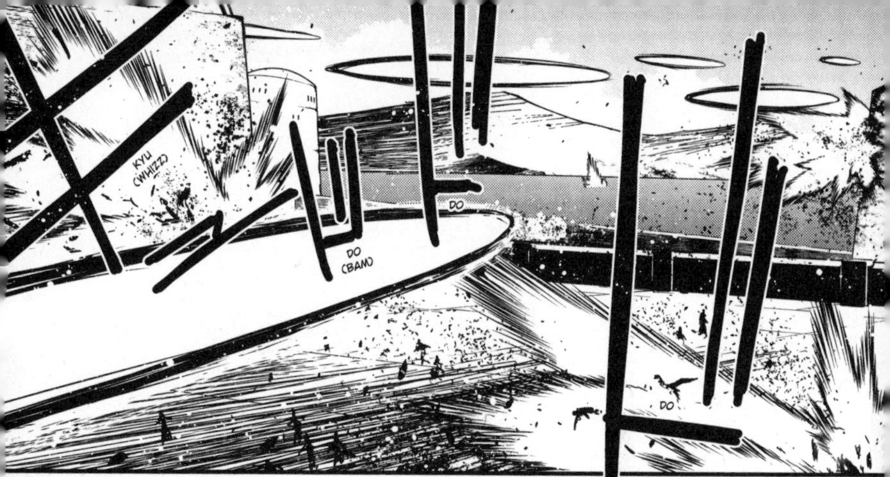
DO
DO
DO
(BAM)
KYU
(WHIZZ)
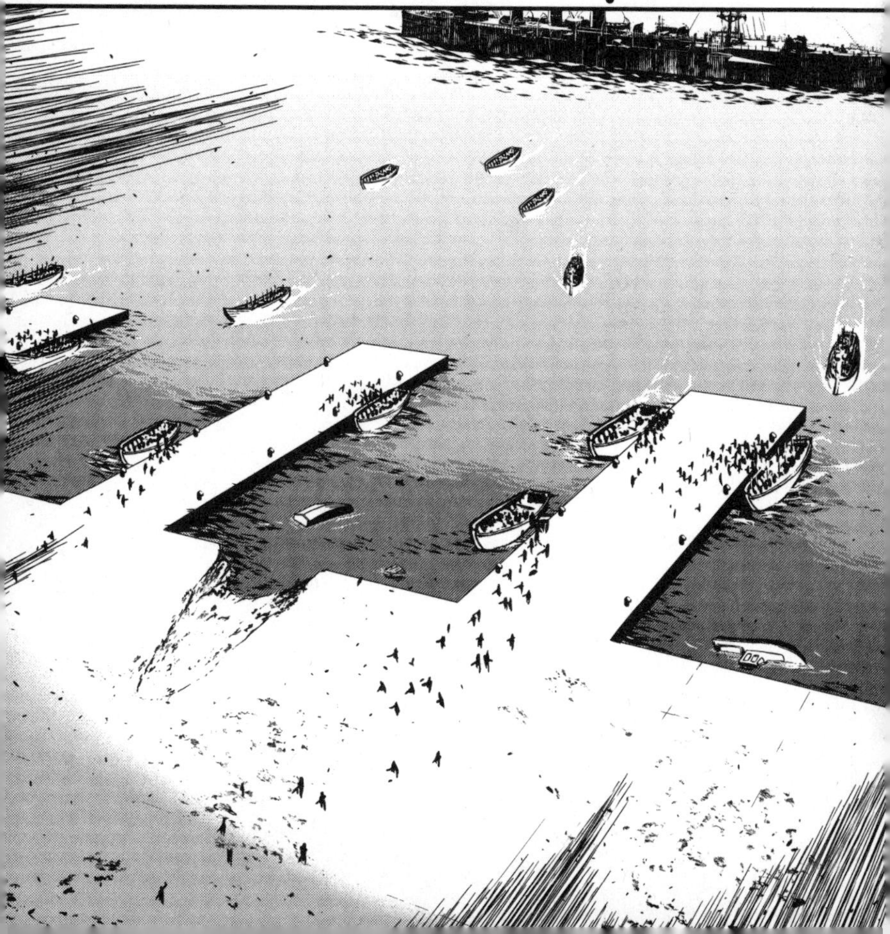

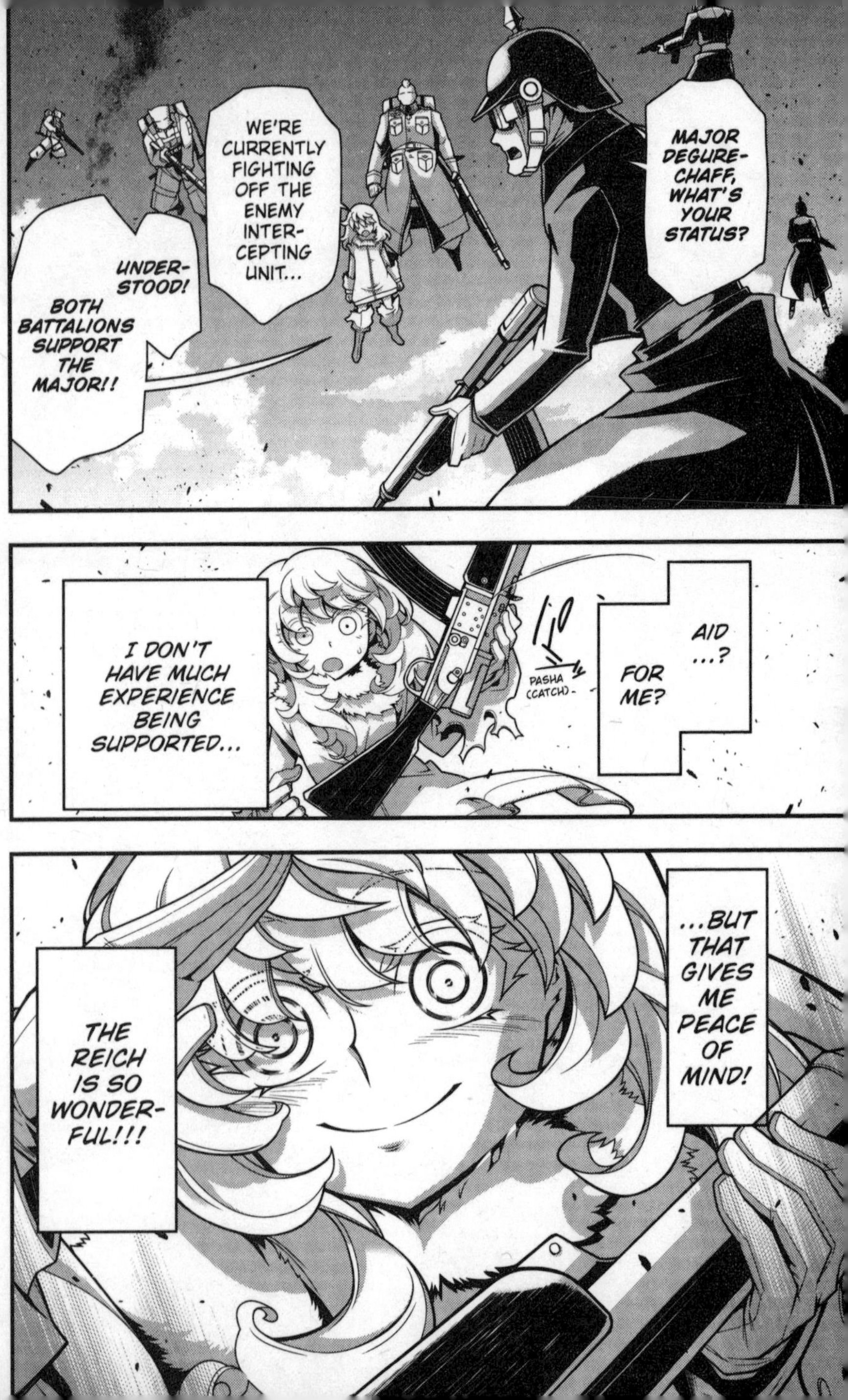
MAJOR DEGURECHAFF, WHAT'S YOUR STATUS?
WE'RE CURRENTLY FIGHTING OFF THE ENEMY INTERCEPTING UNIT...
UNDERSTOOD!
BOTH BATTALIONS SUPPORT THE MAJOR!!
AID ...?
FOR ME?
PASHA (CATCH)
I DON'T HAVE MUCH EXPERIENCE BEING SUPPORTED...
...BUT THAT GIVES ME PEACE OF MIND!
THE REICH IS SO WONDERFUL!!!

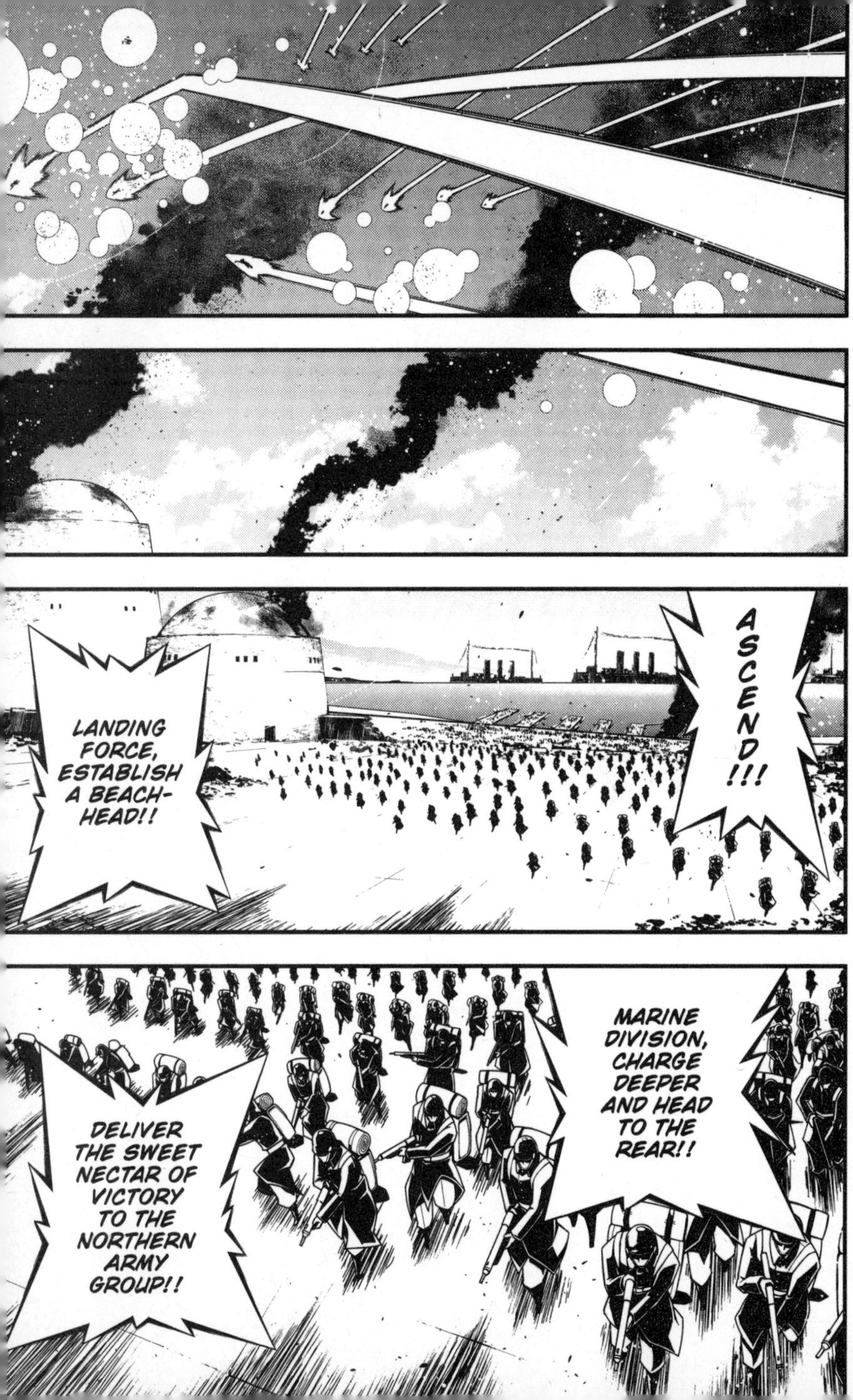
ASCEND!!!
LANDING FORCE, ESTABLISH A BEACH-HEAD!!
MARINE DIVISION, CHARGE DEEPER AND HEAD TO THE REAR!!
DELIVER THE SWEET NECTAR OF VICTORY TO THE NORTHERN ARMY GROUP!!

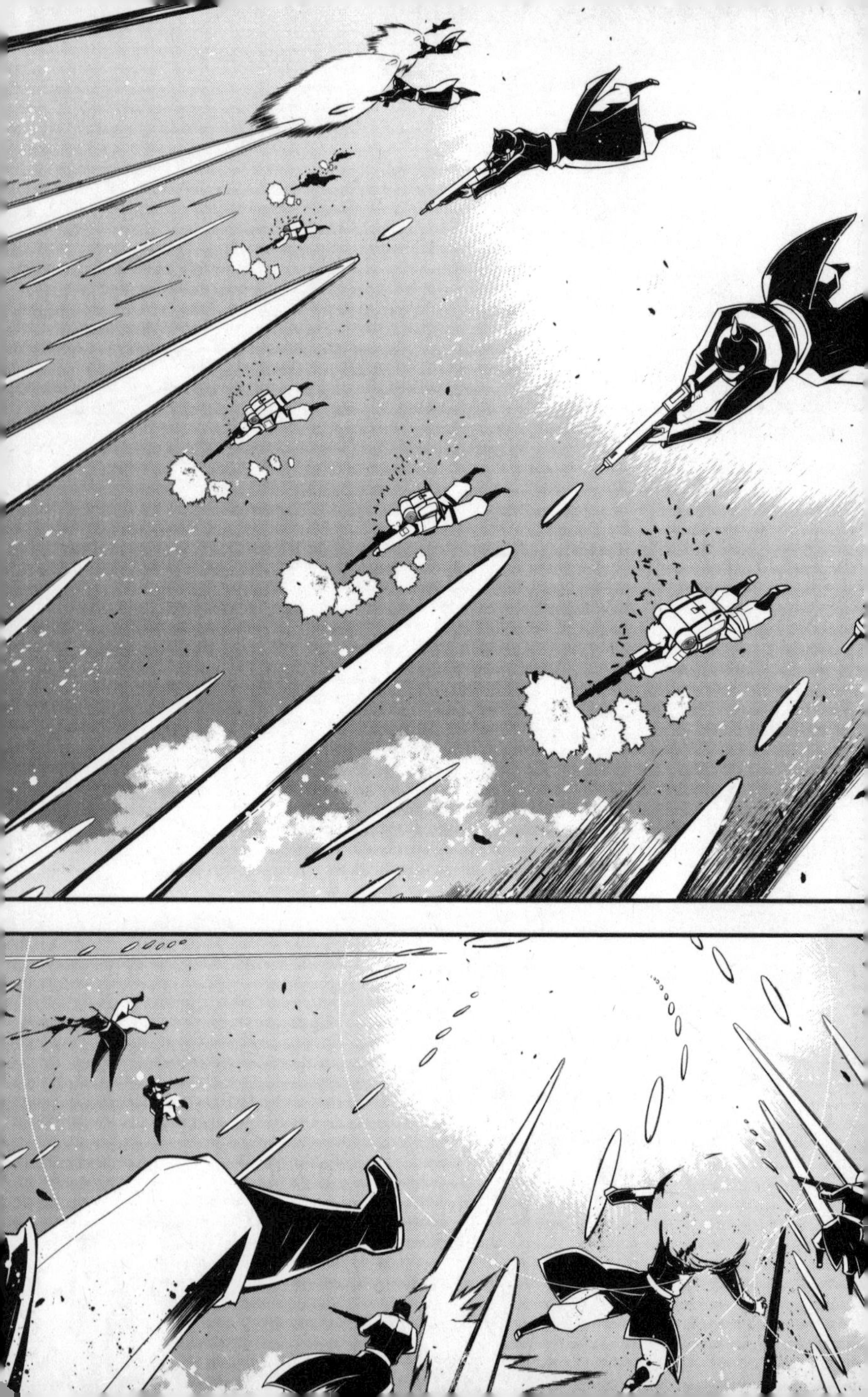

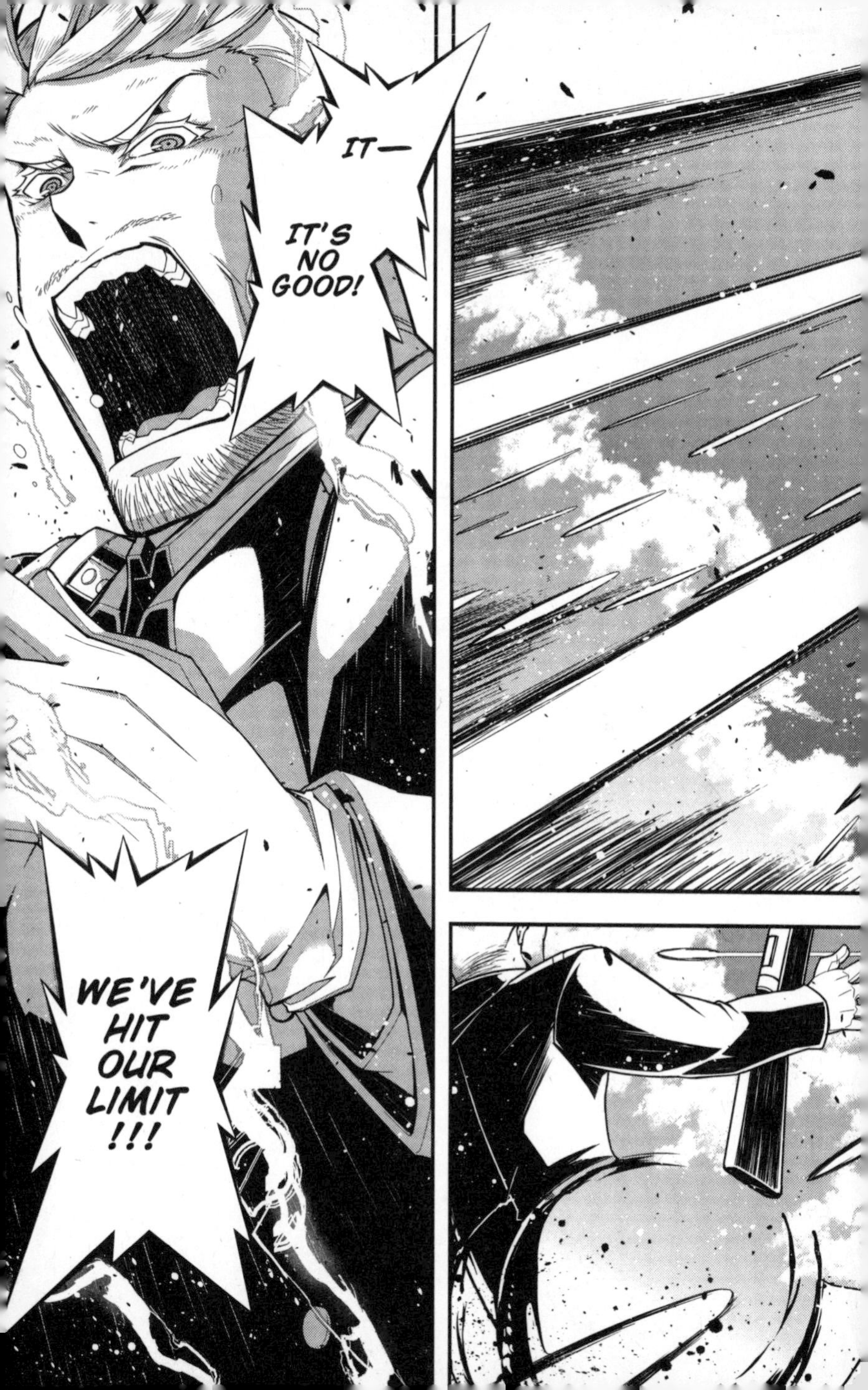
IT—
IT'S NO GOOD!
WE'VE HIT OUR LIMIT!!!

ド゛ル゛…
DODOON
(KABOOM)

オ゛ン

ド゛ォ…
DOON
(BOOM)

Regadonia Entente Alliance Territory
Near Hemholm

Regadonia Entente Alliance
Homeland Defense Main Corps

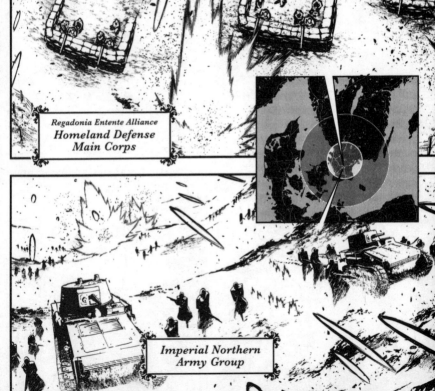

Imperial Northern Army Group

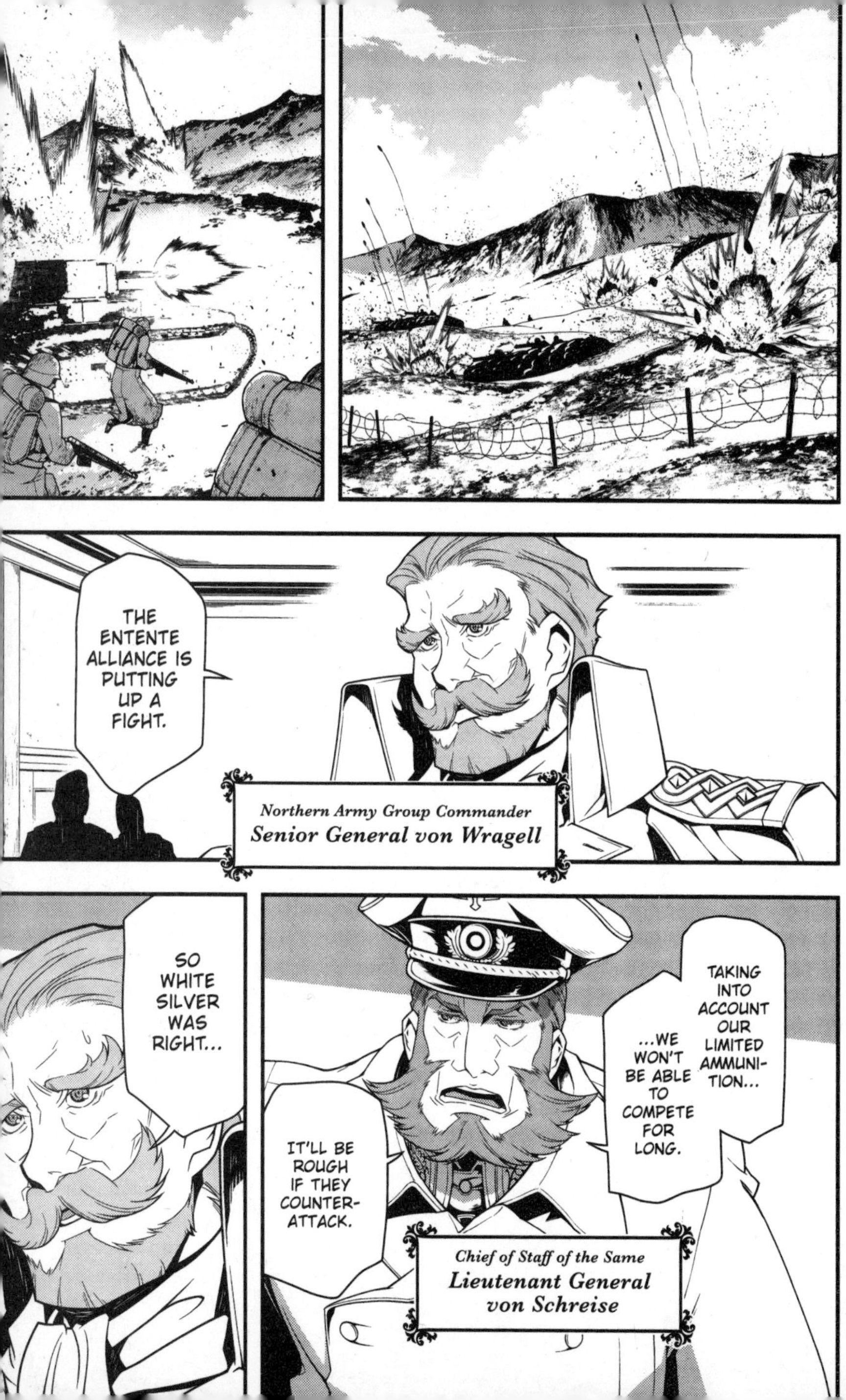
THE ENTENTE ALLIANCE IS PUTTING UP A FIGHT.
Northern Army Group Commander
Senior General von Wragell
TAKING INTO ACCOUNT OUR LIMITED AMMUNITION...
...WE WON'T BE ABLE TO COMPETE FOR LONG.
IT'LL BE ROUGH IF THEY COUNTER-ATTACK.
Chief of Staff of the Same
Lieutenant General von Schreise
SO WHITE SILVER WAS RIGHT...

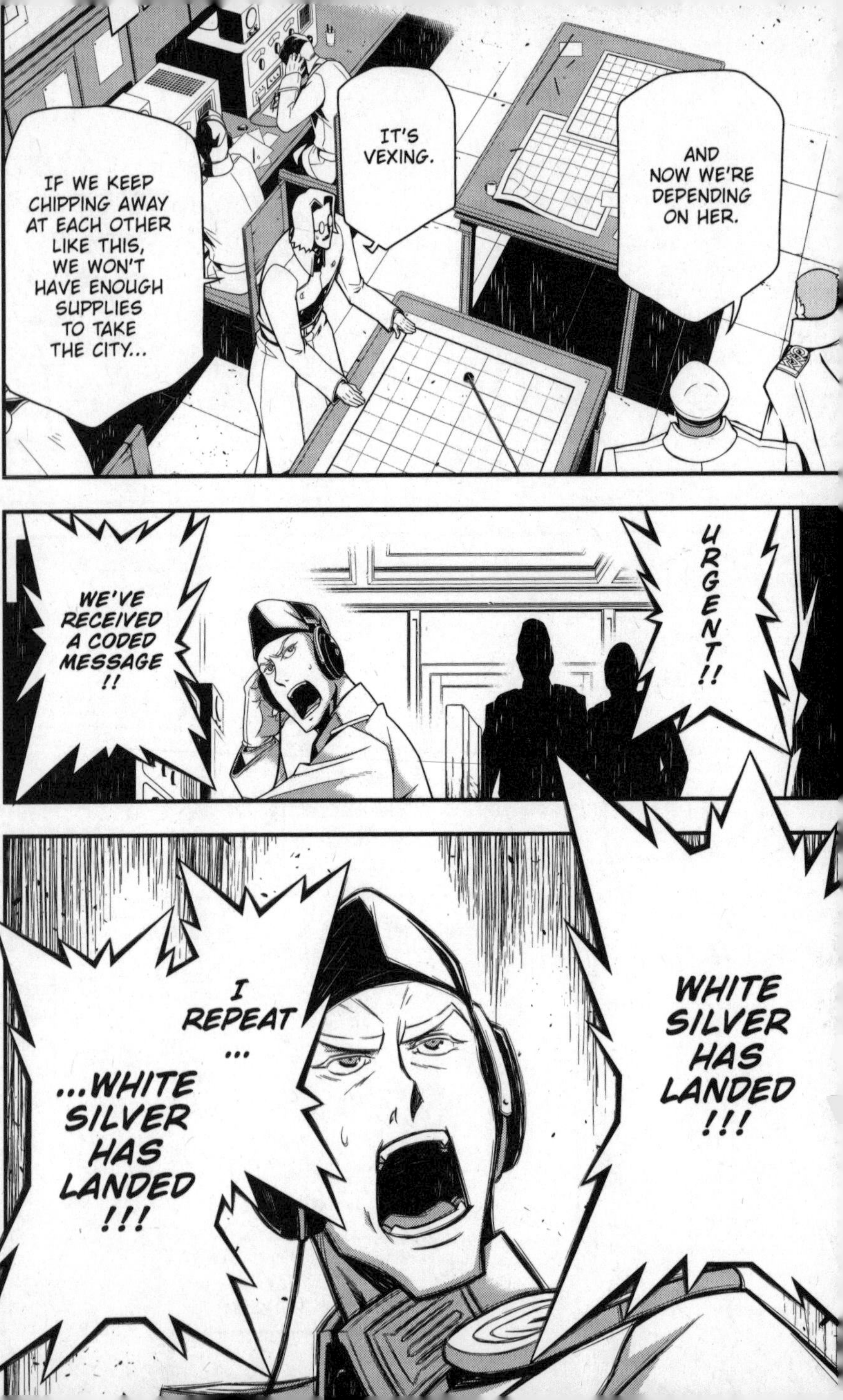
AND NOW WE'RE DEPENDING ON HER.
IT'S VEXING.
IF WE KEEP CHIPPING AWAY AT EACH OTHER LIKE THIS, WE WON'T HAVE ENOUGH SUPPLIES TO TAKE THE CITY...
URGENT!!
WE'VE RECEIVED A CODED MESSAGE!!
WHITE SILVER HAS LANDED!!!
I REPEAT... ...WHITE SILVER HAS LANDED!!!

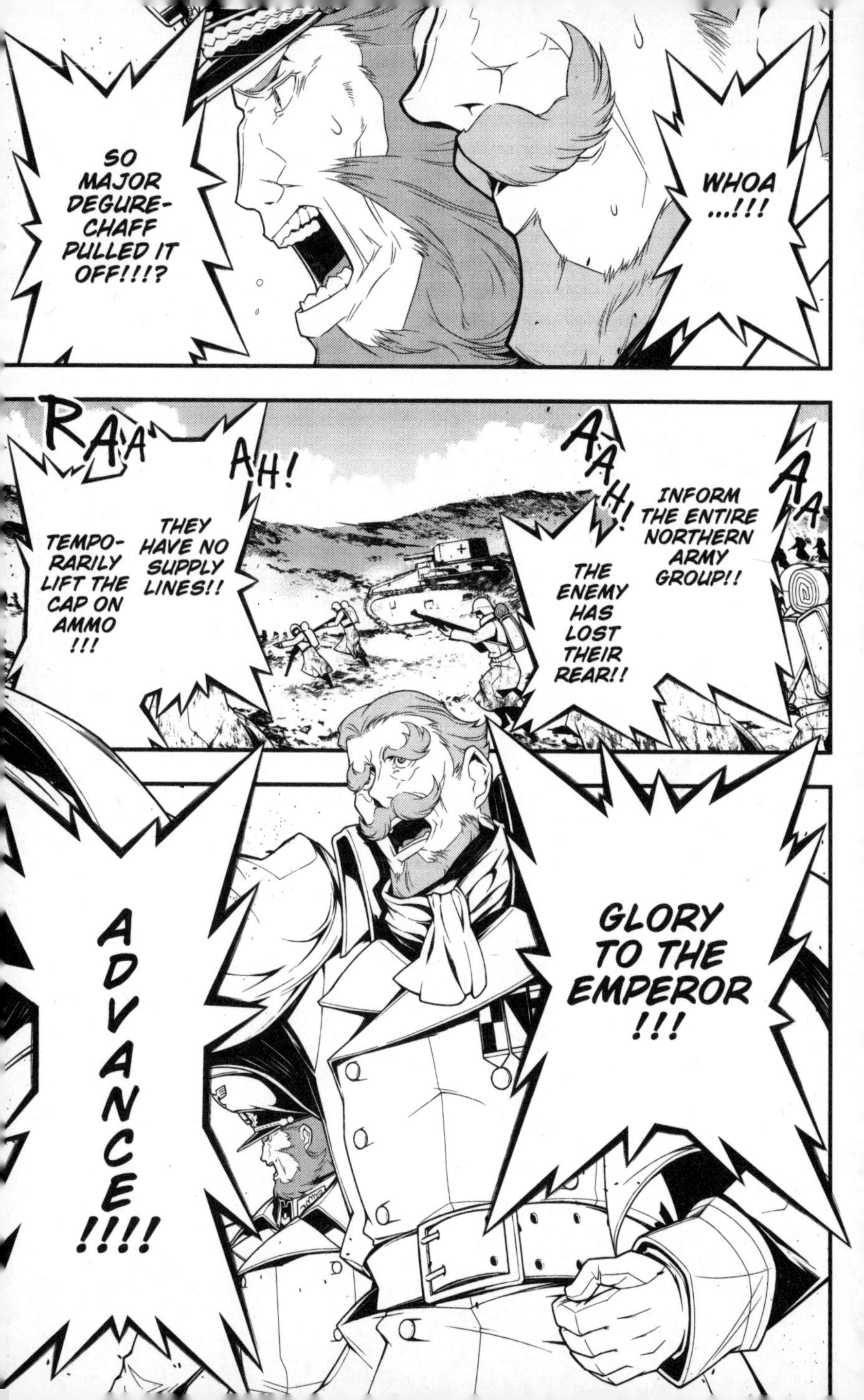
WHOA ...!!!
SO MAJOR DEGURE-CHAFF PULLED IT OFF!!!?
AAA
AAH!
INFORM THE ENTIRE NORTHERN ARMY GROUP!!
THE ENEMY HAS LOST THEIR REAR!!
AH!
THEY HAVE NO SUPPLY LINES!!
RAAA
TEMPO-RARILY LIFT THE CAP ON AMMO !!!
GLORY TO THE EMPEROR !!!
ADVANCE!!!!

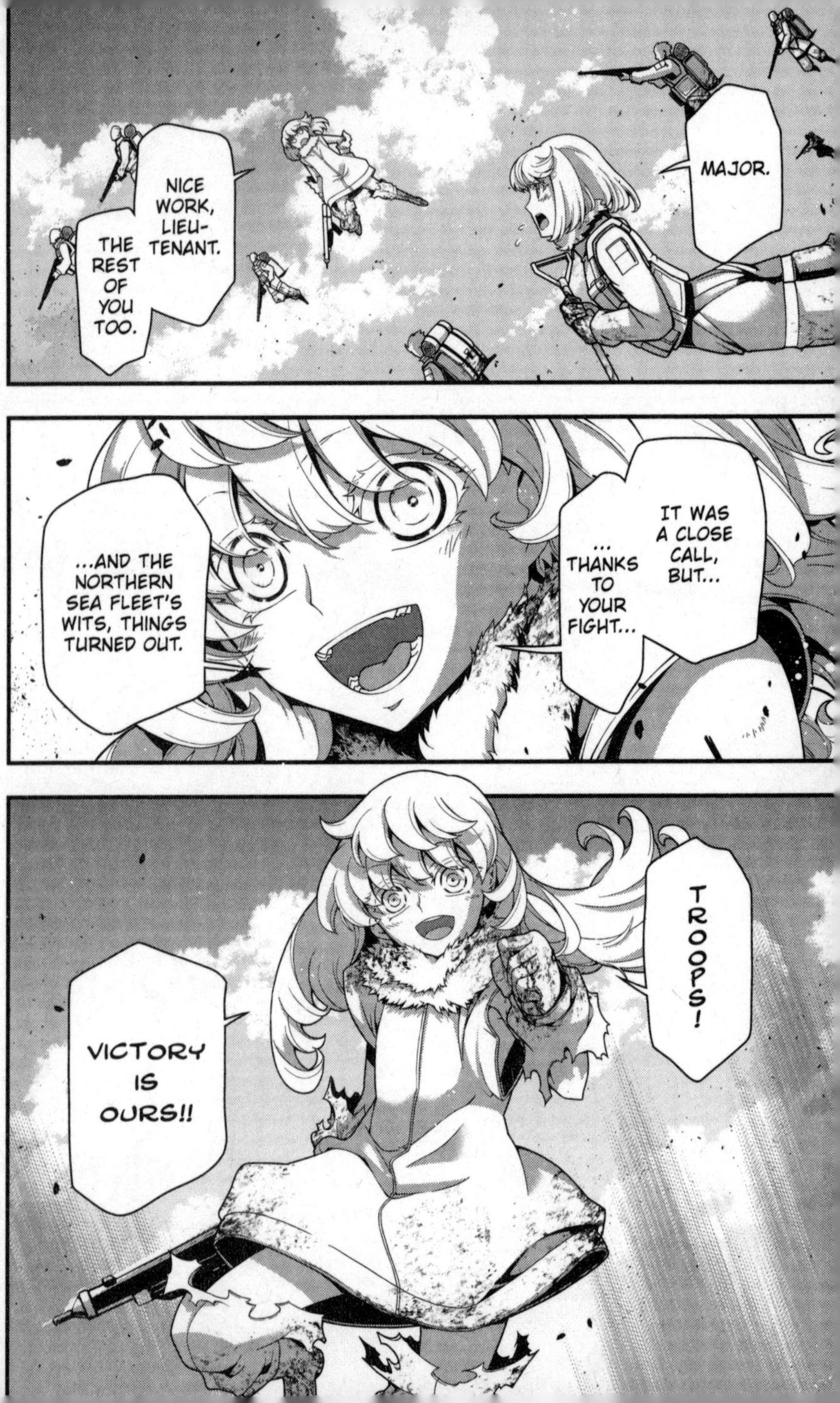
MAJOR.
NICE WORK, LIEU-TENANT.
THE REST OF YOU TOO.
IT WAS A CLOSE CALL, BUT...
...THANKS TO YOUR FIGHT...
...AND THE NORTHERN SEA FLEET'S WITS, THINGS TURNED OUT.
TROOPS!
VICTORY IS OURS!!

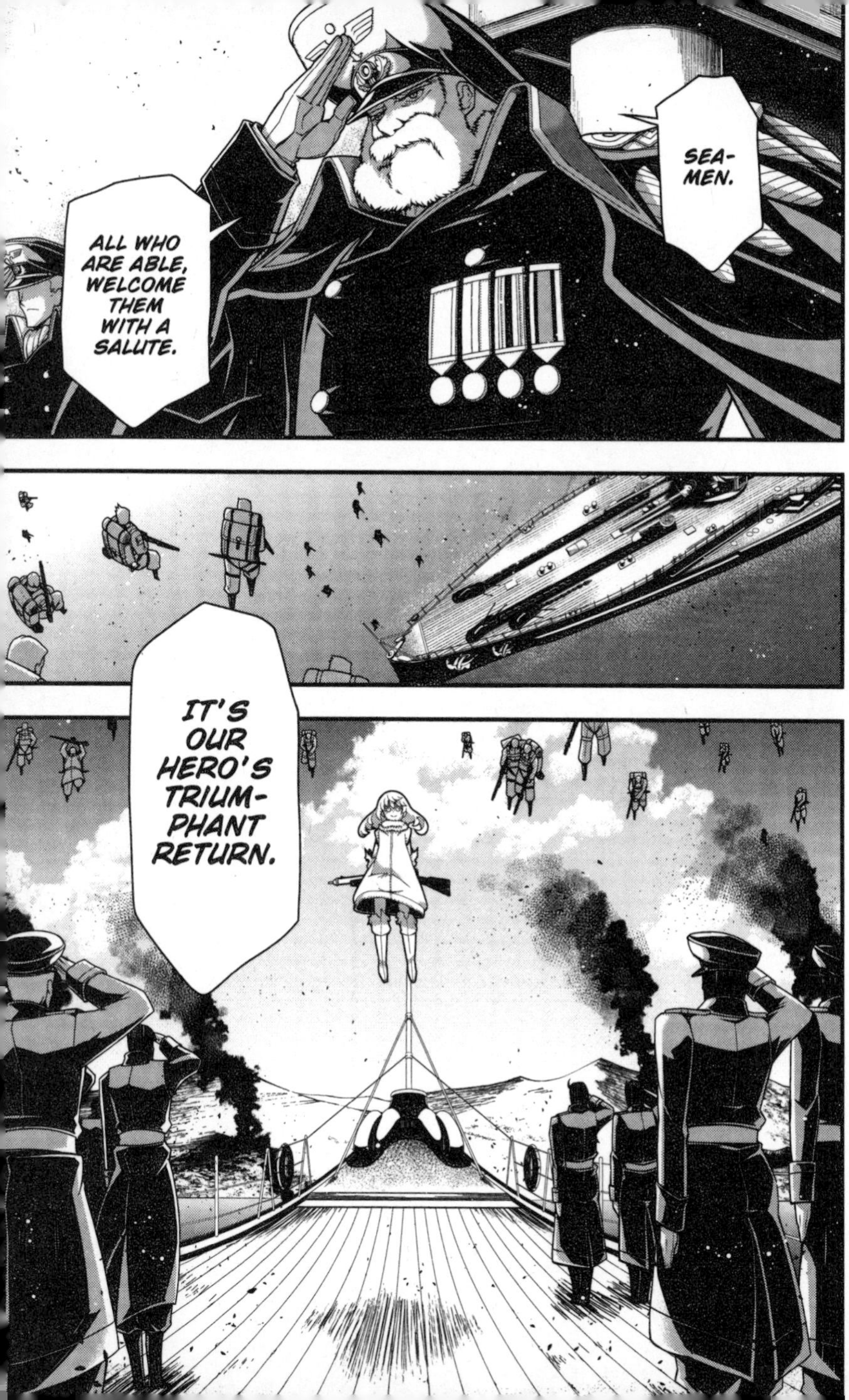
SEA-MEN.
ALL WHO ARE ABLE, WELCOME THEM WITH A SALUTE.
IT'S OUR HERO'S TRIUMPHANT RETURN.

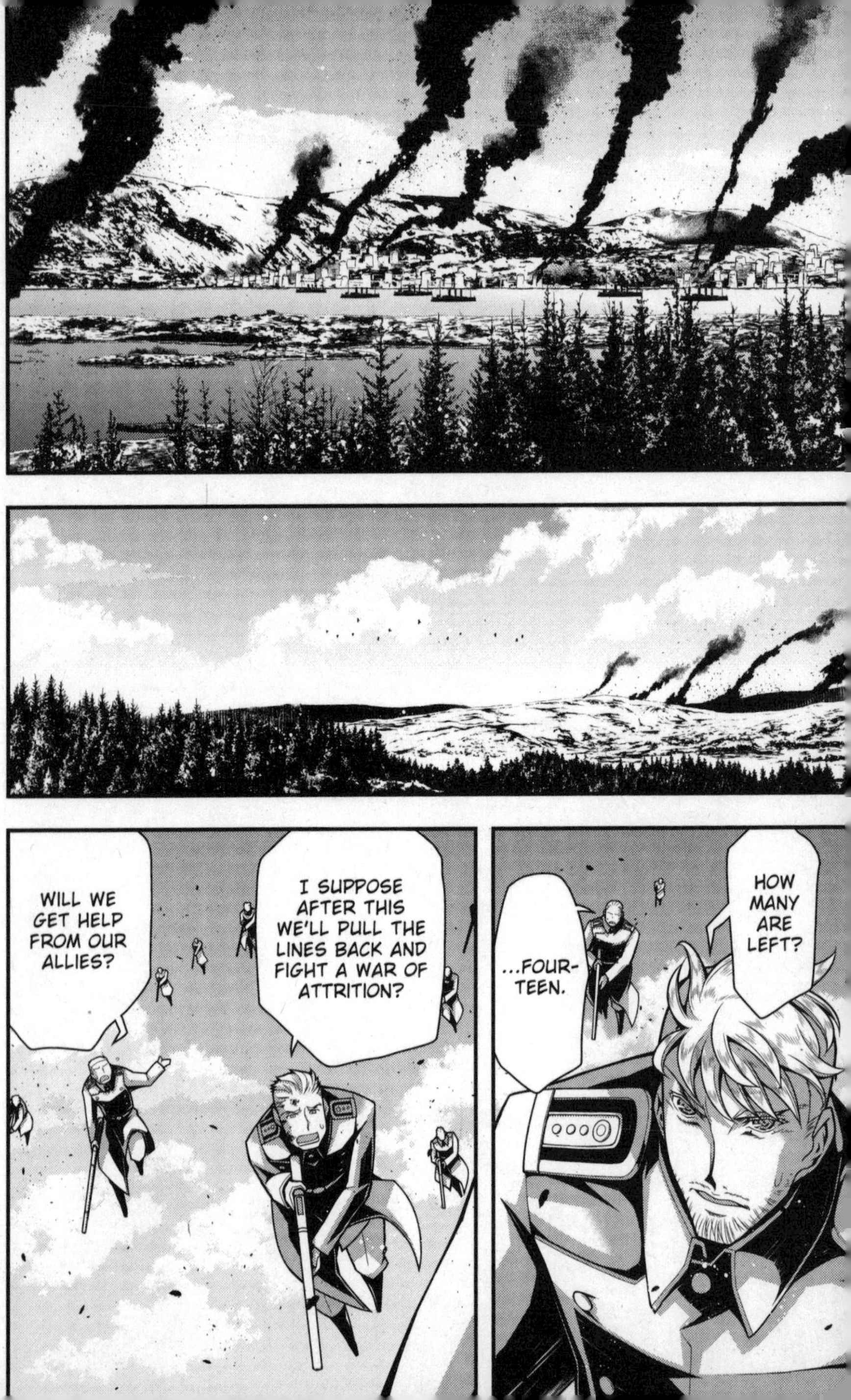
HOW MANY ARE LEFT?
...FOUR-TEEN.
I SUPPOSE AFTER THIS WE'LL PULL THE LINES BACK AND FIGHT A WAR OF ATTRITION?
WILL WE GET HELP FROM OUR ALLIES?

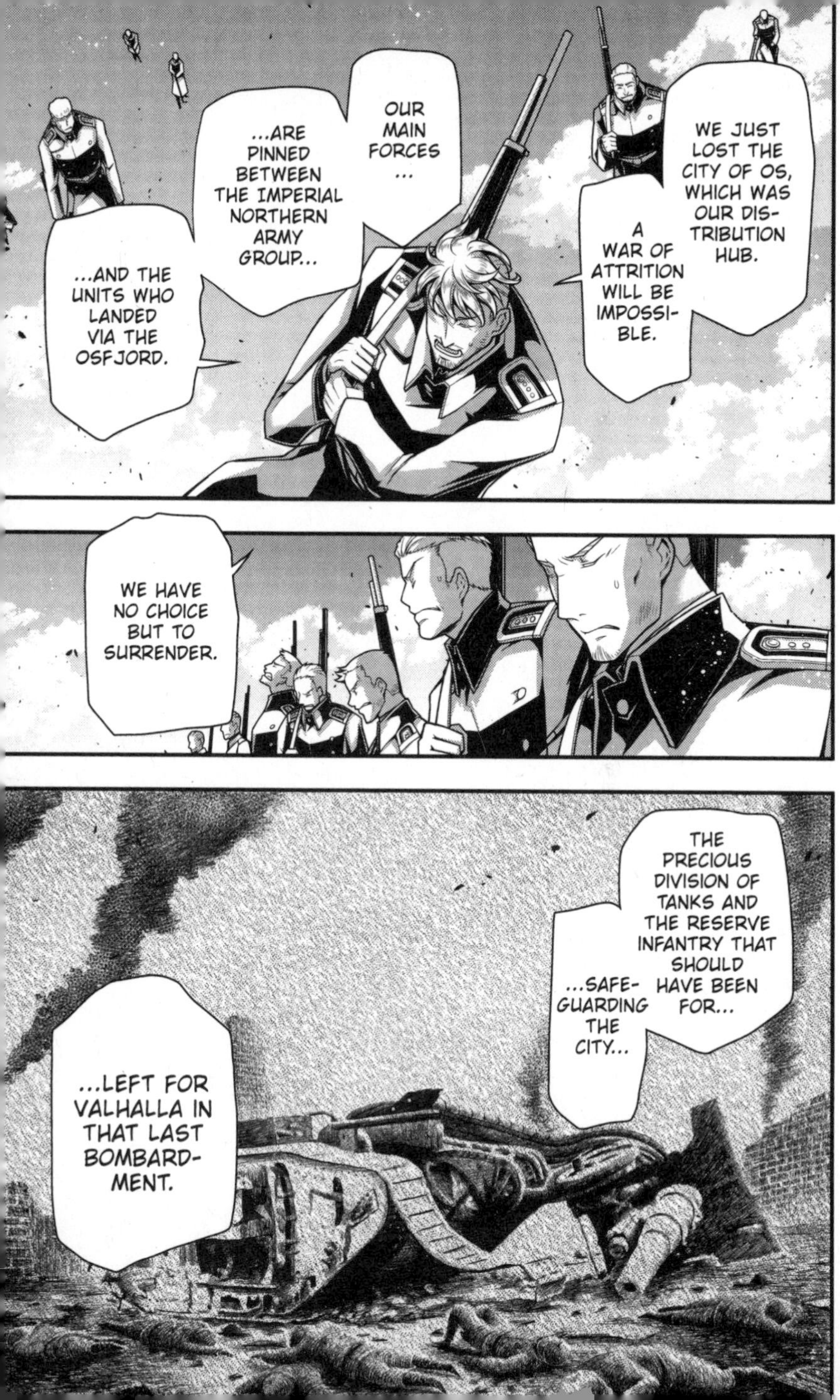
WE JUST LOST THE CITY OF OS, WHICH WAS OUR DISTRIBUTION HUB.
A WAR OF ATTRITION WILL BE IMPOSSIBLE.
OUR MAIN FORCES...
...ARE PINNED BETWEEN THE IMPERIAL NORTHERN ARMY GROUP...
...AND THE UNITS WHO LANDED VIA THE OSFJORD.
WE HAVE NO CHOICE BUT TO SURRENDER.
THE PRECIOUS DIVISION OF TANKS AND THE RESERVE INFANTRY THAT SHOULD HAVE BEEN FOR...
...SAFEGUARDING THE CITY...
...LEFT FOR VALHALLA IN THAT LAST BOMBARDMENT.

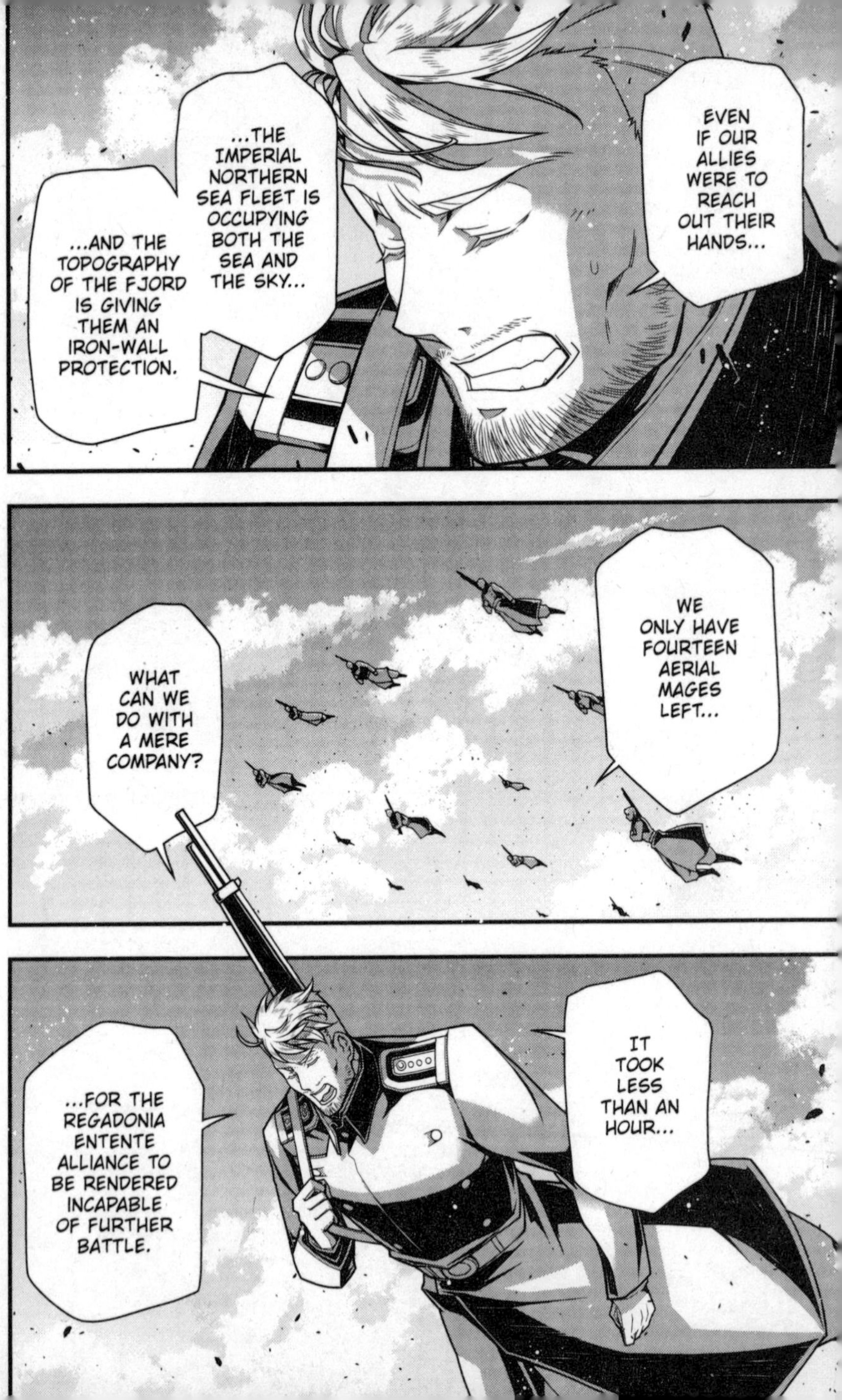
EVEN IF OUR ALLIES WERE TO REACH OUT THEIR HANDS...
...THE IMPERIAL NORTHERN SEA FLEET IS OCCUPYING BOTH THE SEA AND THE SKY...
...AND THE TOPOGRAPHY OF THE FJORD IS GIVING THEM AN IRON-WALL PROTECTION.
WE ONLY HAVE FOURTEEN AERIAL MAGES LEFT...
WHAT CAN WE DO WITH A MERE COMPANY?
IT TOOK LESS THAN AN HOUR...
...FOR THE REGADONIA ENTENTE ALLIANCE TO BE RENDERED INCAPABLE OF FURTHER BATTLE.

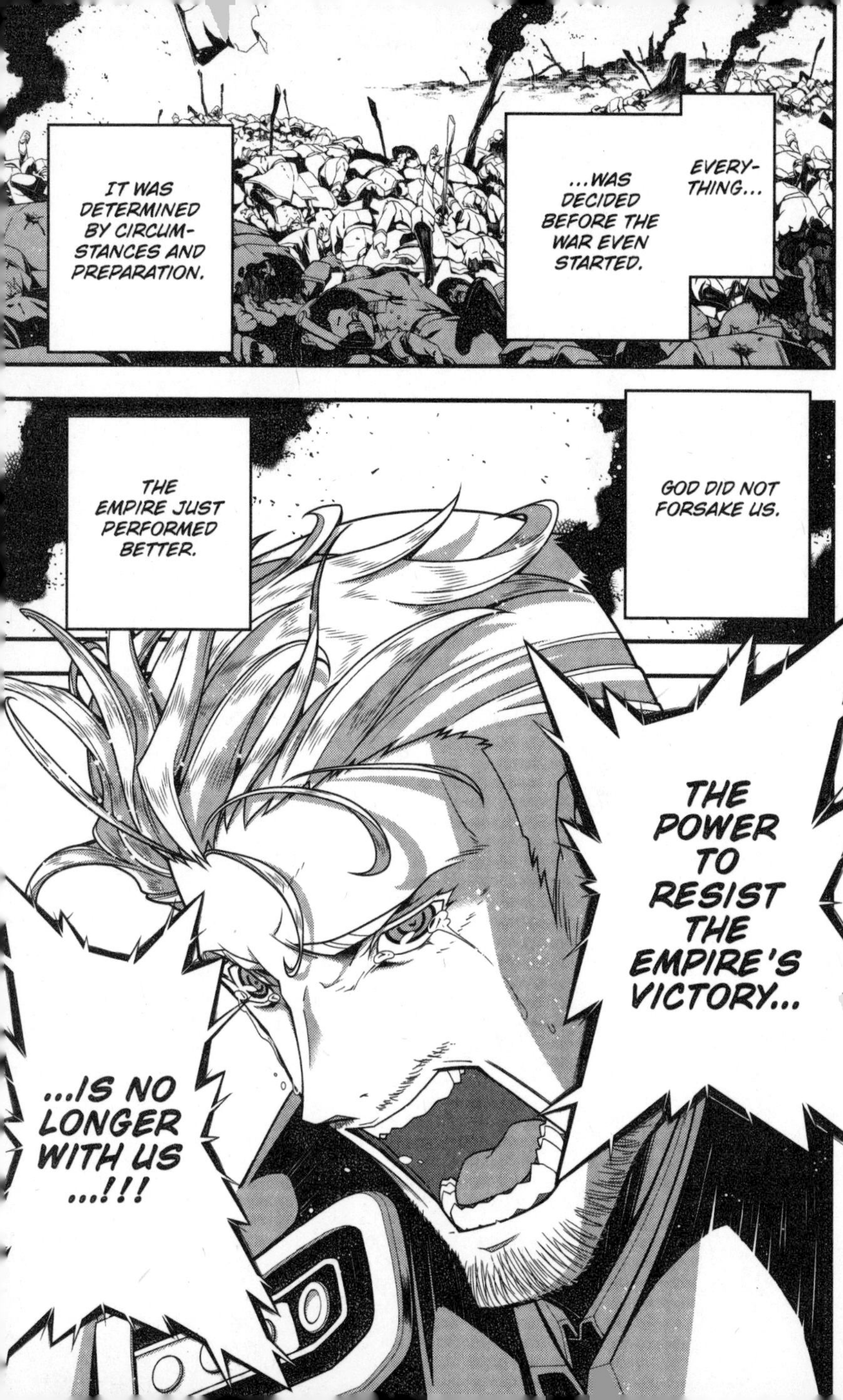
EVERYTHING...
...WAS DECIDED BEFORE THE WAR EVEN STARTED.
IT WAS DETERMINED BY CIRCUMSTANCES AND PREPARATION.
GOD DID NOT FORSAKE US.
THE EMPIRE JUST PERFORMED BETTER.
THE POWER TO RESIST THE EMPIRE'S VICTORY...
...IS NO LONGER WITH US ...!!!

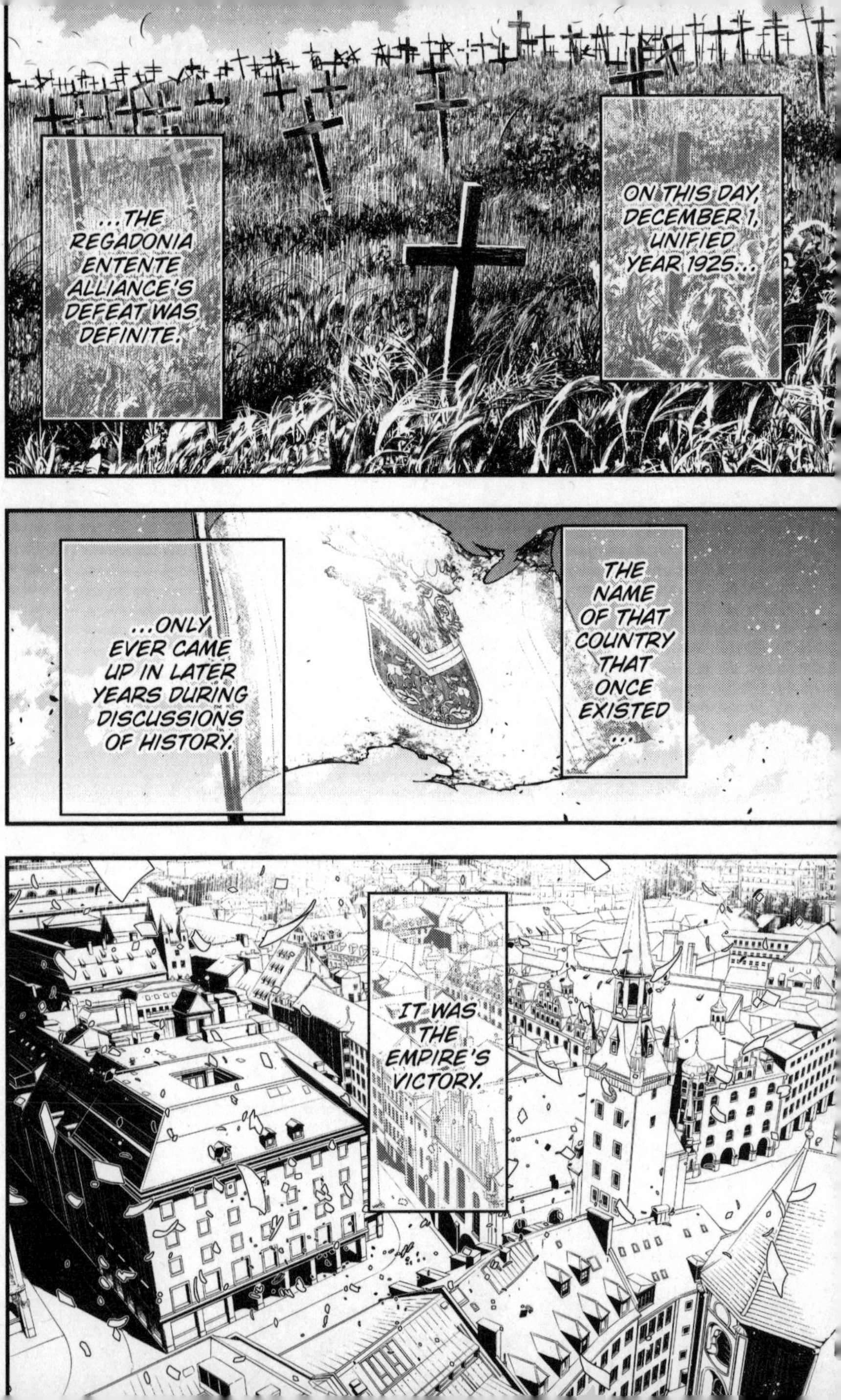
ON THIS DAY, DECEMBER 1, UNIFIED YEAR 1925...
...THE REGADONIA ENTENTE ALLIANCE'S DEFEAT WAS DEFINITE.
THE NAME OF THAT COUNTRY THAT ONCE EXISTED...
...ONLY EVER CAME UP IN LATER YEARS DURING DISCUSSIONS OF HISTORY.
IT WAS THE EMPIRE'S VICTORY.

December 4, Unified Year 1925
The Albion Commonwealth

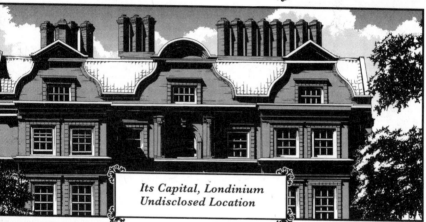

Its Capital, Londinium
Undisclosed Location

Commonwealth Intelligence
Major General Habergram

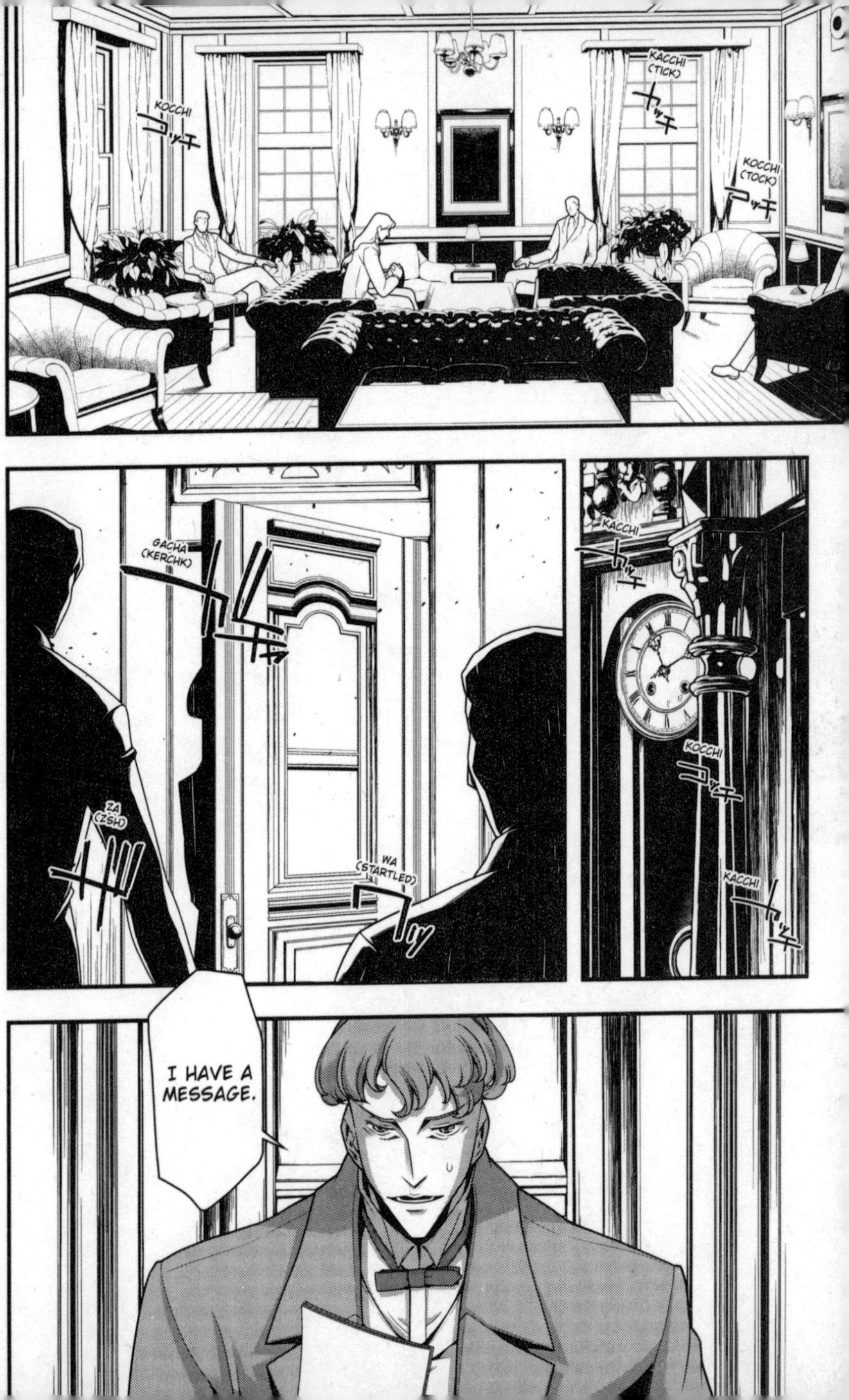
KACCHI (TICK)
KOCCHI (TOCK)
KOCCHI
KACCHI
KOCCHI
KACCHI
GACHA (KERCHK)
WA (STARTLED)
ZA (ZSH)
I HAVE A MESSAGE.

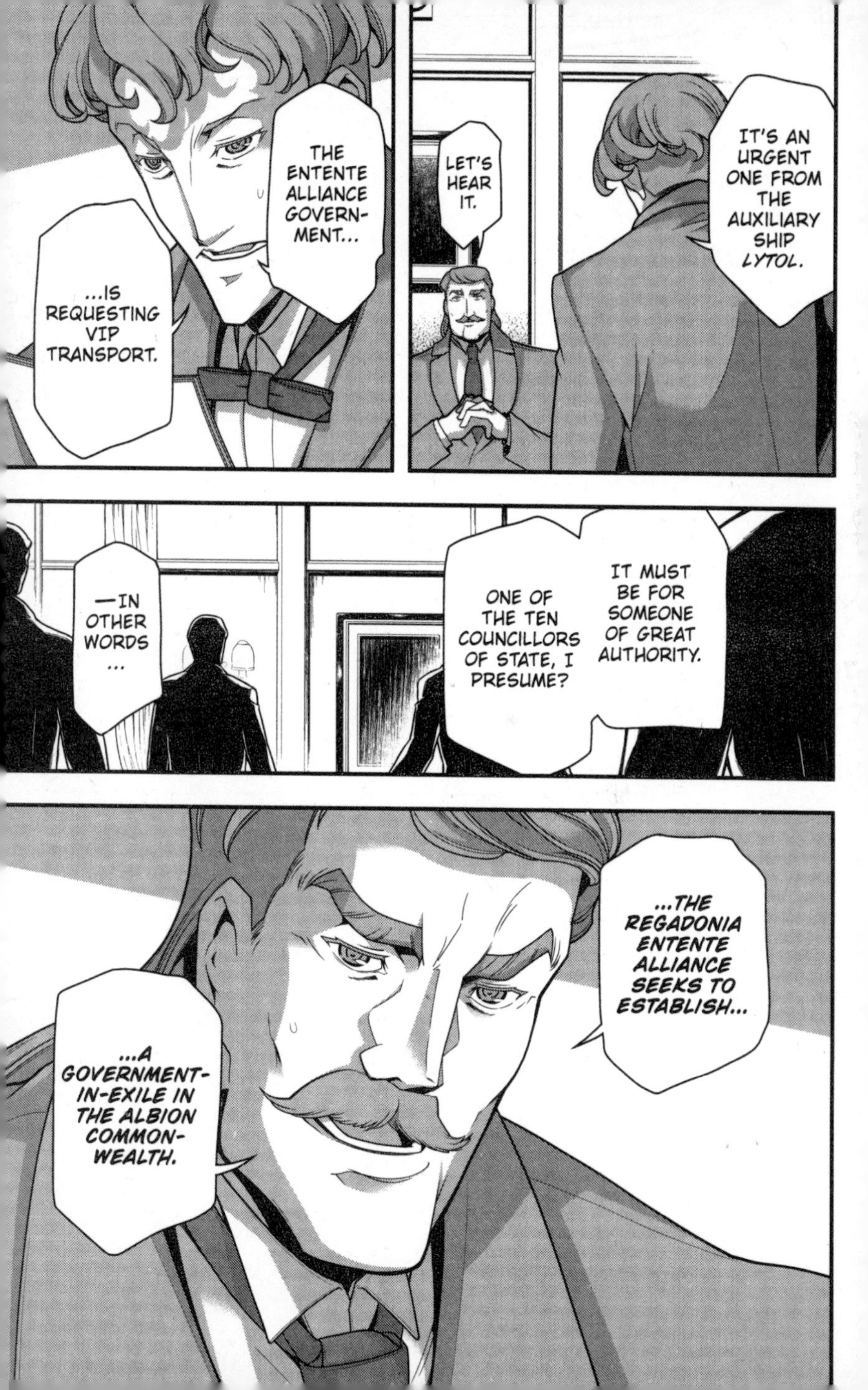
IT'S AN URGENT ONE FROM THE AUXILIARY SHIP *LYTOL*.
LET'S HEAR IT.
THE ENTENTE ALLIANCE GOVERN-MENT...
...IS REQUESTING VIP TRANSPORT.
IT MUST BE FOR SOMEONE OF GREAT AUTHORITY.
ONE OF THE TEN COUNCILLORS OF STATE, I PRESUME?
—IN OTHER WORDS...
...THE REGADONIA ENTENTE ALLIANCE SEEKS TO ESTABLISH...
...A GOVERNMENT-IN-EXILE IN THE ALBION COMMON-WEALTH.

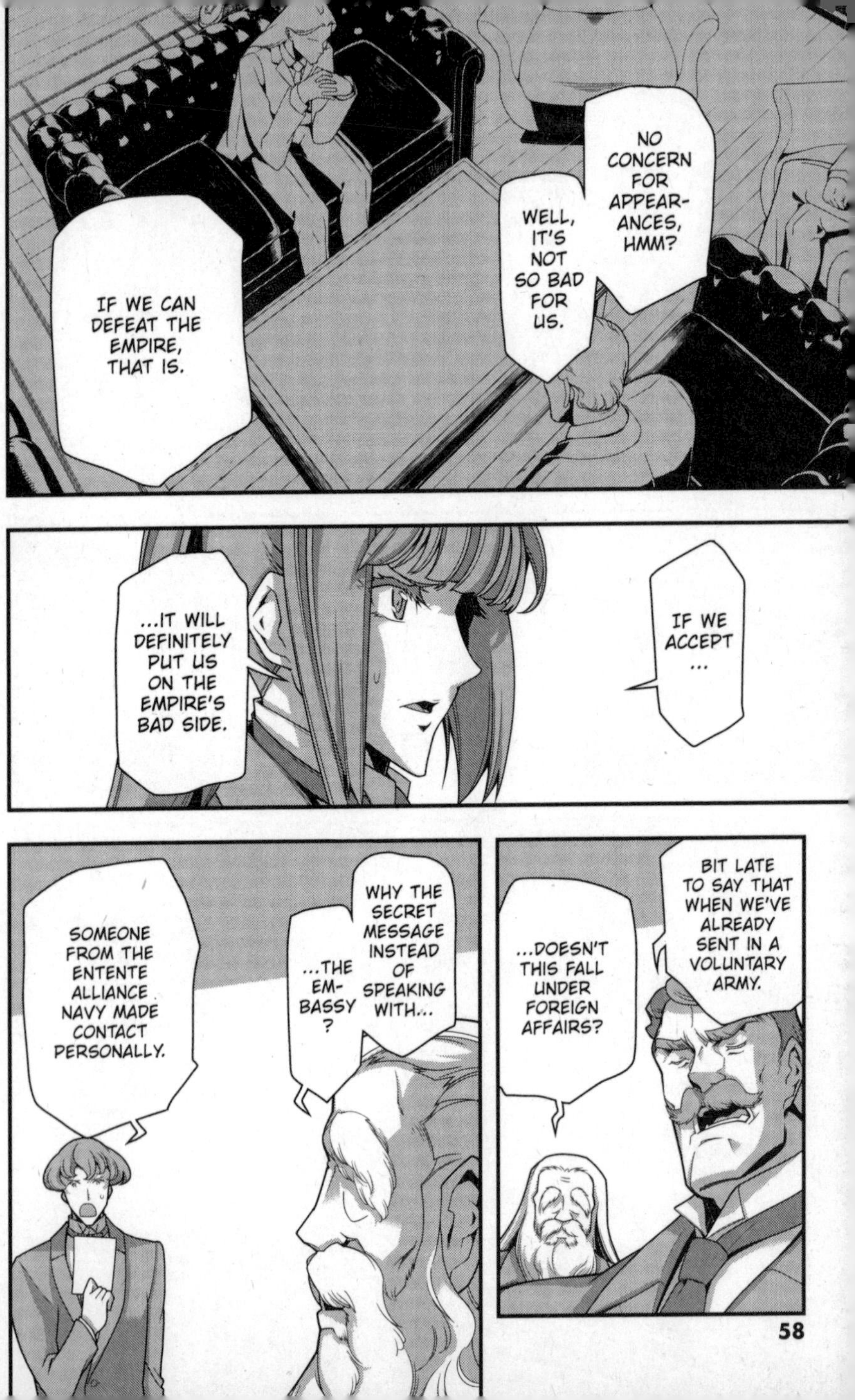
NO CONCERN FOR APPEARANCES, HMM?
WELL, IT'S NOT SO BAD FOR US.
IF WE CAN DEFEAT THE EMPIRE, THAT IS.
IF WE ACCEPT...
...IT WILL DEFINITELY PUT US ON THE EMPIRE'S BAD SIDE.
BIT LATE TO SAY THAT WHEN WE'VE ALREADY SENT IN A VOLUNTARY ARMY.
...DOESN'T THIS FALL UNDER FOREIGN AFFAIRS?
WHY THE SECRET MESSAGE INSTEAD OF SPEAKING WITH...
...THE EMBASSY?
SOMEONE FROM THE ENTENTE ALLIANCE NAVY MADE CONTACT PERSONALLY.

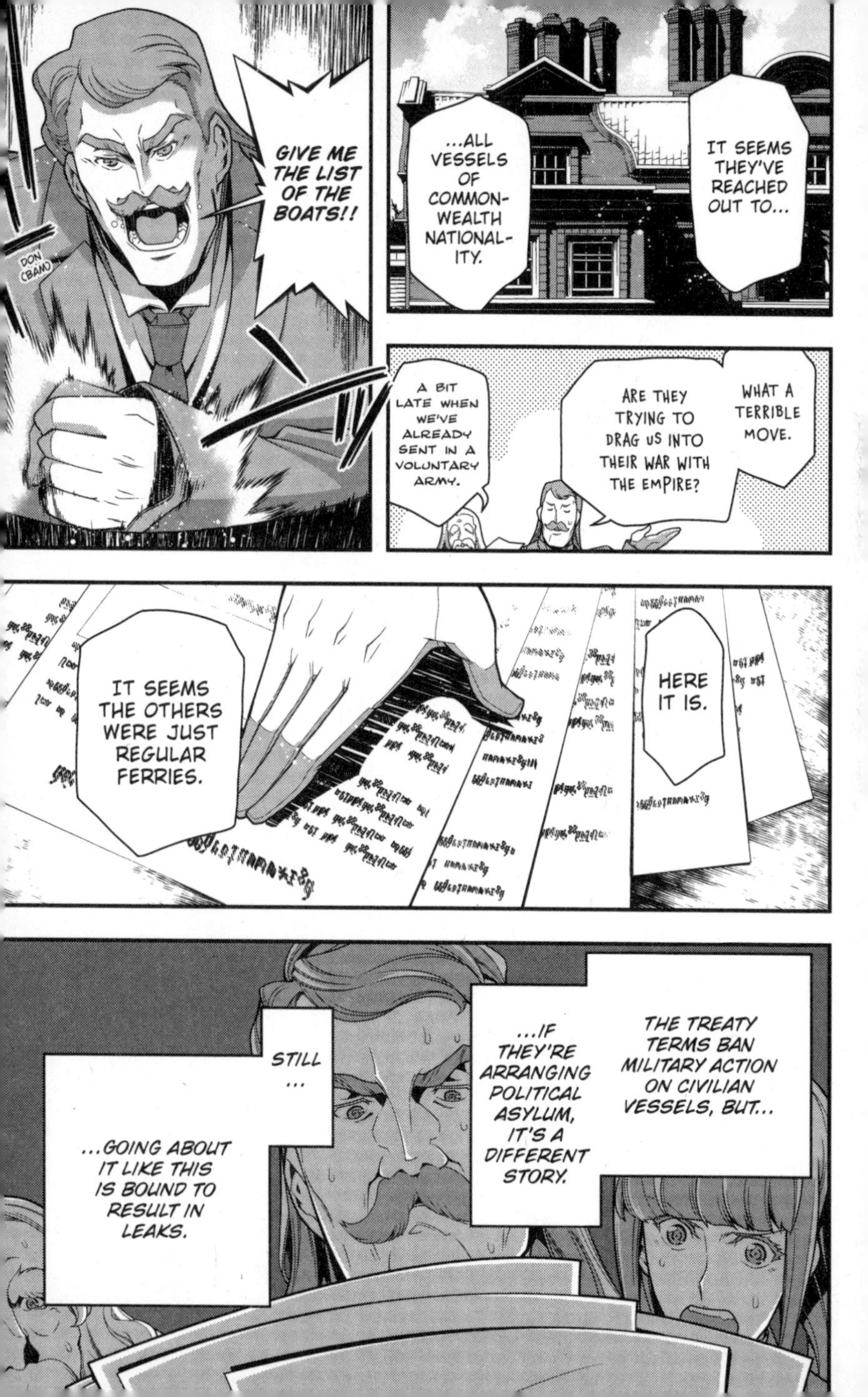
IT SEEMS THEY'VE REACHED OUT TO...
...ALL VESSELS OF COMMONWEALTH NATIONALITY.
WHAT A TERRIBLE MOVE.
ARE THEY TRYING TO DRAG US INTO THEIR WAR WITH THE EMPIRE?
A BIT LATE WHEN WE'VE ALREADY SENT IN A VOLUNTARY ARMY.
GIVE ME THE LIST OF THE BOATS!!
DON (BAM)
HERE IT IS.
IT SEEMS THE OTHERS WERE JUST REGULAR FERRIES.
THE TREATY TERMS BAN MILITARY ACTION ON CIVILIAN VESSELS, BUT...
...IF THEY'RE ARRANGING POLITICAL ASYLUM, IT'S A DIFFERENT STORY.
STILL...
...GOING ABOUT IT LIKE THIS IS BOUND TO RESULT IN LEAKS.

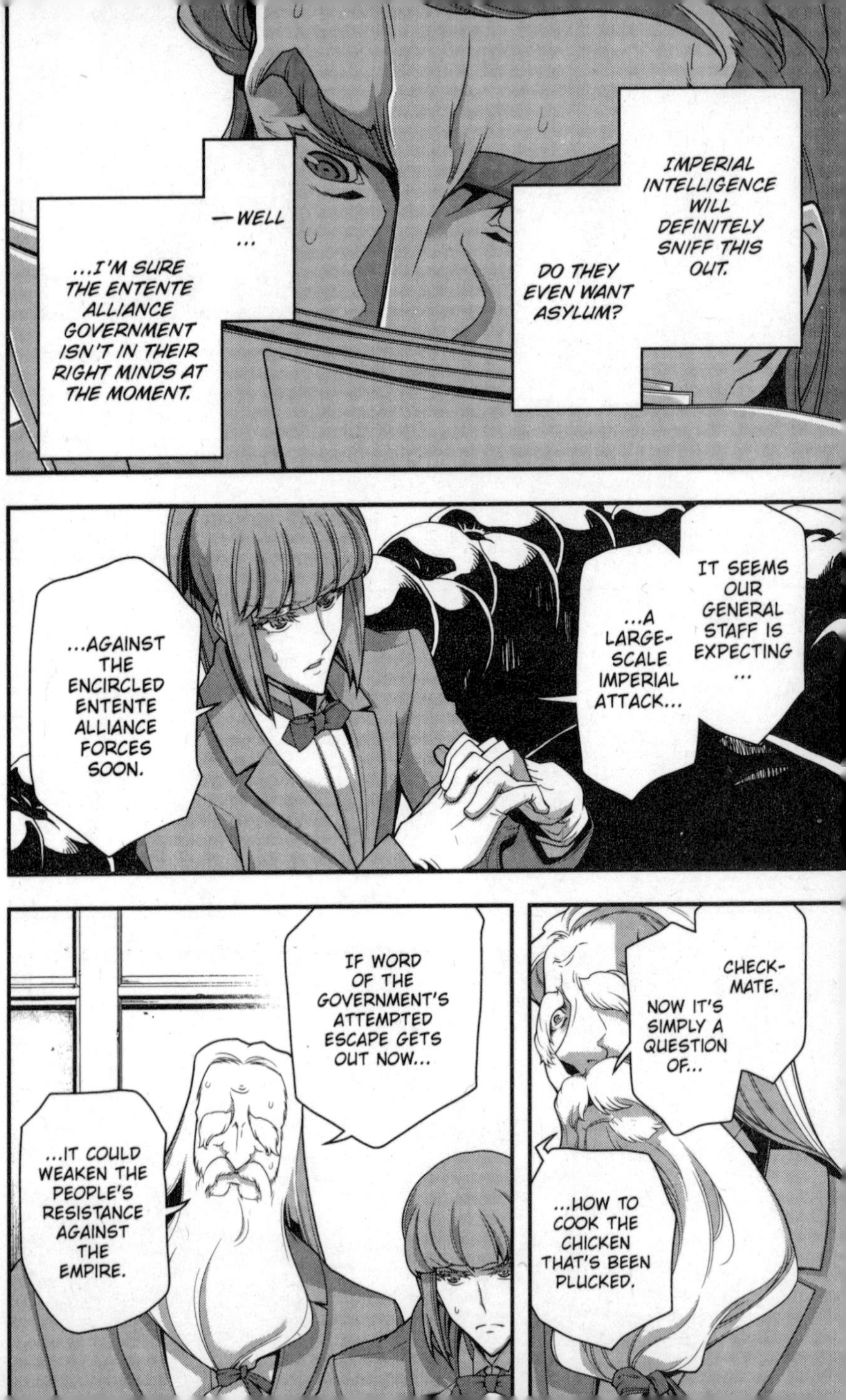
IMPERIAL INTELLIGENCE WILL DEFINITELY SNIFF THIS OUT.
DO THEY EVEN WANT ASYLUM?
—WELL ...
...I'M SURE THE ENTENTE ALLIANCE GOVERNMENT ISN'T IN THEIR RIGHT MINDS AT THE MOMENT.
IT SEEMS OUR GENERAL STAFF IS EXPECTING ...
...A LARGE-SCALE IMPERIAL ATTACK...
...AGAINST THE ENCIRCLED ENTENTE ALLIANCE FORCES SOON.
CHECK-MATE.
NOW IT'S SIMPLY A QUESTION OF...
...HOW TO COOK THE CHICKEN THAT'S BEEN PLUCKED.
IF WORD OF THE GOVERNMENT'S ATTEMPTED ESCAPE GETS OUT NOW...
...IT COULD WEAKEN THE PEOPLE'S RESISTANCE AGAINST THE EMPIRE.

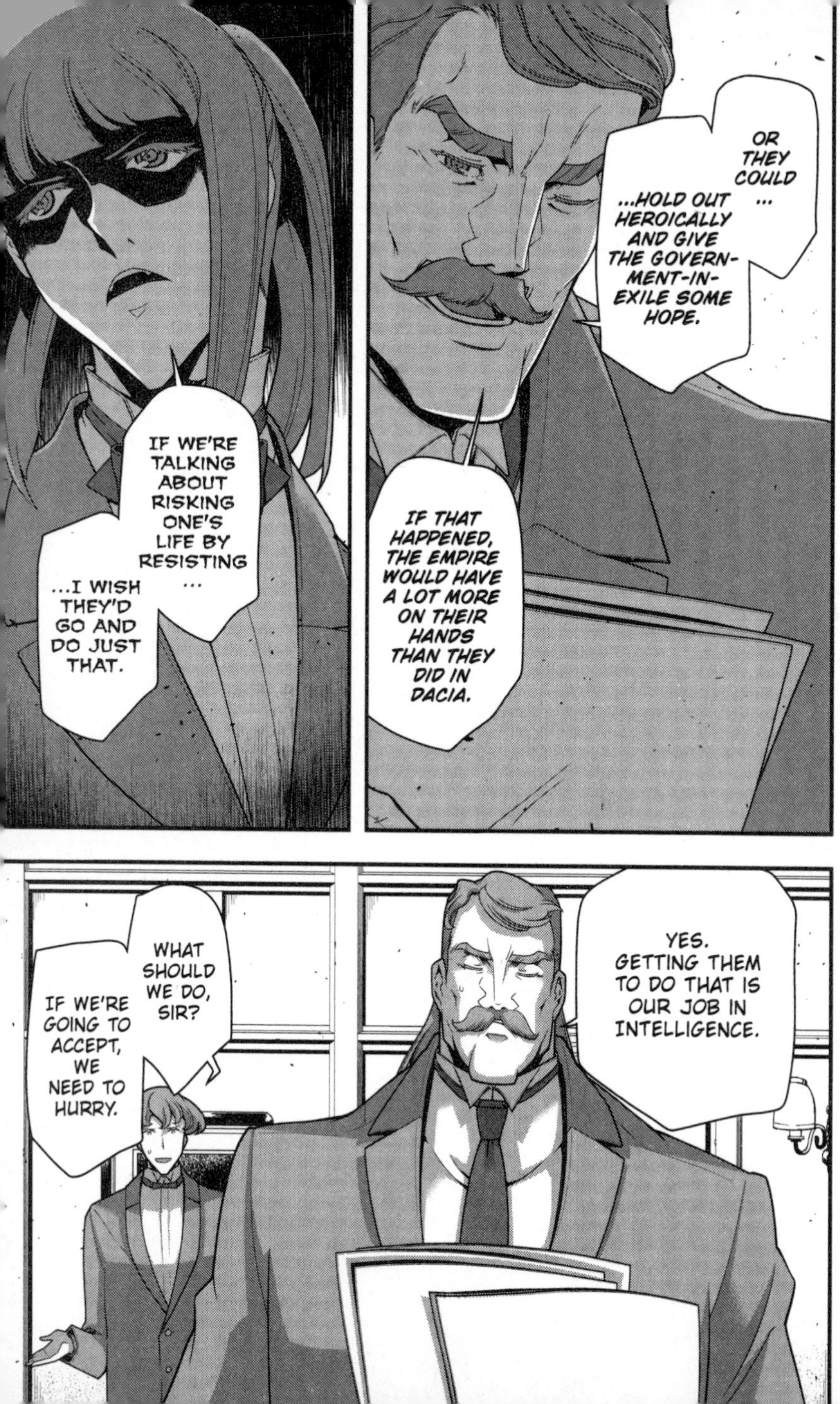
OR THEY COULD ...
...HOLD OUT HEROICALLY AND GIVE THE GOVERN-MENT-IN-EXILE SOME HOPE.
IF THAT HAPPENED, THE EMPIRE WOULD HAVE A LOT MORE ON THEIR HANDS THAN THEY DID IN DACIA.
IF WE'RE TALKING ABOUT RISKING ONE'S LIFE BY RESISTING ...
...I WISH THEY'D GO AND DO JUST THAT.
YES. GETTING THEM TO DO THAT IS OUR JOB IN INTELLIGENCE.
WHAT SHOULD WE DO, SIR?
IF WE'RE GOING TO ACCEPT, WE NEED TO HURRY.

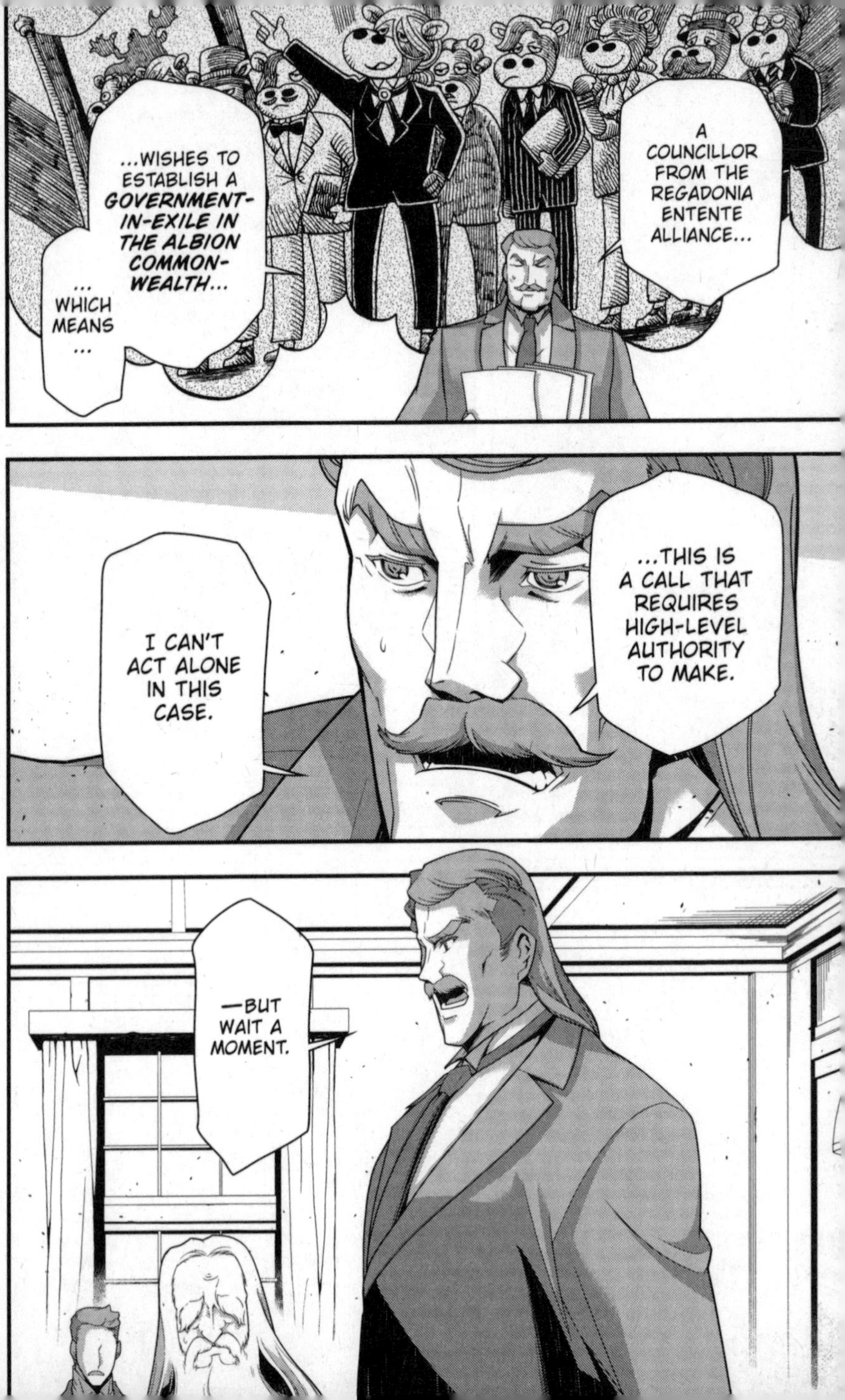
A COUNCILLOR FROM THE REGADONIA ENTENTE ALLIANCE...
...WISHES TO ESTABLISH A *GOVERNMENT-IN-EXILE IN THE ALBION COMMONWEALTH...*
... WHICH MEANS ...
...THIS IS A CALL THAT REQUIRES HIGH-LEVEL AUTHORITY TO MAKE.
I CAN'T ACT ALONE IN THIS CASE.
—BUT WAIT A MOMENT.

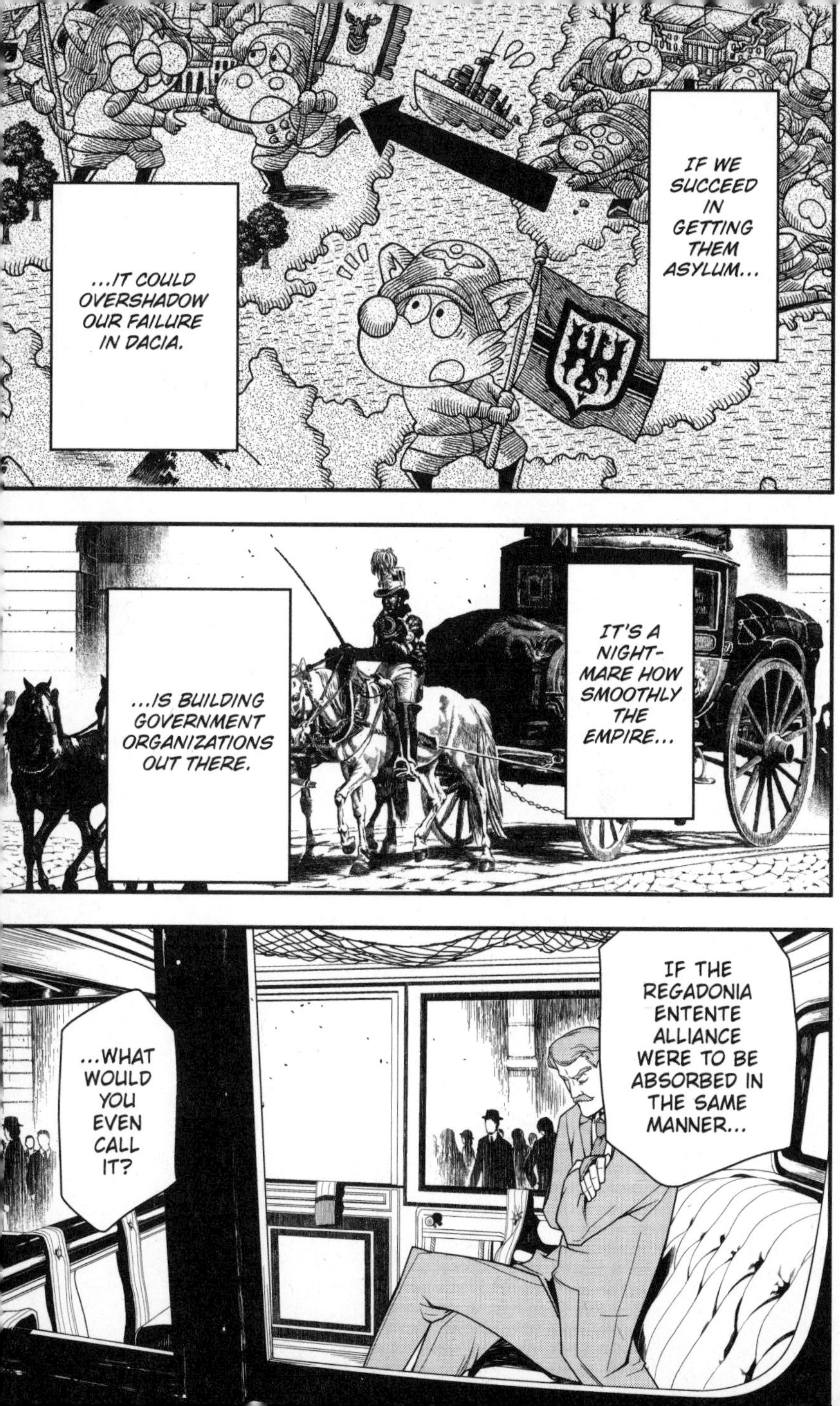
IF WE SUCCEED IN GETTING THEM ASYLUM...
...IT COULD OVERSHADOW OUR FAILURE IN DACIA.
IT'S A NIGHT-MARE HOW SMOOTHLY THE EMPIRE...
...IS BUILDING GOVERNMENT ORGANIZATIONS OUT THERE.
IF THE REGADONIA ENTENTE ALLIANCE WERE TO BE ABSORBED IN THE SAME MANNER...
...WHAT WOULD YOU EVEN CALL IT?

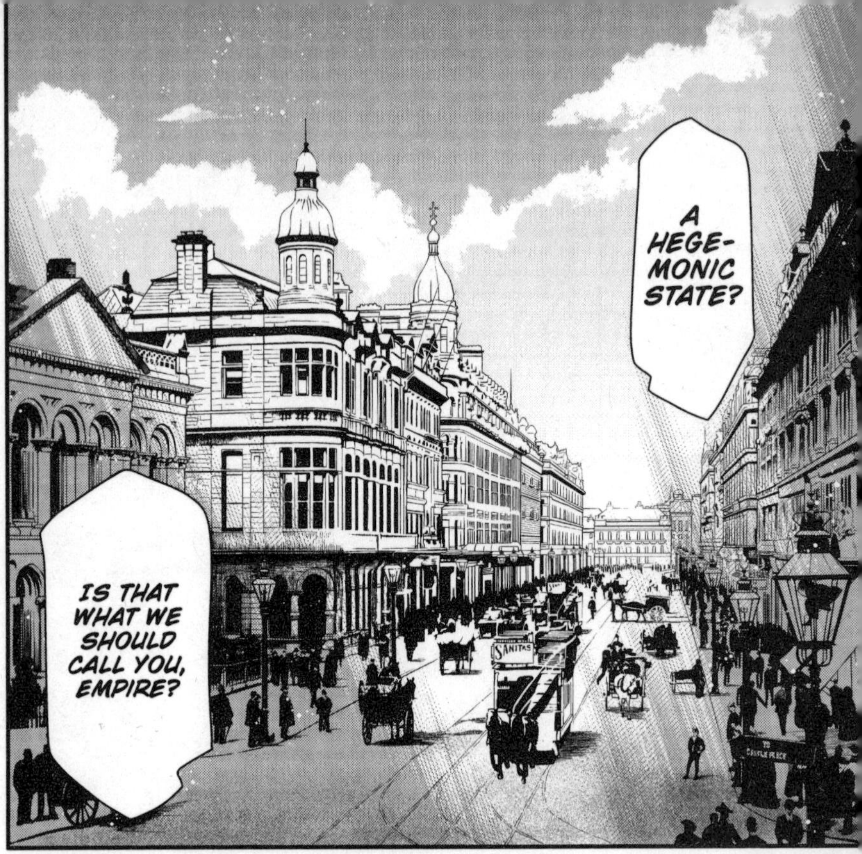
A HEGE-MONIC STATE?
IS THAT WHAT WE SHOULD CALL YOU, EMPIRE?
SANITAS

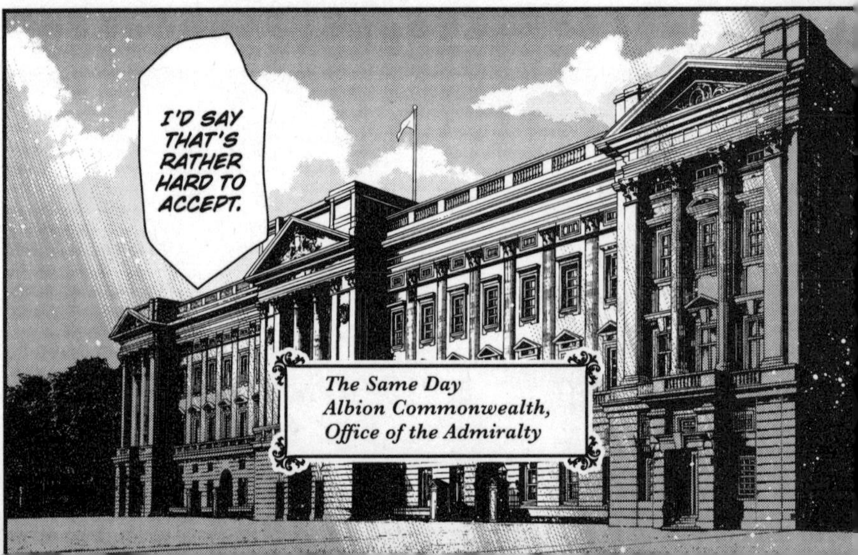
I'D SAY THAT'S RATHER HARD TO ACCEPT.
The Same Day
Albion Commonwealth,
Office of the Admiralty

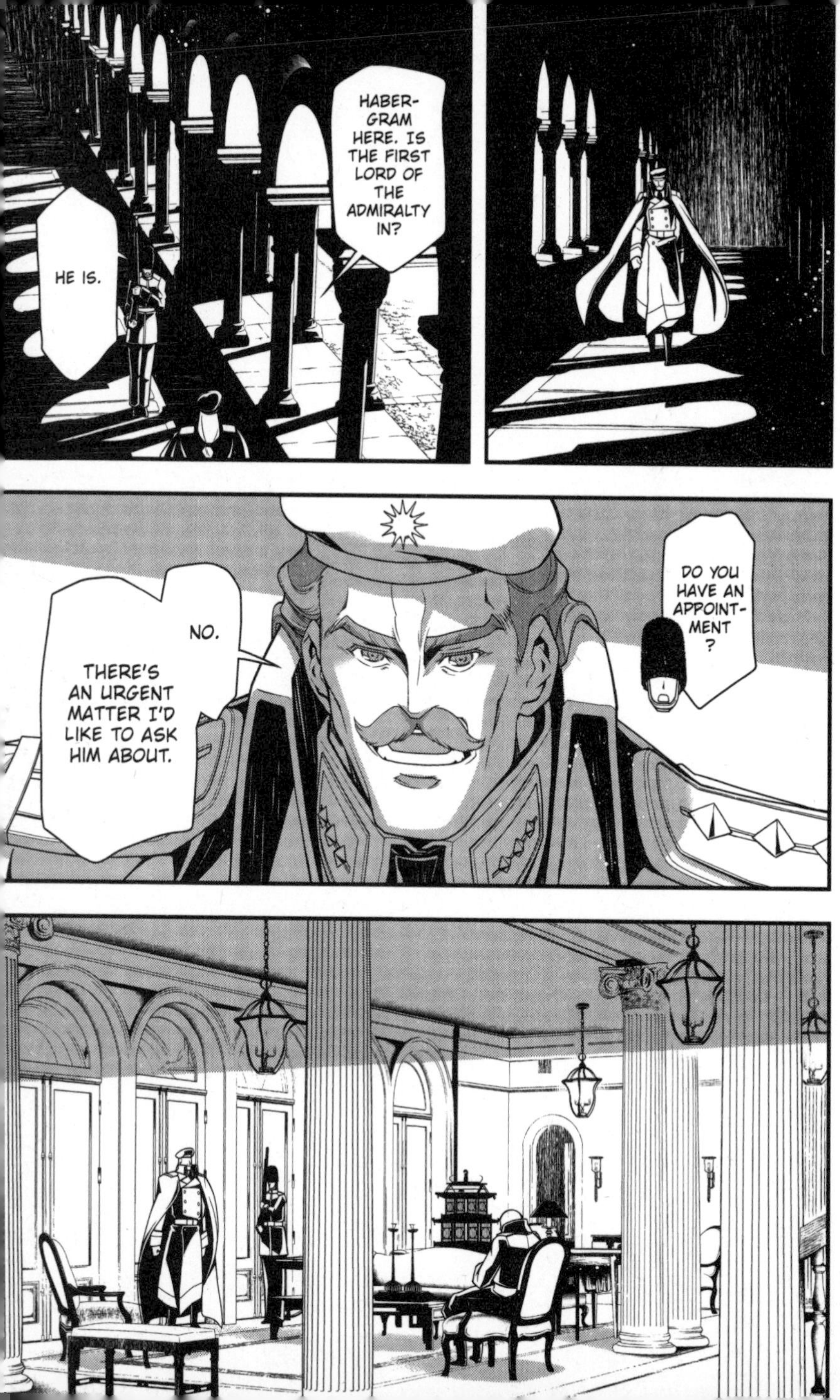
HABER-GRAM HERE. IS THE FIRST LORD OF THE ADMIRALTY IN?
HE IS.
DO YOU HAVE AN APPOINT-MENT?
NO.
THERE'S AN URGENT MATTER I'D LIKE TO ASK HIM ABOUT.

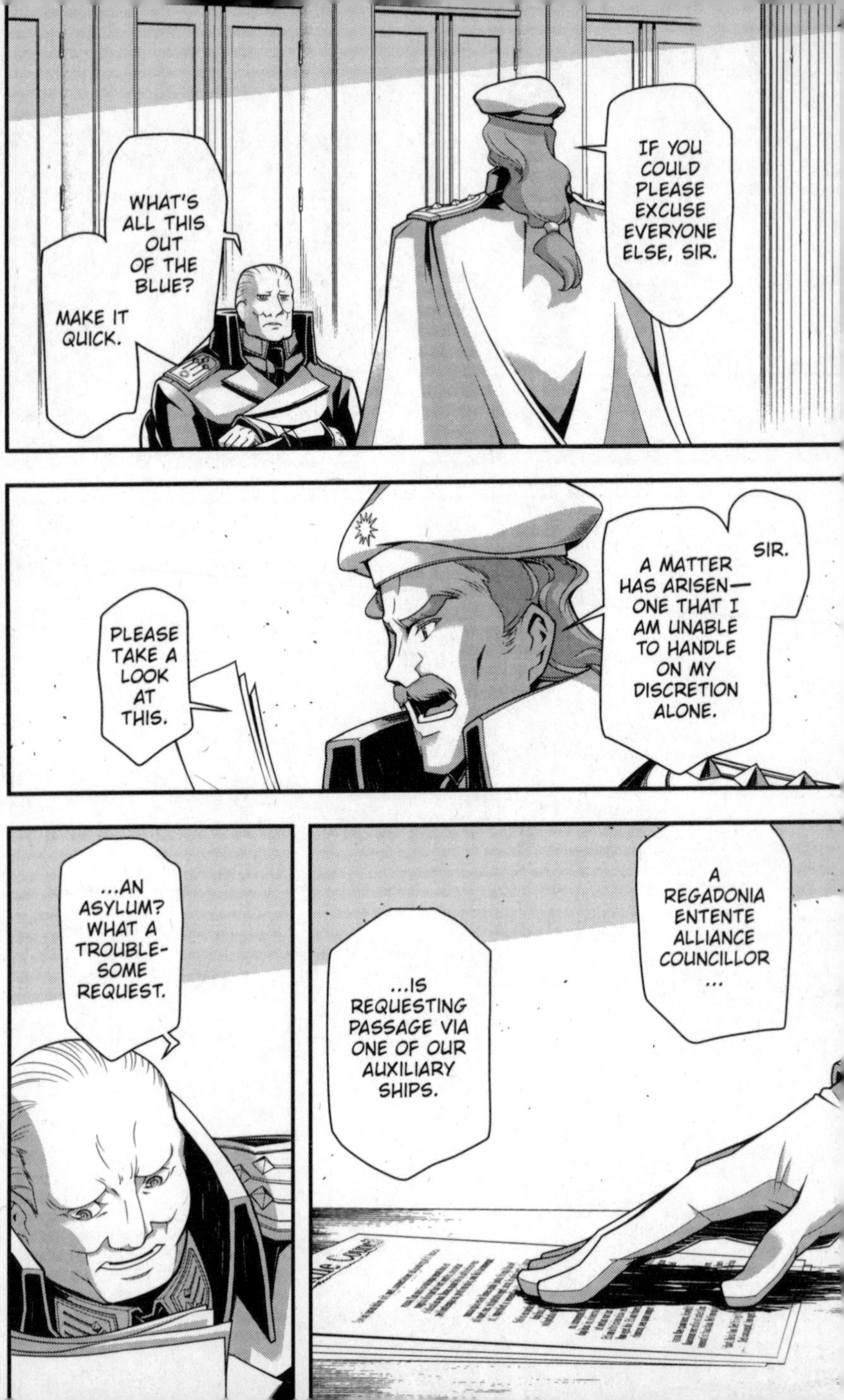
IF YOU COULD PLEASE EXCUSE EVERYONE ELSE, SIR.
WHAT'S ALL THIS OUT OF THE BLUE?
MAKE IT QUICK.
SIR. A MATTER HAS ARISEN—ONE THAT I AM UNABLE TO HANDLE ON MY DISCRETION ALONE.
PLEASE TAKE A LOOK AT THIS.
A REGADONIA ENTENTE ALLIANCE COUNCILLOR...
...IS REQUESTING PASSAGE VIA ONE OF OUR AUXILIARY SHIPS.
...AN ASYLUM? WHAT A TROUBLESOME REQUEST.

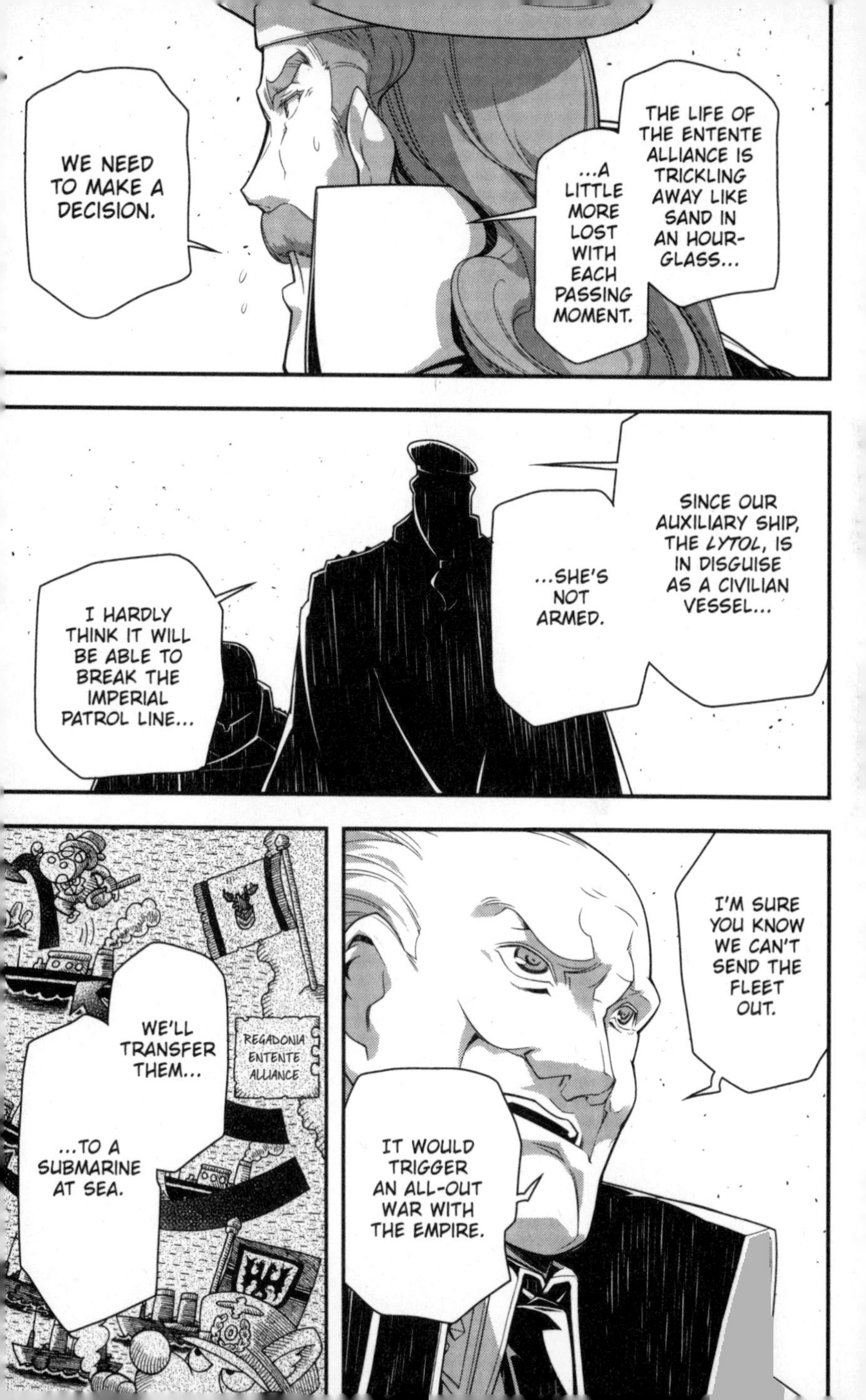
THE LIFE OF THE ENTENTE ALLIANCE IS TRICKLING AWAY LIKE SAND IN AN HOUR-GLASS...
...A LITTLE MORE LOST WITH EACH PASSING MOMENT.
WE NEED TO MAKE A DECISION.
SINCE OUR AUXILIARY SHIP, THE *LYTOL*, IS IN DISGUISE AS A CIVILIAN VESSEL...
...SHE'S NOT ARMED.
I HARDLY THINK IT WILL BE ABLE TO BREAK THE IMPERIAL PATROL LINE...
I'M SURE YOU KNOW WE CAN'T SEND THE FLEET OUT.
IT WOULD TRIGGER AN ALL-OUT WAR WITH THE EMPIRE.
WE'LL TRANSFER THEM...
REGADONIA ENTENTE ALLIANCE
...TO A SUBMARINE AT SEA.

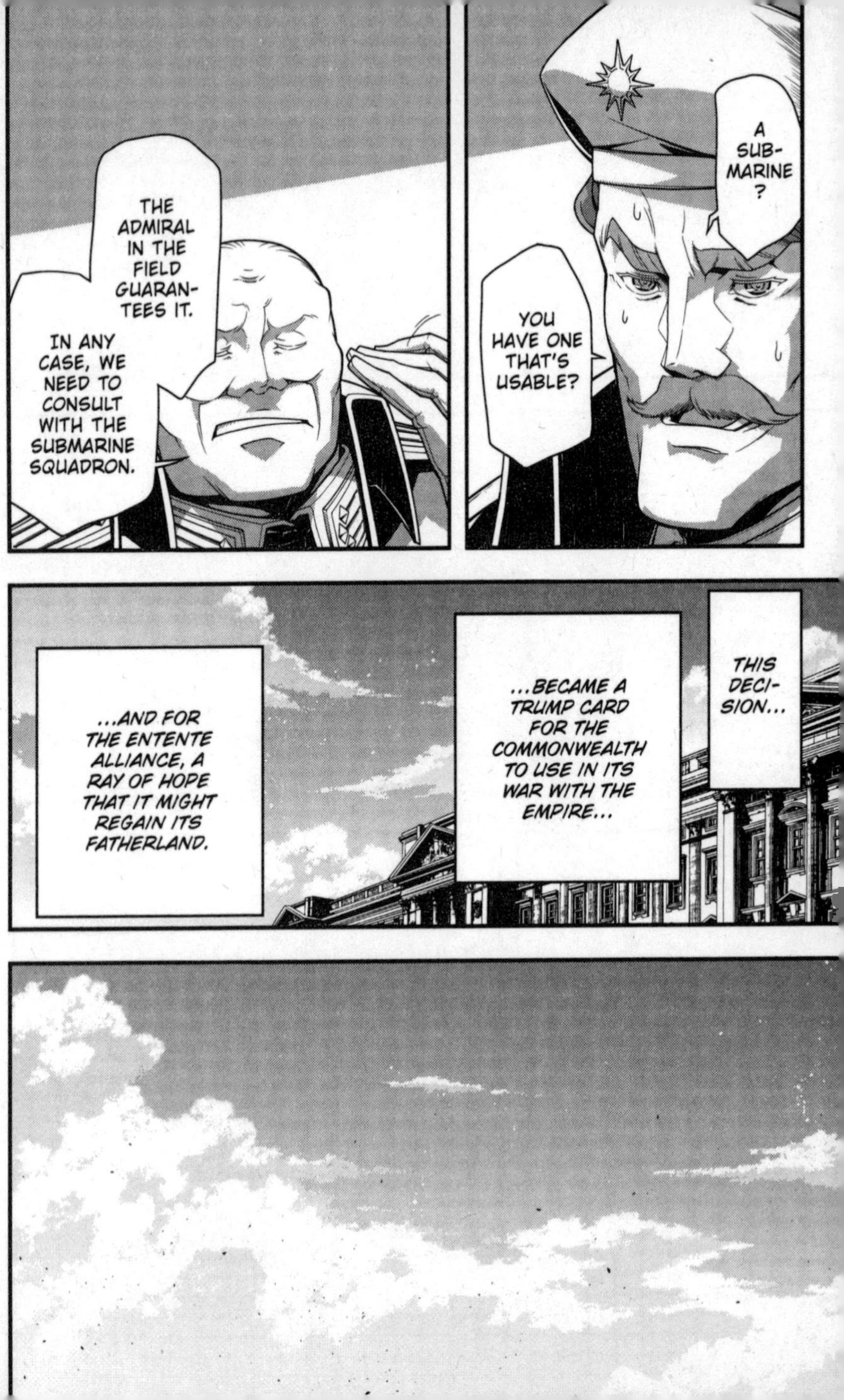
A SUB-MARINE?
YOU HAVE ONE THAT'S USABLE?
THE ADMIRAL IN THE FIELD GUARAN-TEES IT.
IN ANY CASE, WE NEED TO CONSULT WITH THE SUBMARINE SQUADRON.
THIS DECI-SION...
...BECAME A TRUMP CARD FOR THE COMMONWEALTH TO USE IN ITS WAR WITH THE EMPIRE...
...AND FOR THE ENTENTE ALLIANCE, A RAY OF HOPE THAT IT MIGHT REGAIN ITS FATHERLAND.

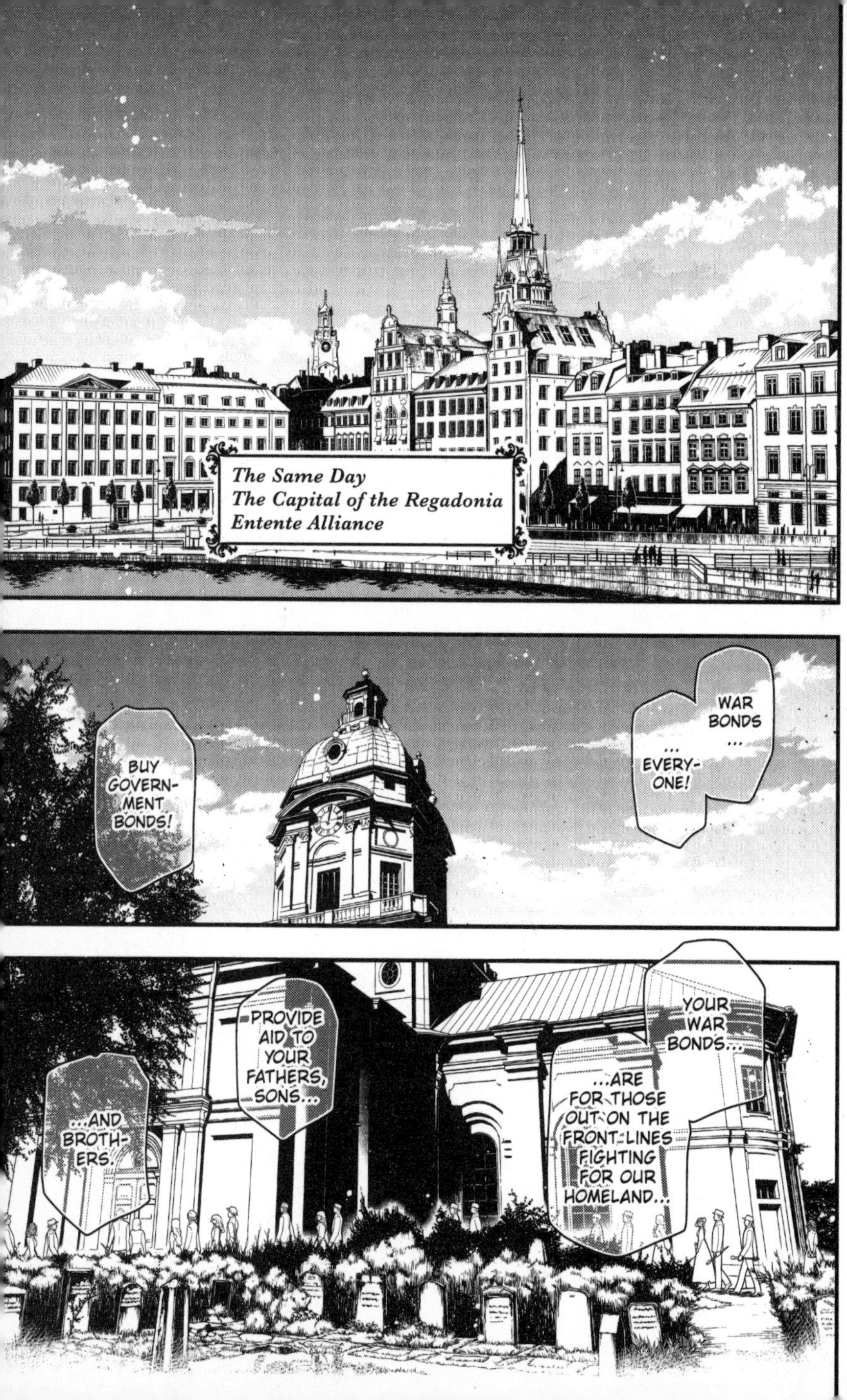
The Same Day
The Capital of the Regadonia Entente Alliance
WAR BONDS ... ... EVERY-ONE!
BUY GOVERN-MENT BONDS!
YOUR WAR BONDS...
...ARE FOR THOSE OUT ON THE FRONT LINES FIGHTING FOR OUR HOMELAND...
PROVIDE AID TO YOUR FATHERS, SONS...
...AND BROTHERS.

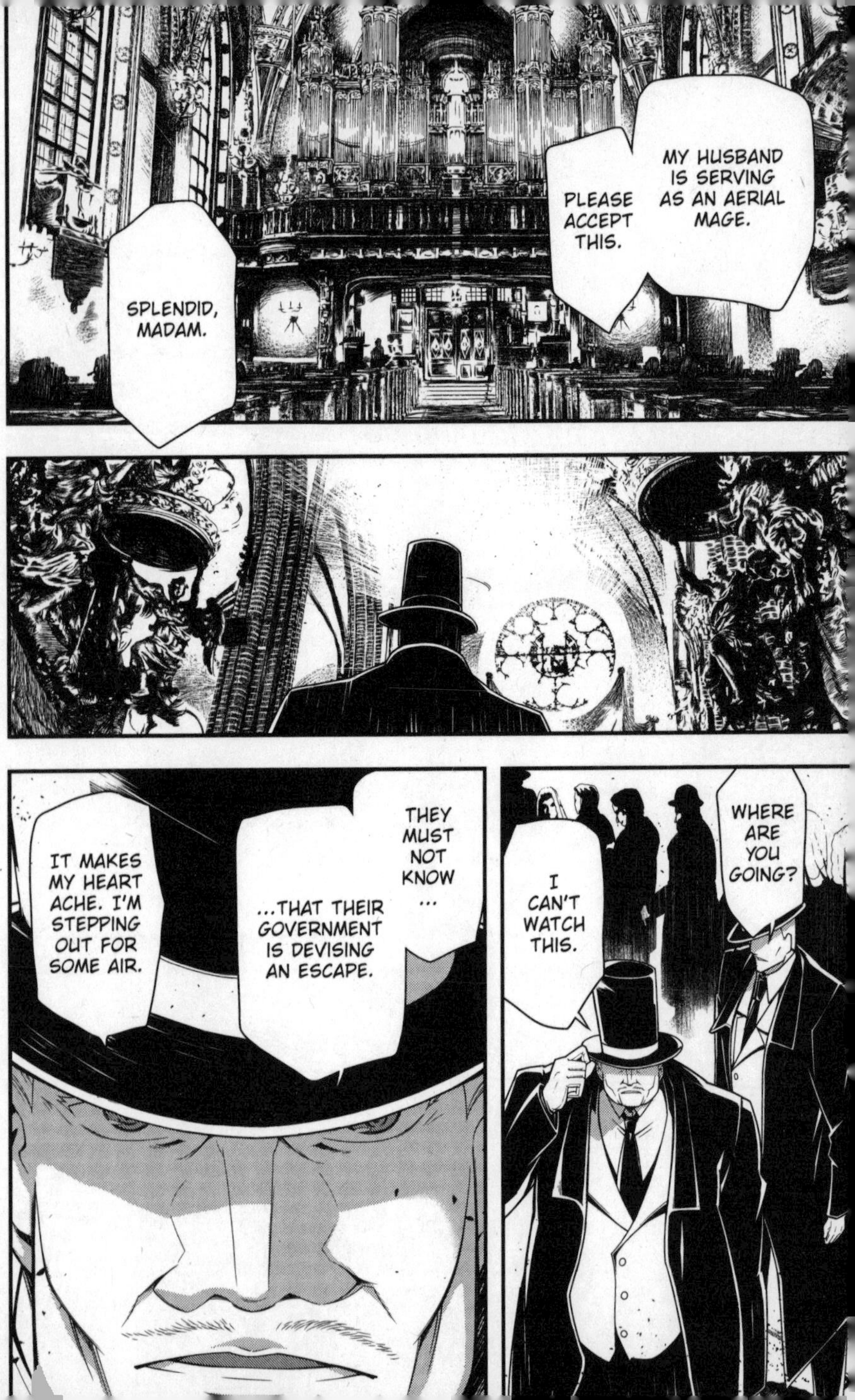
MY HUSBAND IS SERVING AS AN AERIAL MAGE.
PLEASE ACCEPT THIS.
SPLENDID, MADAM.
WHERE ARE YOU GOING?
I CAN'T WATCH THIS.
THEY MUST NOT KNOW...
...THAT THEIR GOVERNMENT IS DEVISING AN ESCAPE.
IT MAKES MY HEART ACHE. I'M STEPPING OUT FOR SOME AIR.

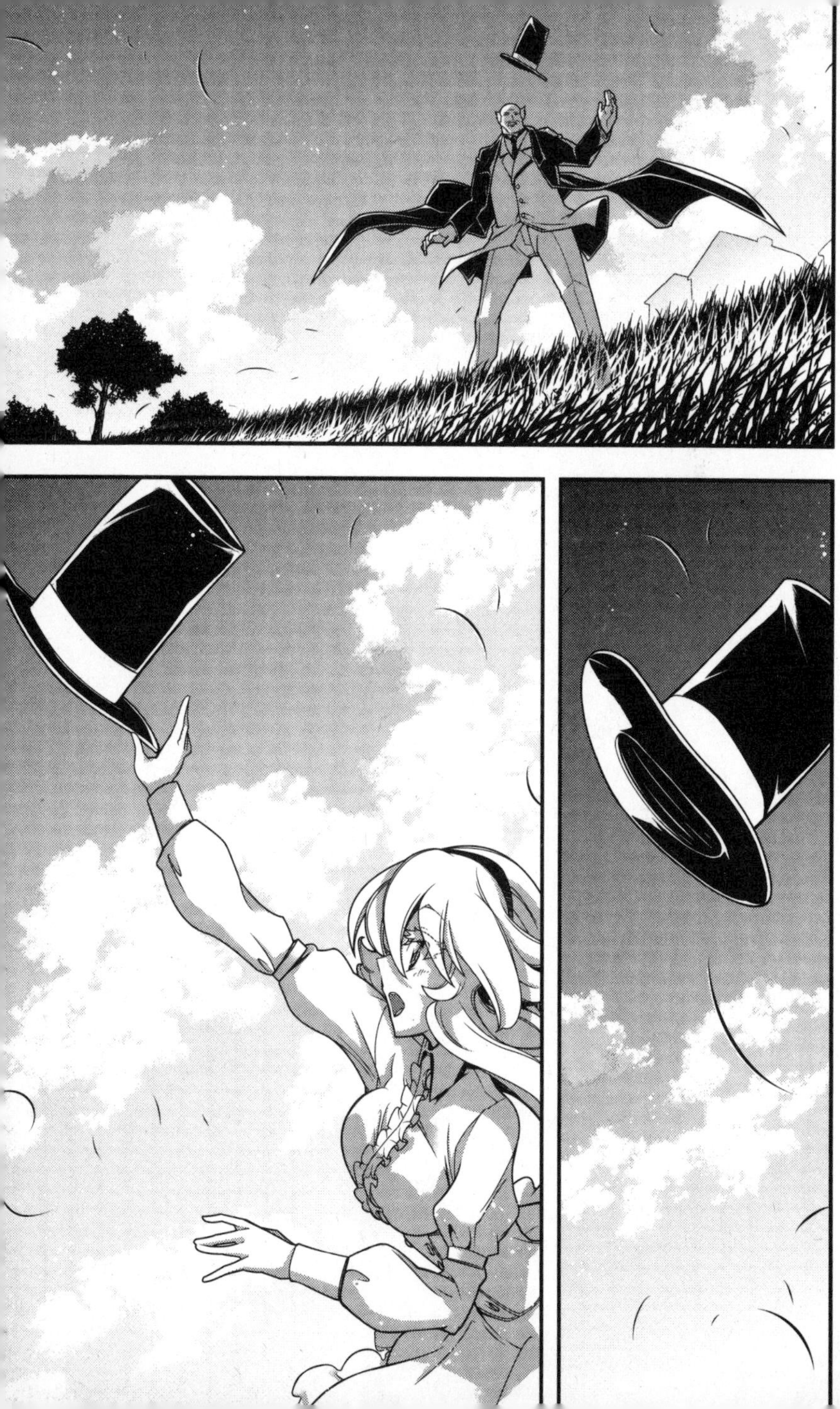

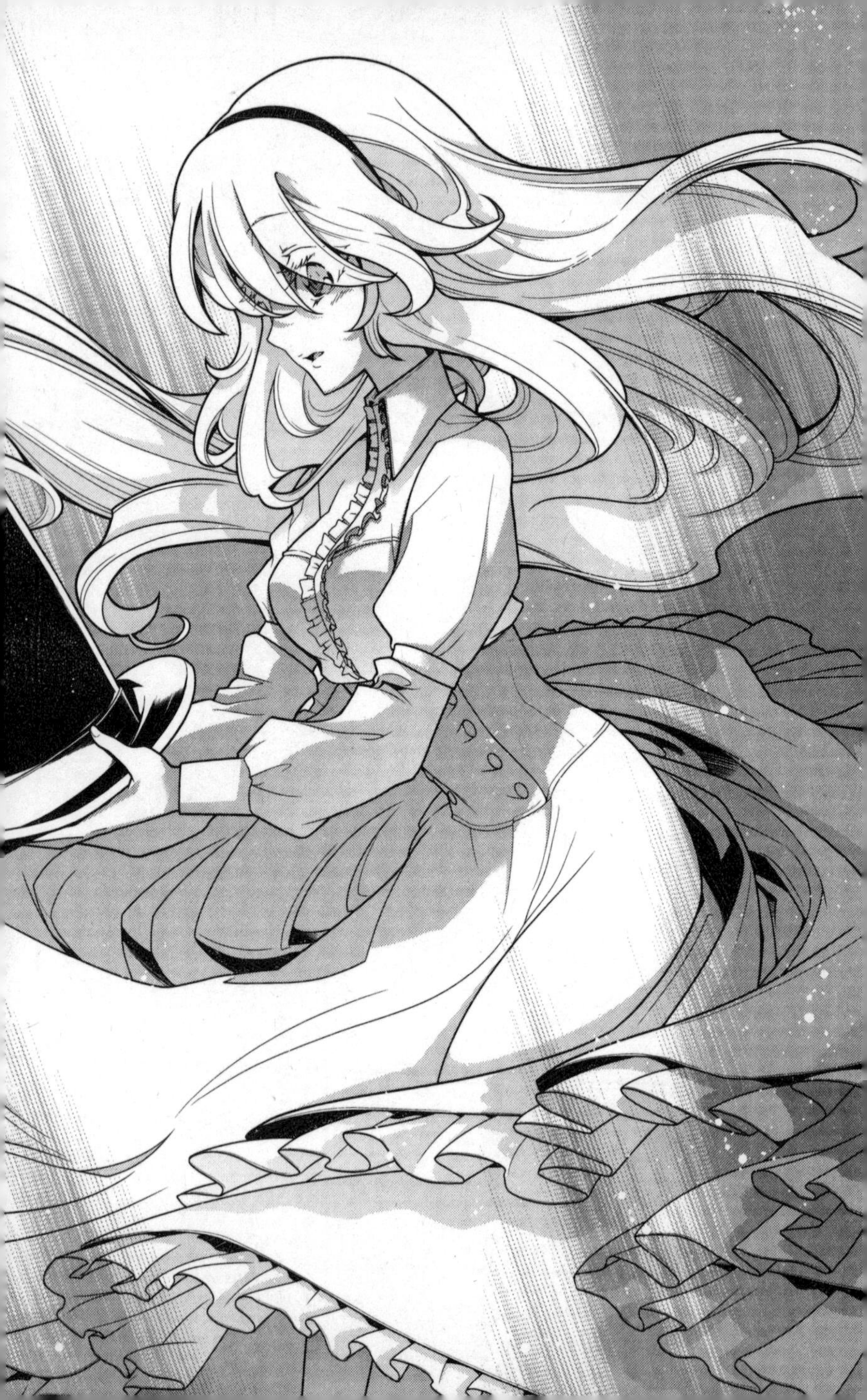

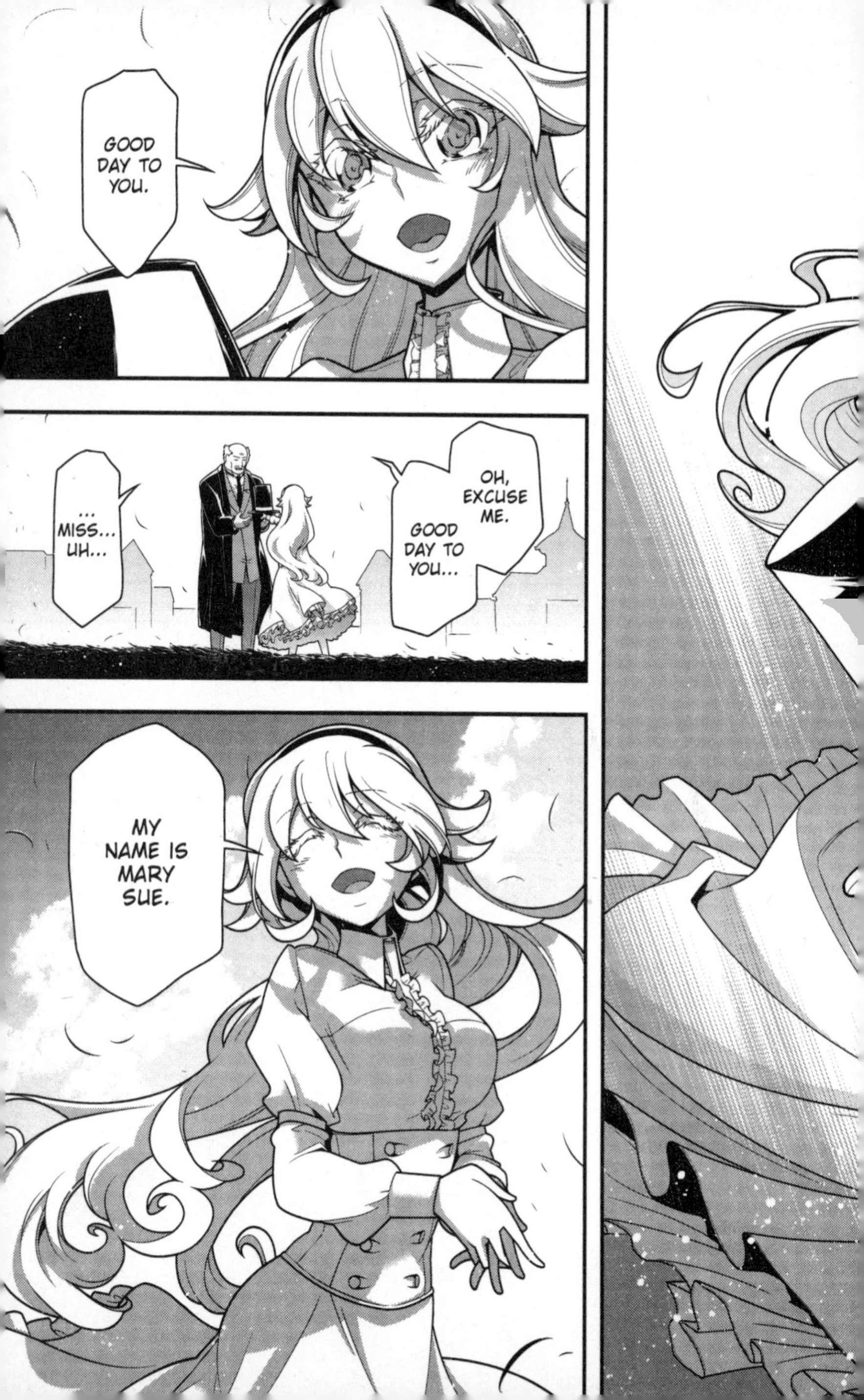
GOOD DAY TO YOU.
OH, EXCUSE ME.
GOOD DAY TO YOU...
... MISS... UH...
MY NAME IS MARY SUE.

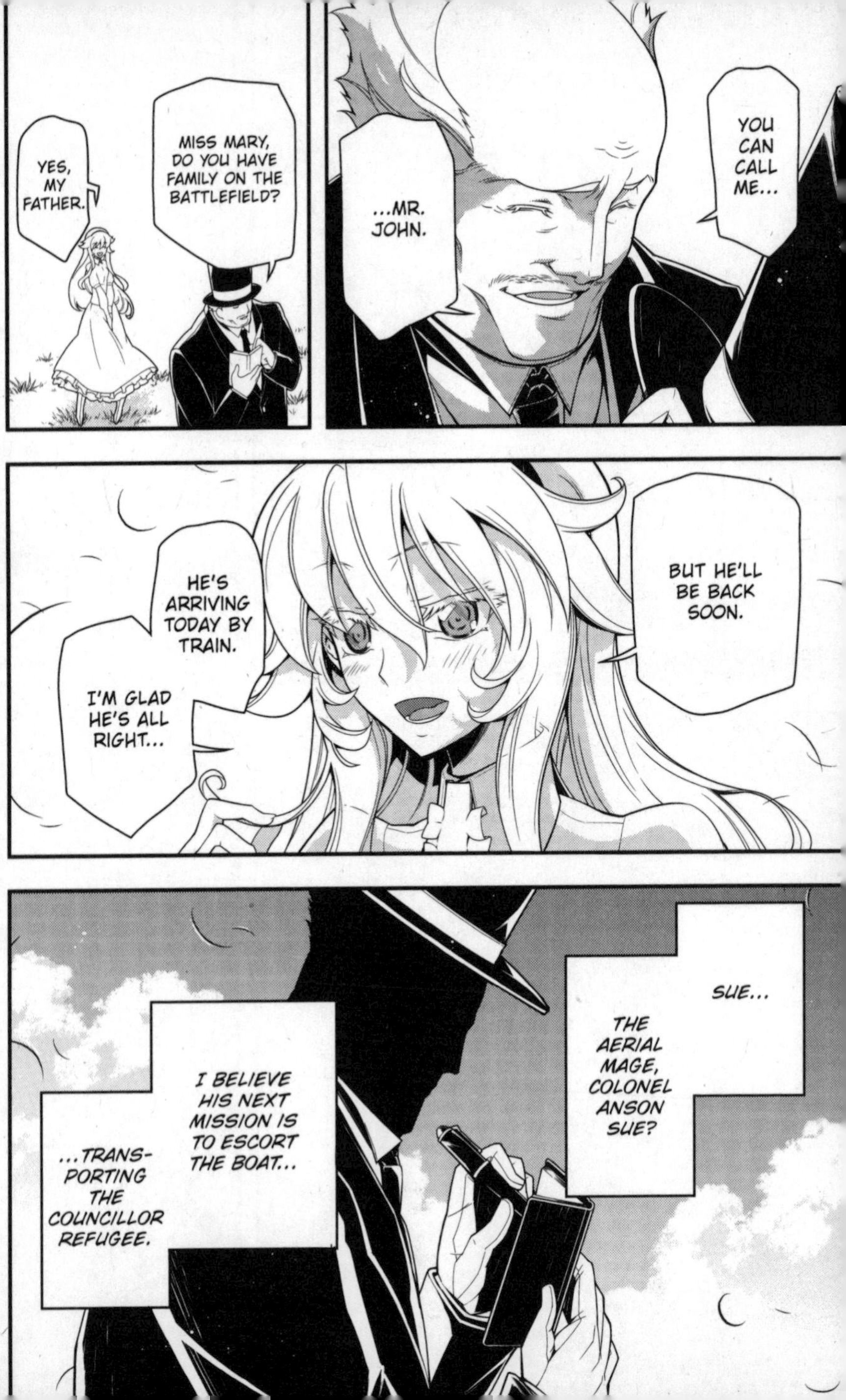
YOU CAN CALL ME...
...MR. JOHN.
MISS MARY, DO YOU HAVE FAMILY ON THE BATTLEFIELD?
YES, MY FATHER.
BUT HE'LL BE BACK SOON.
HE'S ARRIVING TODAY BY TRAIN.
I'M GLAD HE'S ALL RIGHT...
SUE...
THE AERIAL MAGE, COLONEL ANSON SUE?
I BELIEVE HIS NEXT MISSION IS TO ESCORT THE BOAT...
...TRANS-PORTING THE COUNCILLOR REFUGEE.

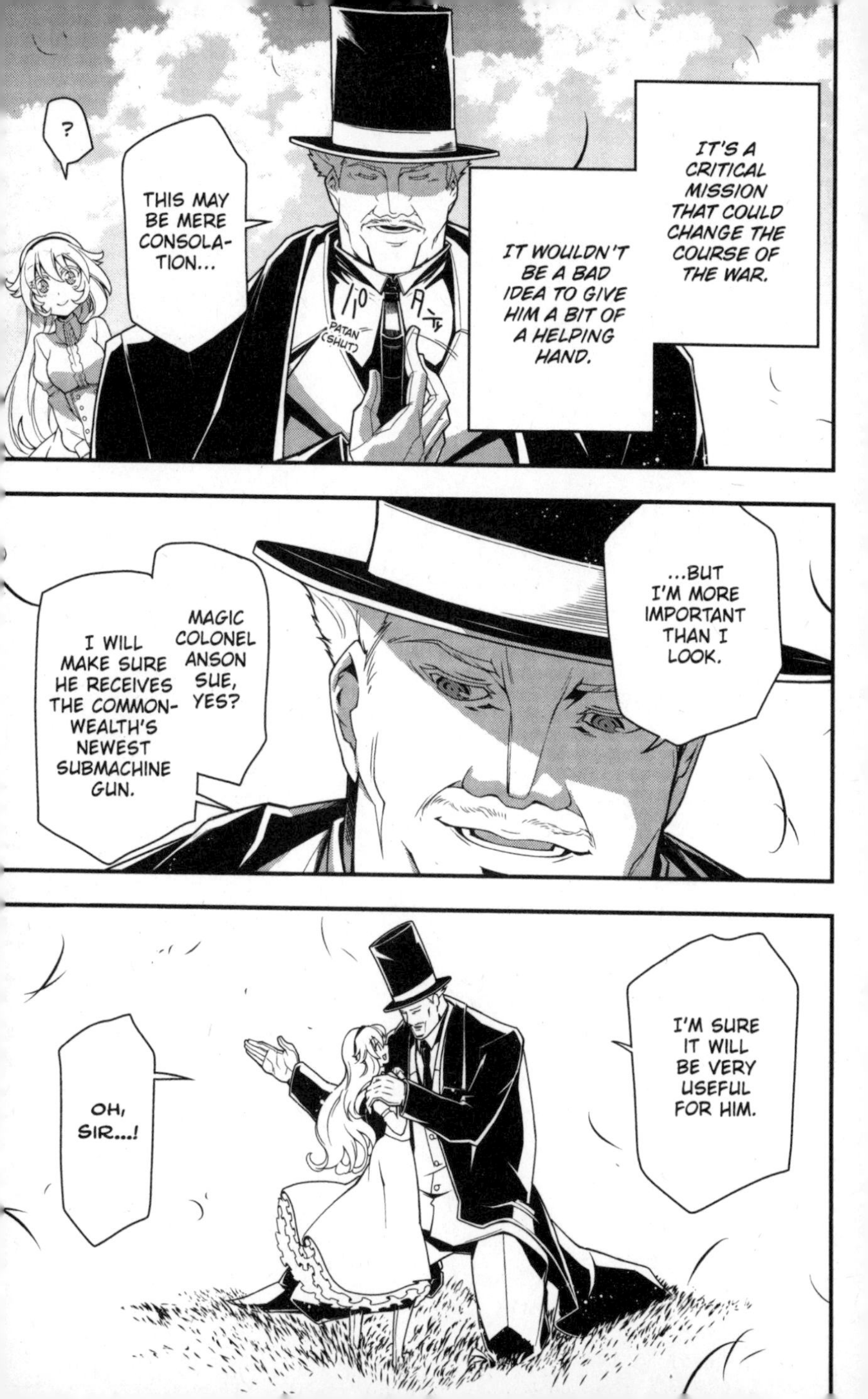
IT'S A CRITICAL MISSION THAT COULD CHANGE THE COURSE OF THE WAR.
IT WOULDN'T BE A BAD IDEA TO GIVE HIM A BIT OF A HELPING HAND.
PATAN (SHUT)
THIS MAY BE MERE CONSOLATION...
?
...BUT I'M MORE IMPORTANT THAN I LOOK.
MAGIC COLONEL ANSON SUE, YES?
I WILL MAKE SURE HE RECEIVES THE COMMONWEALTH'S NEWEST SUBMACHINE GUN.
I'M SURE IT WILL BE VERY USEFUL FOR HIM.
OH, SIR...!

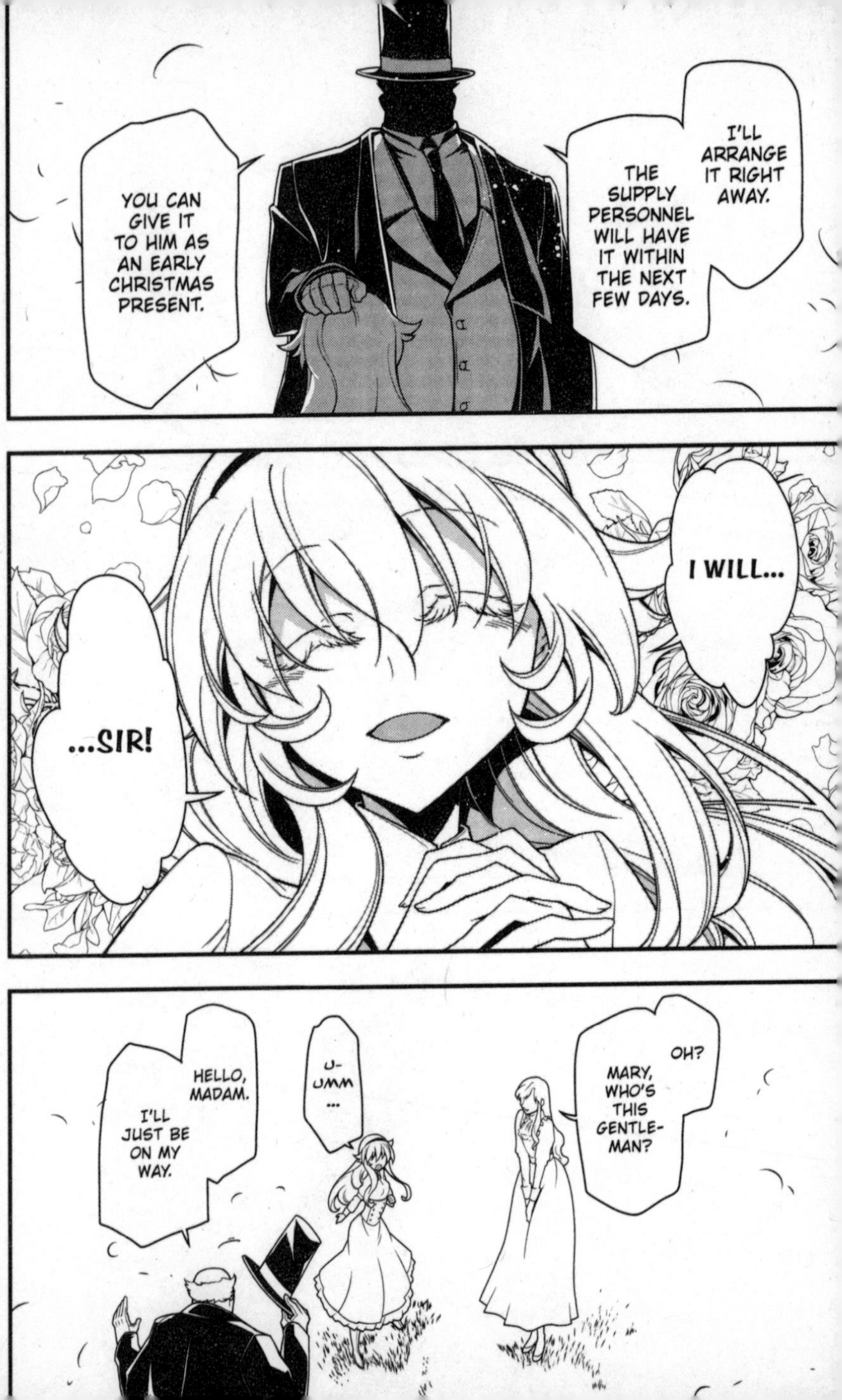
I'LL ARRANGE IT RIGHT AWAY.
THE SUPPLY PERSONNEL WILL HAVE IT WITHIN THE NEXT FEW DAYS.
YOU CAN GIVE IT TO HIM AS AN EARLY CHRISTMAS PRESENT.
I WILL...
...SIR!
OH?
MARY, WHO'S THIS GENTLE-MAN?
U-UMM...
HELLO, MADAM.
I'LL JUST BE ON MY WAY.

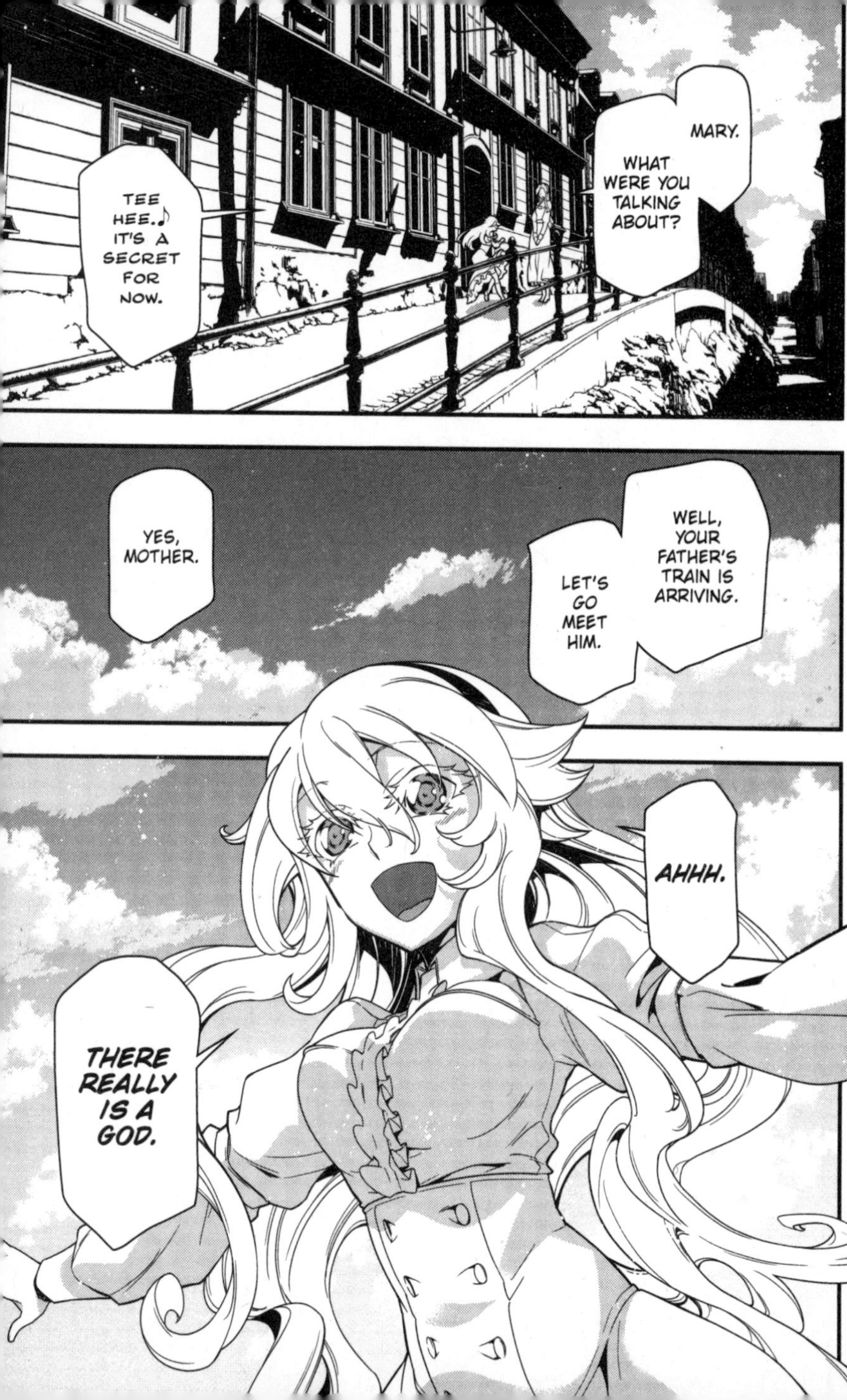
MARY.
WHAT WERE YOU TALKING ABOUT?
TEE HEE.♪ IT'S A SECRET FOR NOW.
WELL, YOUR FATHER'S TRAIN IS ARRIVING.
LET'S GO MEET HIM.
YES, MOTHER.
AHHH.
THERE REALLY IS A GOD.

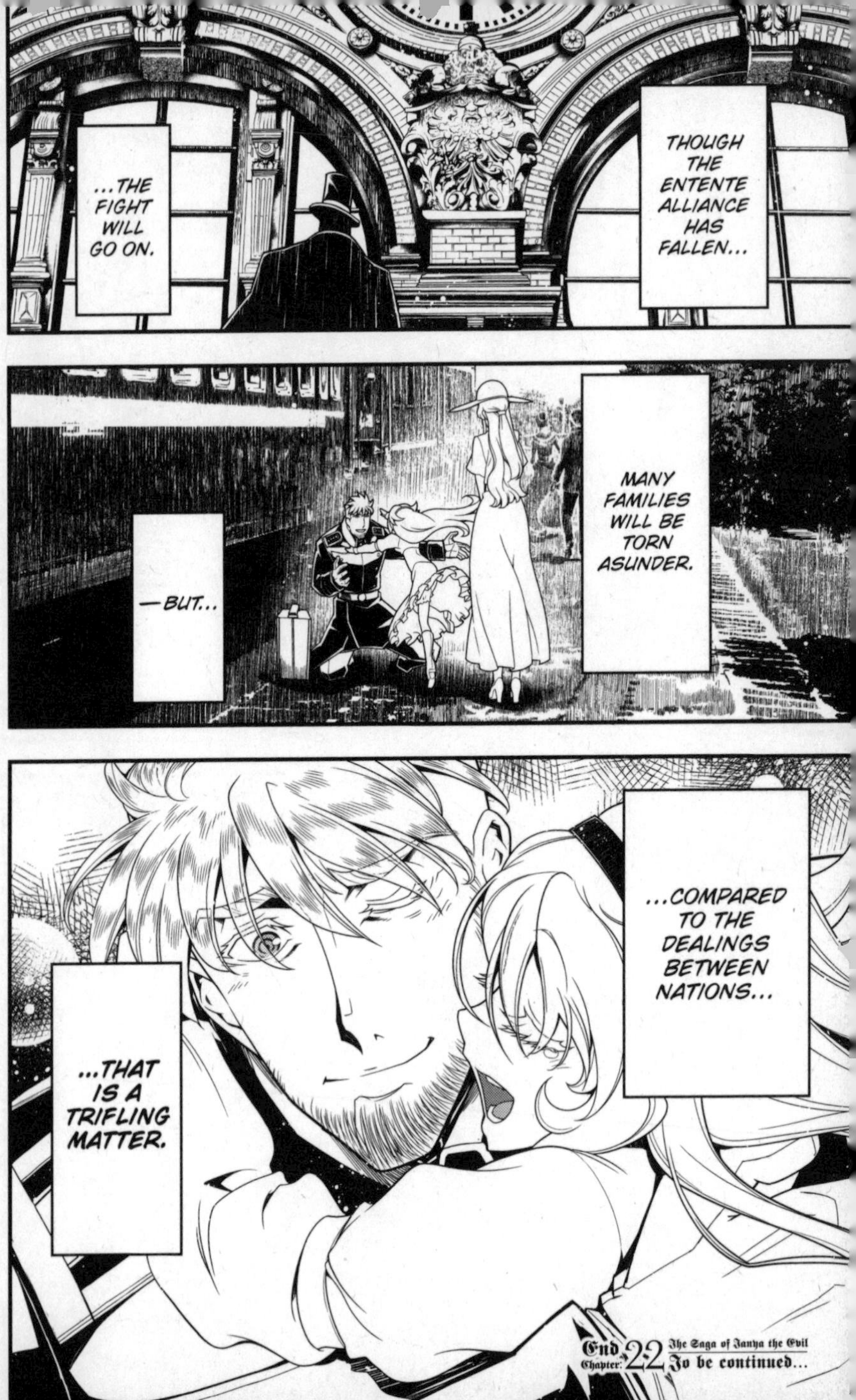
THOUGH THE ENTENTE ALLIANCE HAS FALLEN...
...THE FIGHT WILL GO ON.
MANY FAMILIES WILL BE TORN ASUNDER.
—BUT...
...COMPARED TO THE DEALINGS BETWEEN NATIONS...
...THAT IS A TRIFLING MATTER.
End Chapter: 22 The Saga of Tanya the Evil To be continued...

Glossary Chapter 27

Landing Force

Naval infantry units.

There are also amphibious units called marines, but they are often a different branch from the navy and usually have a different chain of command from naval infantry. It depends on the country. One may have marines as part of the navy while another may choose to have it assimilated into the naval infantry. Either way, they both started out as units that would board enemy ships for hand-to-hand combat during the age of sail.

In one particular country that had naval infantry, each ship had a designated landing force, and when something came up, they would equip their special landing party gear and carry out the mission. By taking the landing forces from each ship, a regiment-sized joint landing force could be formed.

That country not only had provisional infantry but also had permanent members who performed roles such as base security.

The Empire seems to have both marines and naval infantry. In this operation, the naval infantry landing force was to establish a beachhead while the marines were supposed to advance deeper into enemy territory. If the beachhead were to be surrounded by enemy land troops, the landing troops would be put at a disadvantage, so they must have wanted to expand the lines swiftly to break through any potential encirclement.

From the way the naval infantry and marines, with their different chains of command, operated together so smoothly, you can see how precisely this landing mission was manned. General Rudersdorf must have been in his element.

Fjord Topography

The port that marks the entryway to the city of Os is flanked by sheer cliffs. The entrance route appears to be a long, narrow bay that maintains a near constant width from the entrance all the way in. This type of topography, formed by glaciers eroding the earth, is called a fjord, and it is characteristic of Scandinavia. Since fjord waters are deep, large ships can enter. For this reason, fjords have long been used as natural ports.

Of course, this topography is also great for defense; if you line the cliffs with guns, it's a free-for-all when an invading ship comes along. The Empire managed to take out this port by dropping in mages from Norden in a sneak attack, but that sort of operation is nearly impossible for another country's army with no base nearby. As Colonel Sue said, the Osfjord was probably providing the Empire with iron-wall protection.

Glossary Chapter 28

Council

A meeting for deliberating matters or the organization that holds it.

In the Entente Alliance, the ten-member council is the most powerful political organ. Its inner workings are unclear, but it is very likely that important decisions are settled by consensus and not by a single person. There is no designated head. If there is, they don't seem to have any special authority.

This sort of rule by consensus in a council is rare. There were a few examples of something similar in the Communist Bloc, but in most cases, either the head of the council was essentially head of state, or there was a senate consisting of people from the privileged class that functioned as an advisory body for a head of state.

The reasoning behind the Entente Alliance's total consensus system isn't touched upon here, but it probably has something to do with its name. It must be an alliance that came out of an entente relationship to foster commerce. If the members of the council were familiar with business conventions, no one would agree to anything that wasn't in their interests. Perhaps the consensus system came about naturally to allow for people to find a common ground while encouraging mutual profit.

Intelligence Agency

The department that collects and analyzes information about other countries from the standpoint of national security. Here, they are sometimes called an "intelligence service," (based on England's Secret Intelligence Service) as the Commonwealth was inspired in part by England. They can take on different missions and forms, depending on the country, but are usually concerned with national security. The talent of the intelligence agency can change a nation's fate.

There are many ways an intelligence agency collects information. HUMINT (human intelligence) retrieves information from diplomats and spies, SIGINT (signals intelligence) uses the interception of waves and communications, and IMINT (imagery intelligence) obtains data by analyzing images taken by reconnaissance planes.

Then there's OSINT, which analyzes internal circumstances based on publicly available newspapers, broadcasts, personnel transfer orders, and so on. This type of legal method makes up a larger portion of intelligence work than you might think.

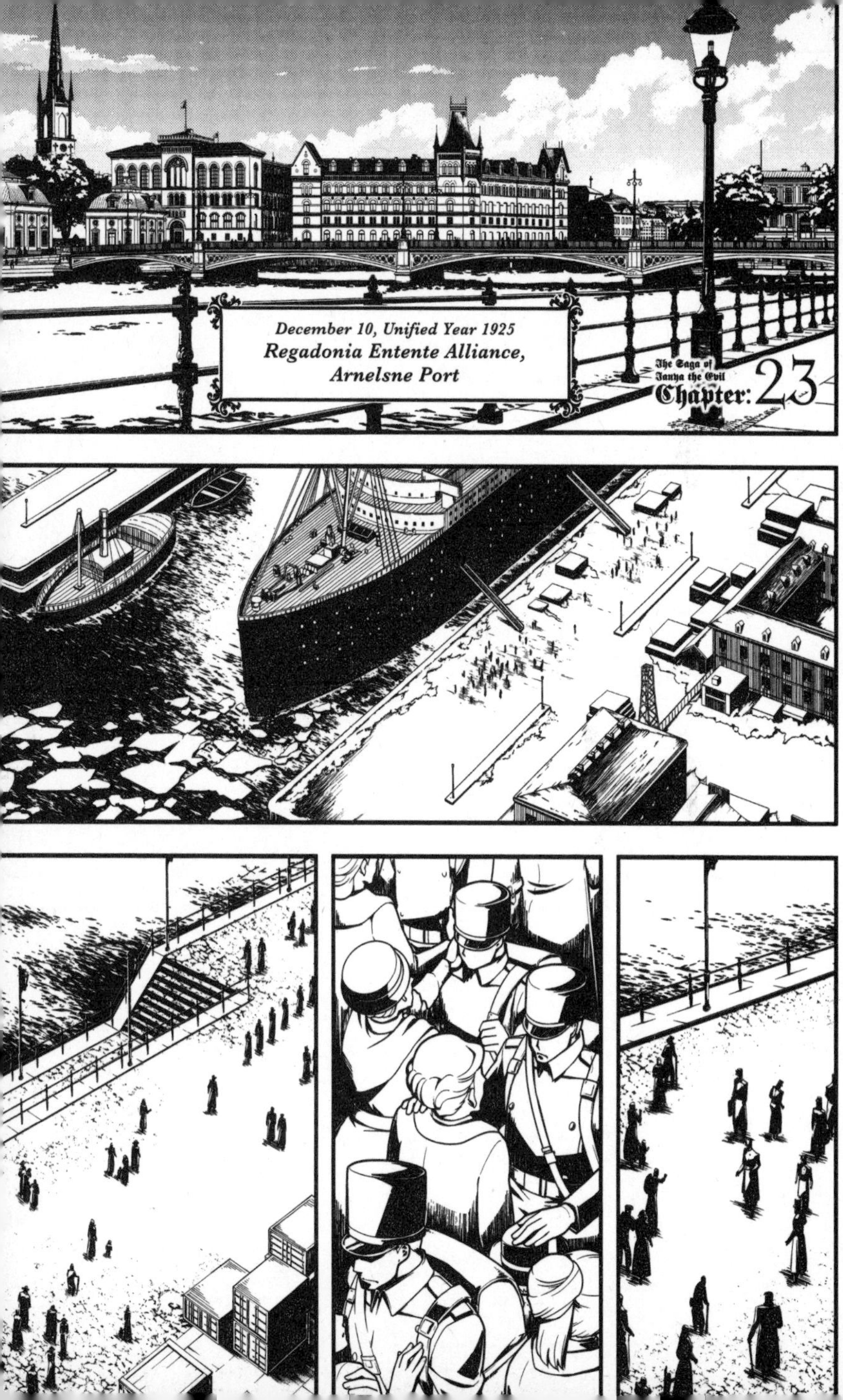
The Saga of Tanya the Evil
Chapter: 23
December 10, Unified Year 1925
Regadonia Entente Alliance, Arnelsne Port

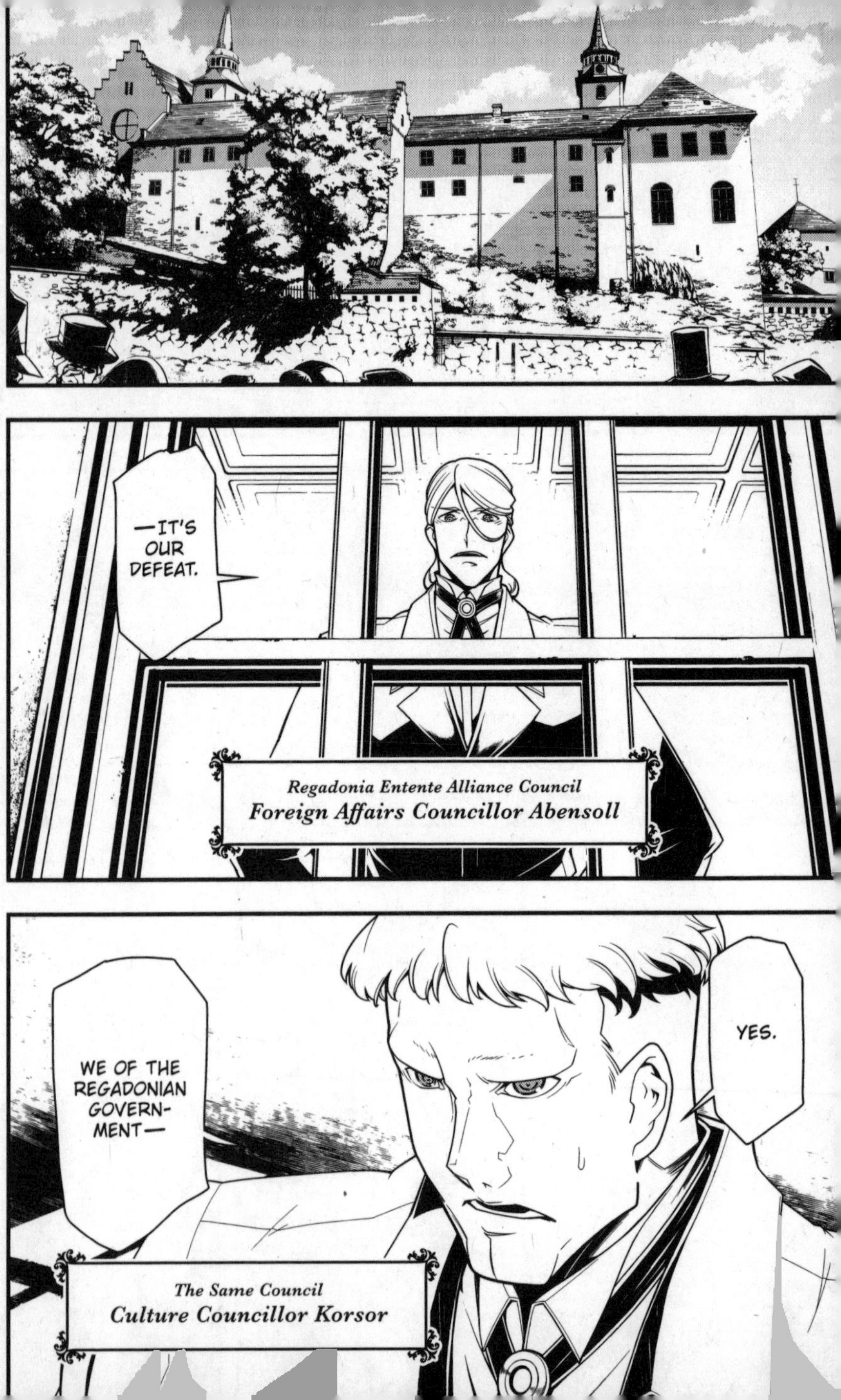
—IT'S OUR DEFEAT.
Regadonia Entente Alliance Council
Foreign Affairs Councillor Abensoll
YES.
WE OF THE REGADONIAN GOVERN-MENT—
The Same Council
Culture Councillor Korsor

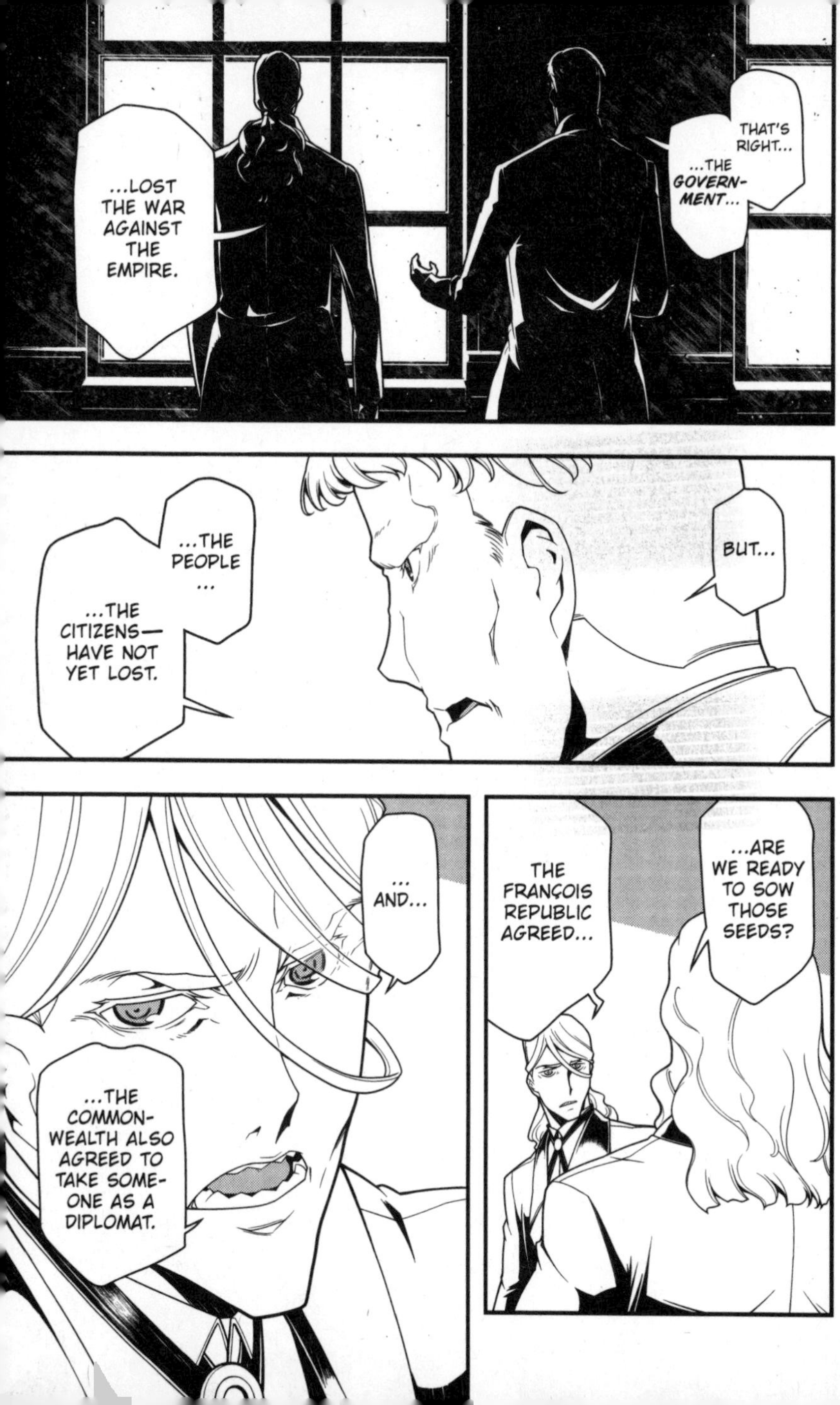
THAT'S RIGHT... ...THE *GOVERNMENT*...
...LOST THE WAR AGAINST THE EMPIRE.
BUT...
...THE PEOPLE...
...THE CITIZENS—HAVE NOT YET LOST.
...ARE WE READY TO SOW THOSE SEEDS?
THE FRANÇOIS REPUBLIC AGREED...
... AND...
...THE COMMONWEALTH ALSO AGREED TO TAKE SOMEONE AS A DIPLOMAT.

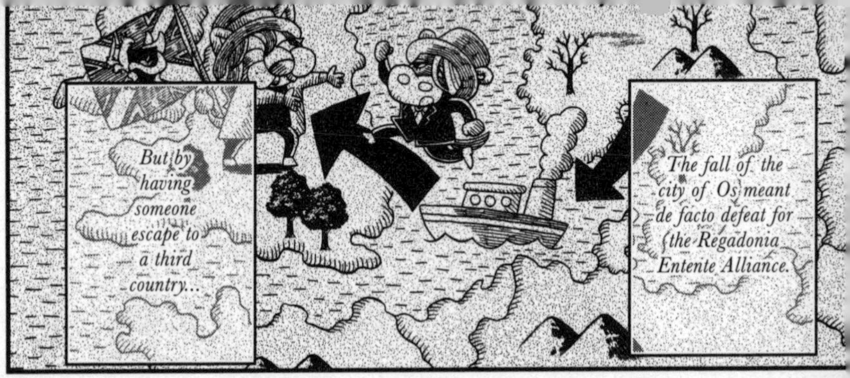
The fall of the city of Os meant de facto defeat for the Regadonia Entente Alliance.
But by having someone escape to a third country...
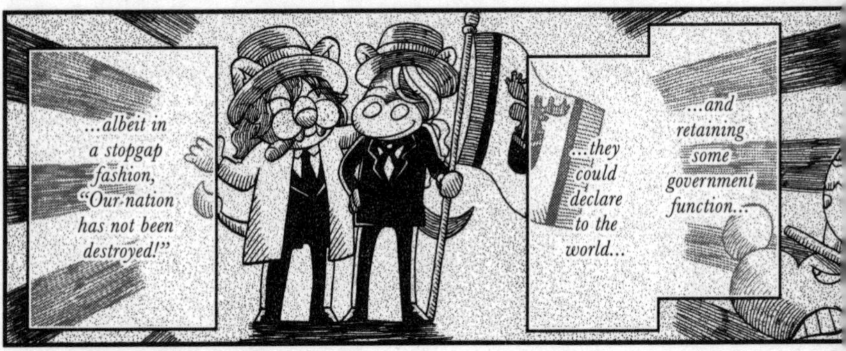
...and retaining some government function...
...they could declare to the world...
...albeit in a stopgap fashion, "Our nation has not been destroyed!"
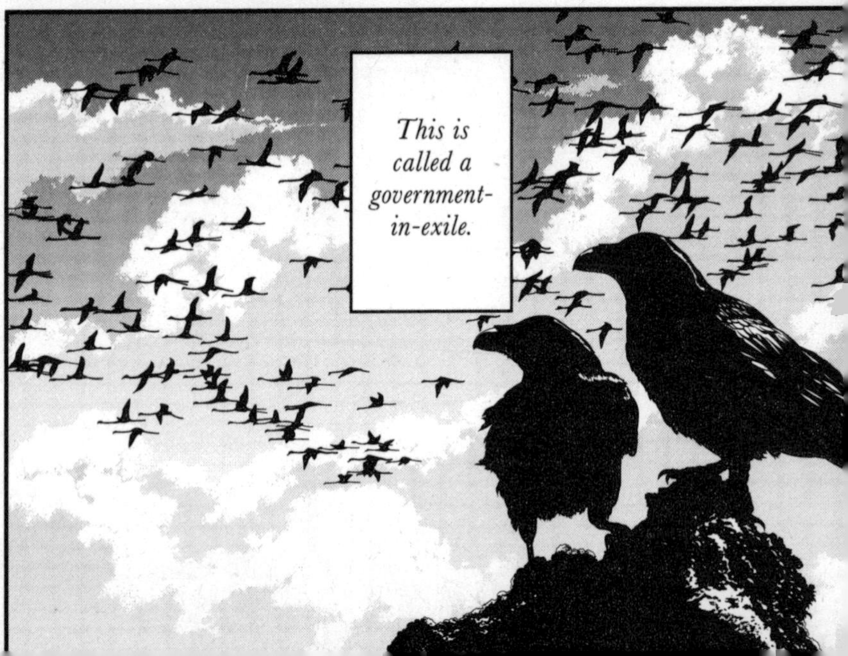
This is called a government-in-exile.

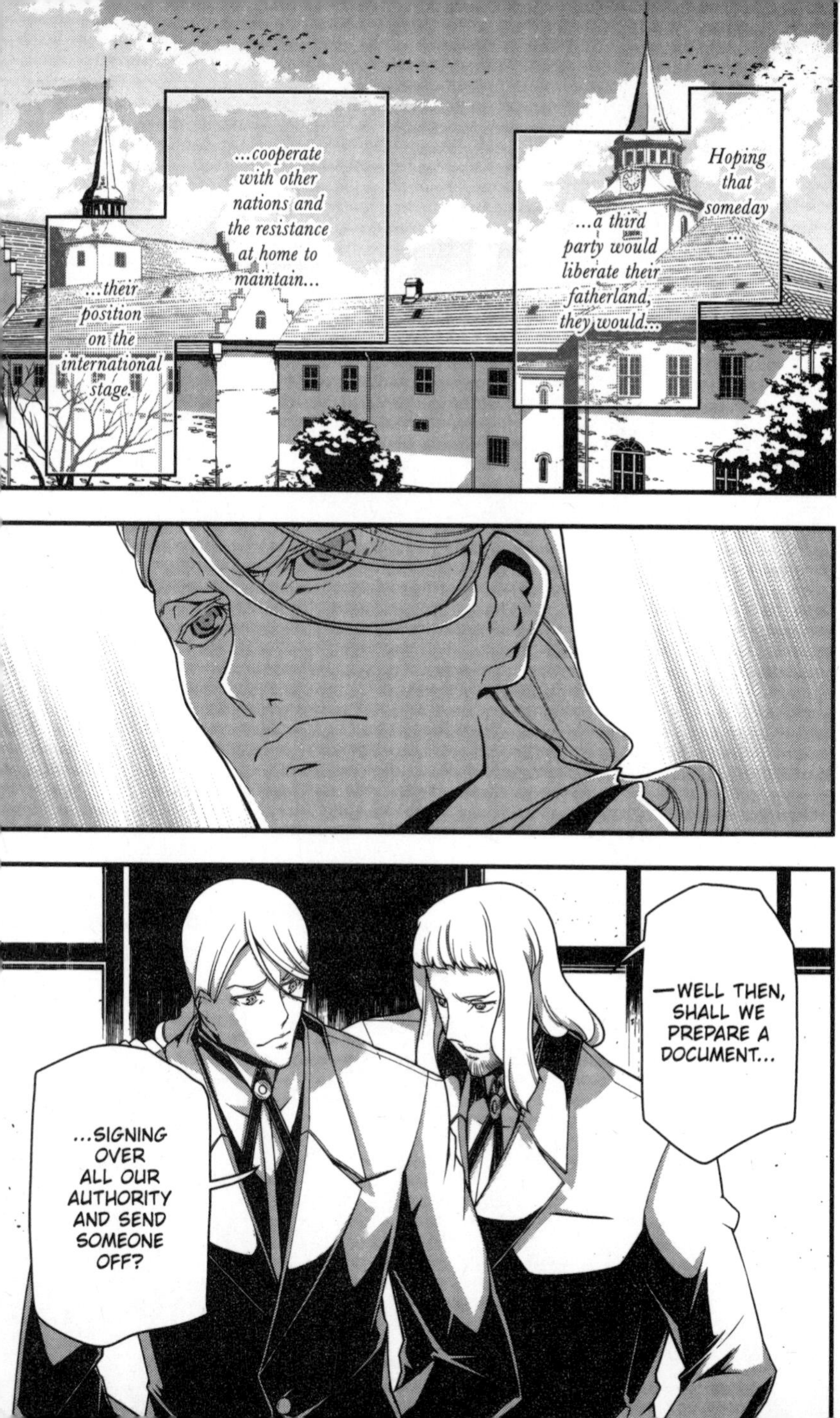
Hoping that someday...
...a third party would liberate their fatherland, they would...
...cooperate with other nations and the resistance at home to maintain...
...their position on the international stage.
—WELL THEN, SHALL WE PREPARE A DOCUMENT...
...SIGNING OVER ALL OUR AUTHORITY AND SEND SOMEONE OFF?

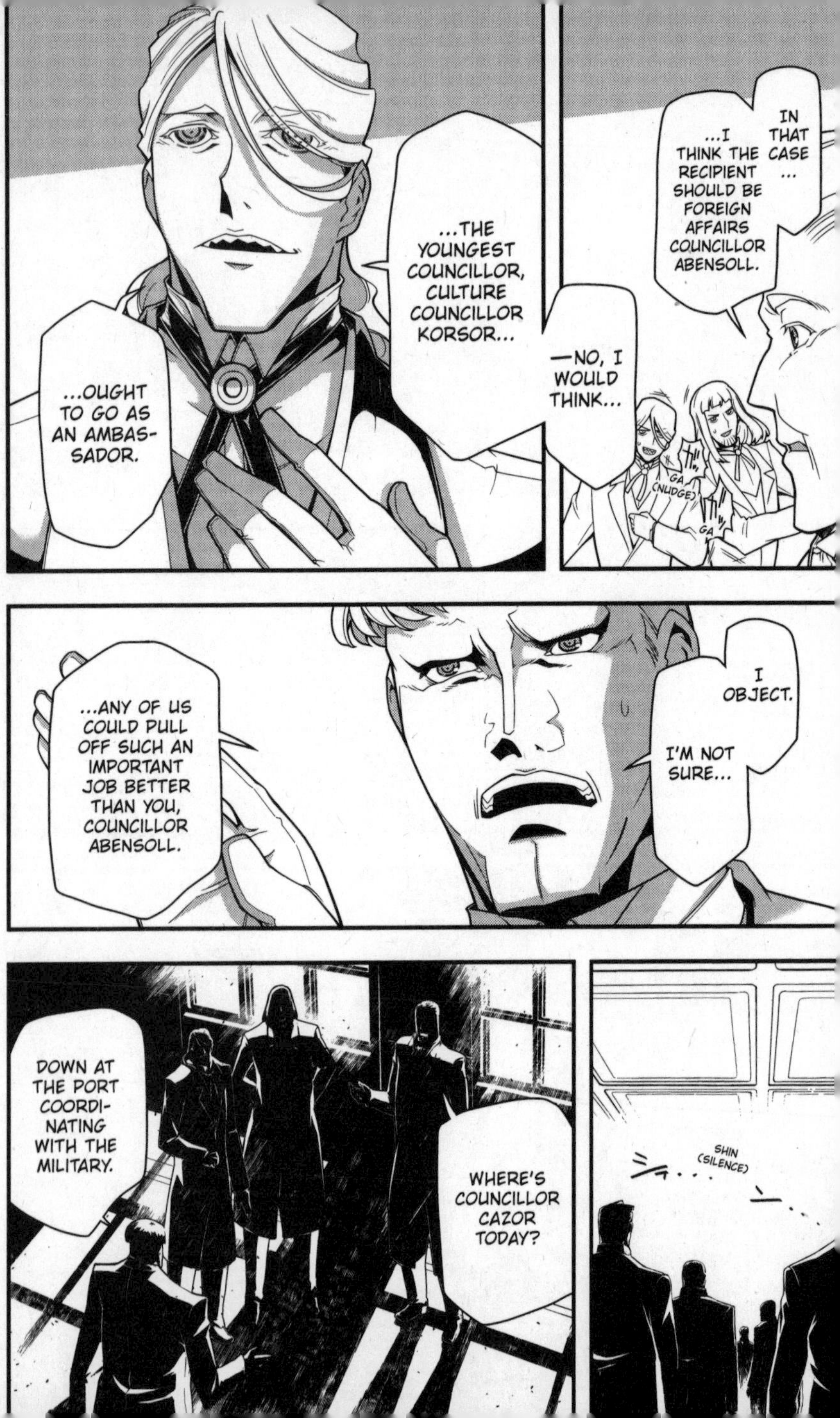
IN THAT CASE...
...I THINK THE RECIPIENT SHOULD BE FOREIGN AFFAIRS COUNCILLOR ABENSOLL.
—NO, I WOULD THINK...
GA (NUDGE)
GA
...THE YOUNGEST COUNCILLOR, CULTURE COUNCILLOR KORSOR...
...OUGHT TO GO AS AN AMBAS-SADOR.
I OBJECT.
I'M NOT SURE...
...ANY OF US COULD PULL OFF SUCH AN IMPORTANT JOB BETTER THAN YOU, COUNCILLOR ABENSOLL.
SHIN (SILENCE)
WHERE'S COUNCILLOR CAZOR TODAY?
DOWN AT THE PORT COORDI-NATING WITH THE MILITARY.

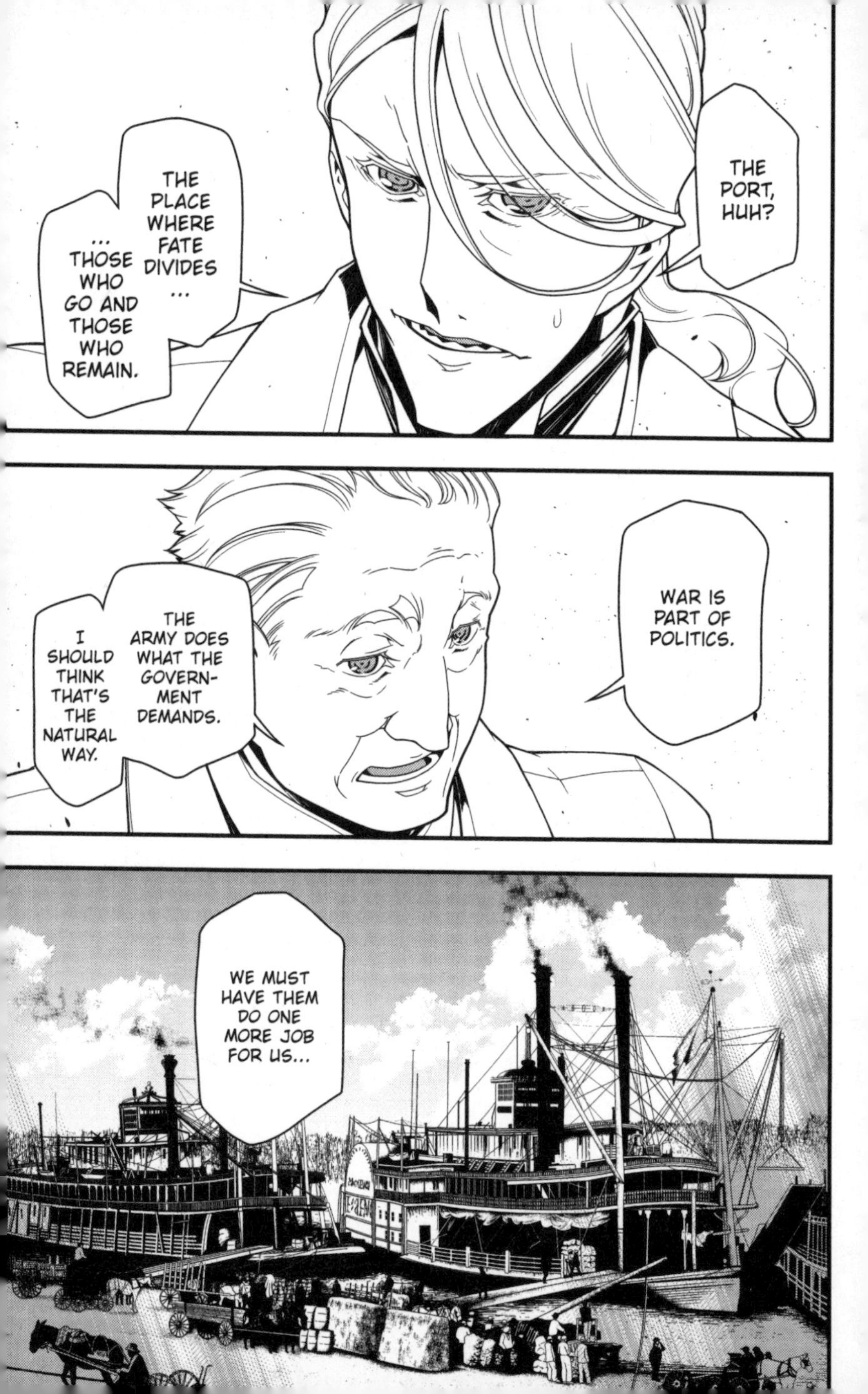
THE PORT, HUH?
THE PLACE WHERE FATE DIVIDES ...
... THOSE WHO GO AND THOSE WHO REMAIN.
WAR IS PART OF POLITICS.
THE ARMY DOES WHAT THE GOVERN-MENT DEMANDS.
I SHOULD THINK THAT'S THE NATURAL WAY.
WE MUST HAVE THEM DO ONE MORE JOB FOR US...

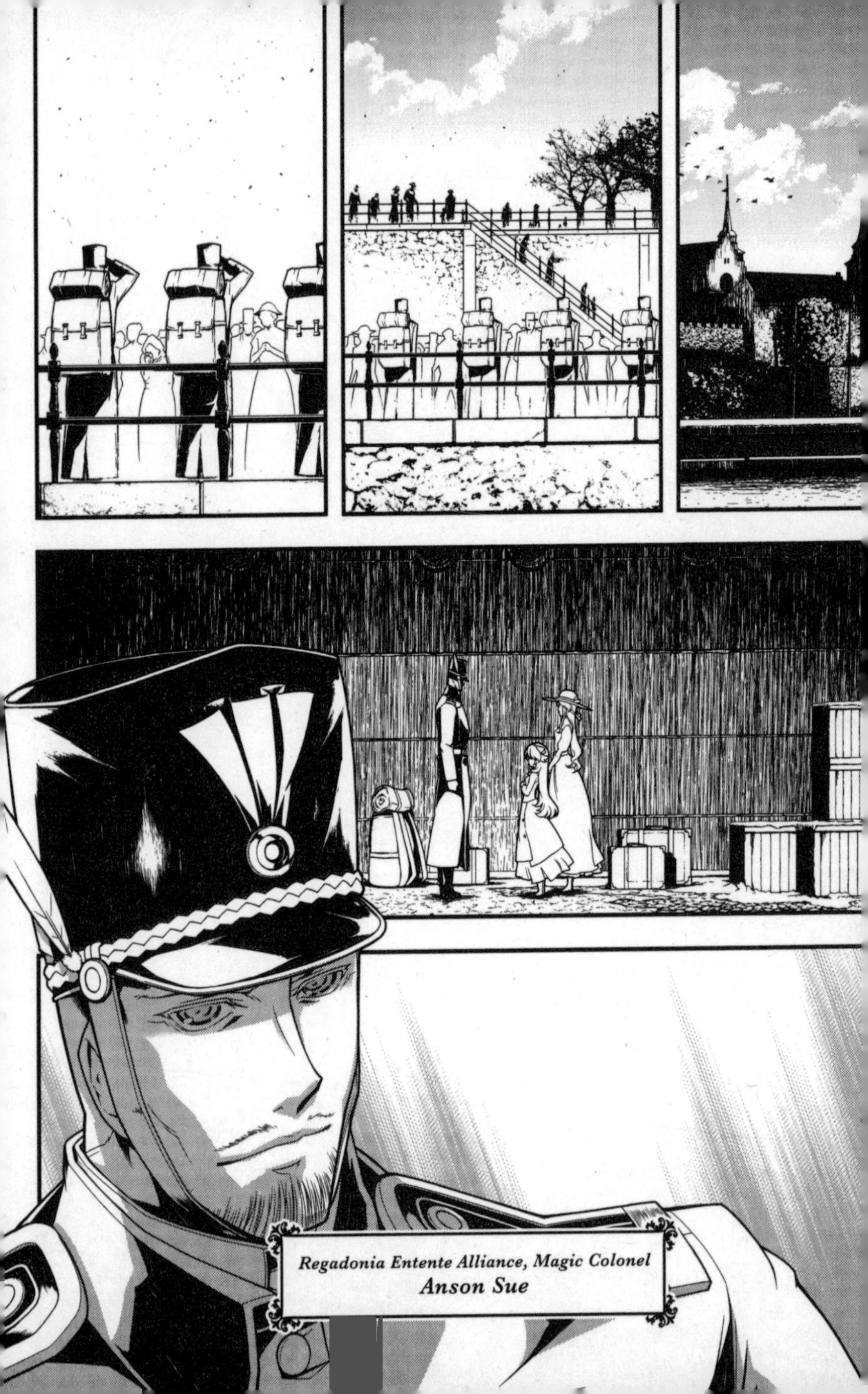
Regadonia Entente Alliance, Magic Colonel
Anson Sue

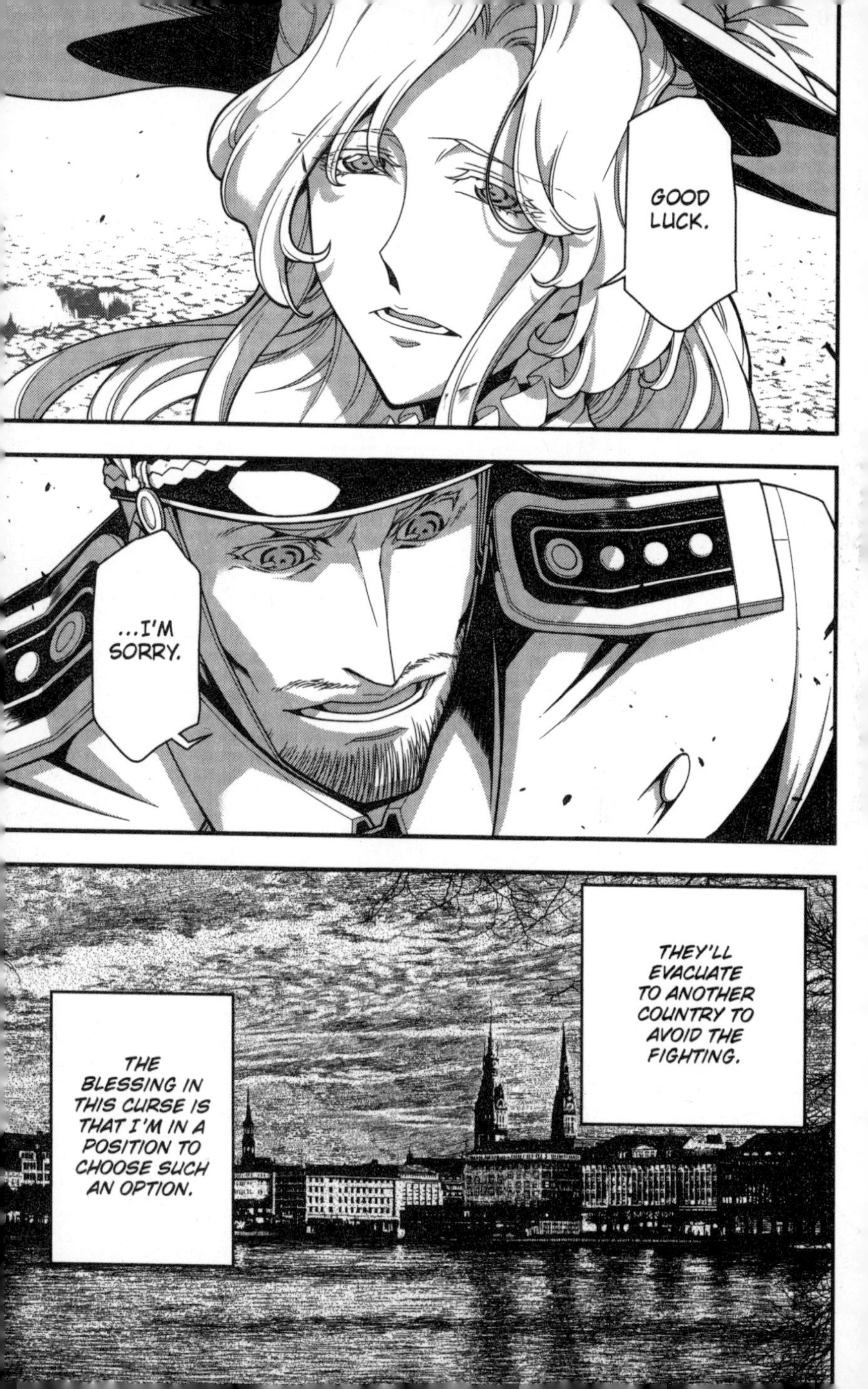
GOOD LUCK.
...I'M SORRY.
THEY'LL EVACUATE TO ANOTHER COUNTRY TO AVOID THE FIGHTING.
THE BLESSING IN THIS CURSE IS THAT I'M IN A POSITION TO CHOOSE SUCH AN OPTION.

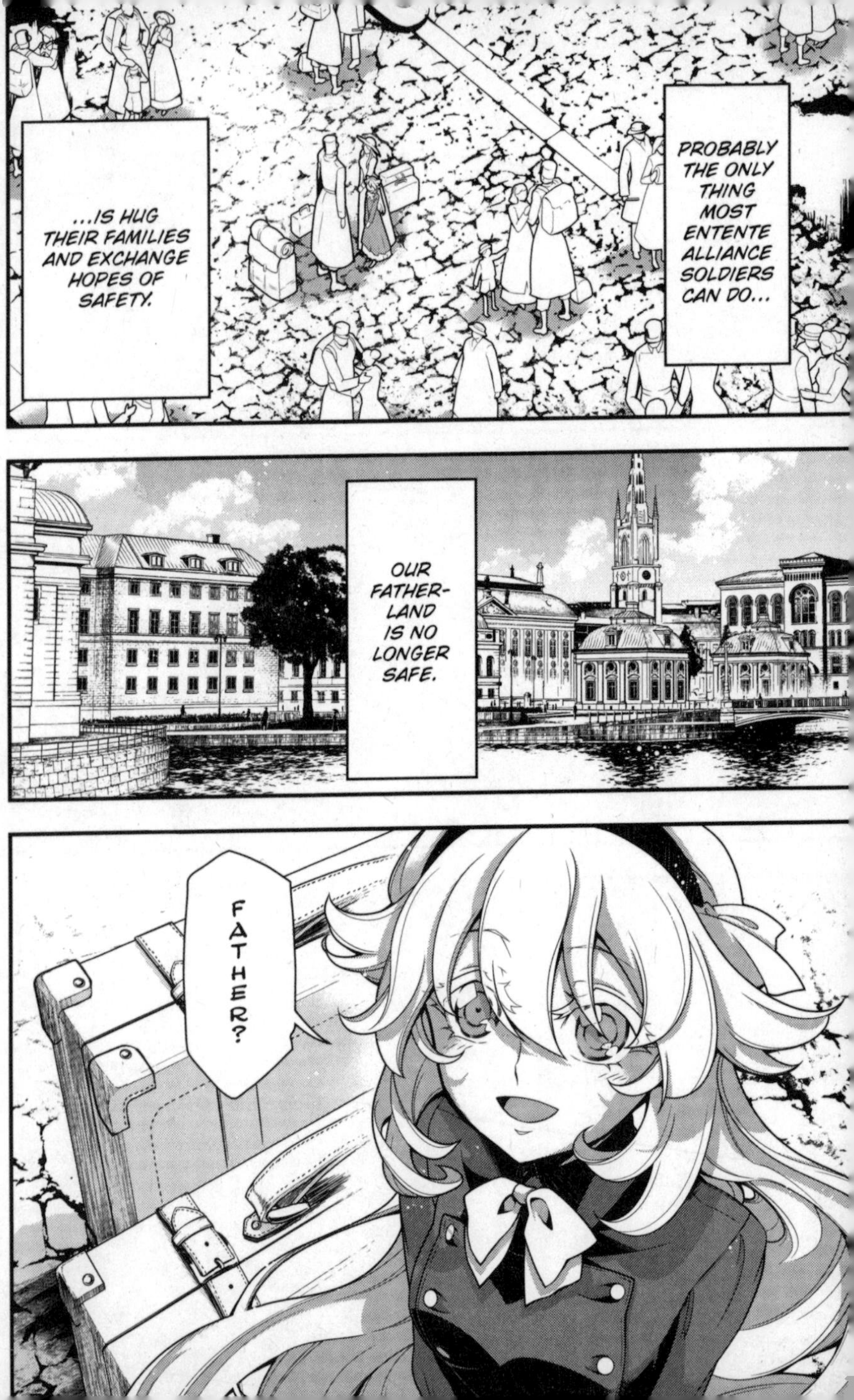
PROBABLY THE ONLY THING MOST ENTENTE ALLIANCE SOLDIERS CAN DO...
...IS HUG THEIR FAMILIES AND EXCHANGE HOPES OF SAFETY.
OUR FATHER-LAND IS NO LONGER SAFE.
FATHER?

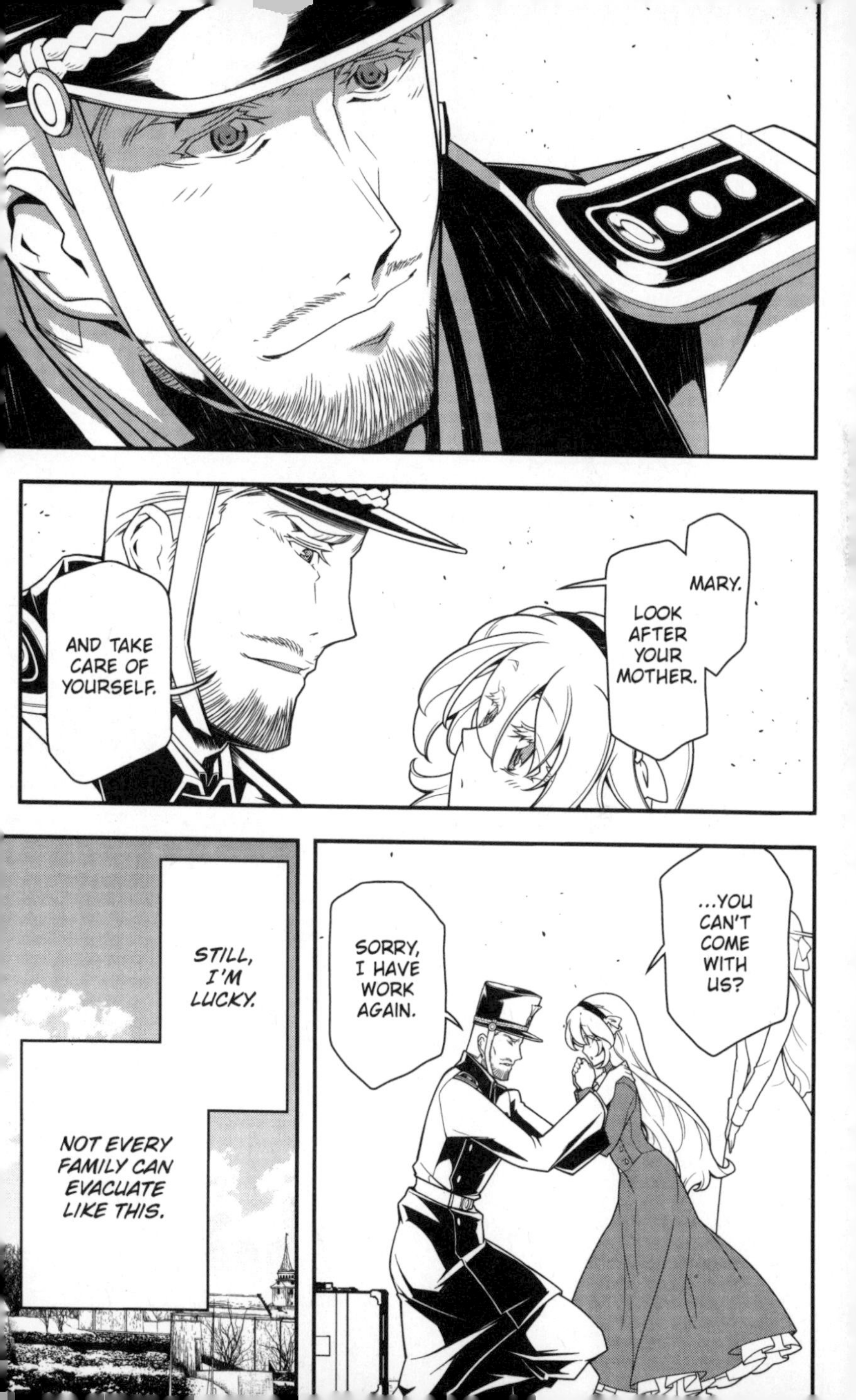
MARY. LOOK AFTER YOUR MOTHER.
AND TAKE CARE OF YOURSELF.
...YOU CAN'T COME WITH US?
SORRY, I HAVE WORK AGAIN.
STILL, I'M LUCKY.
NOT EVERY FAMILY CAN EVACUATE LIKE THIS.

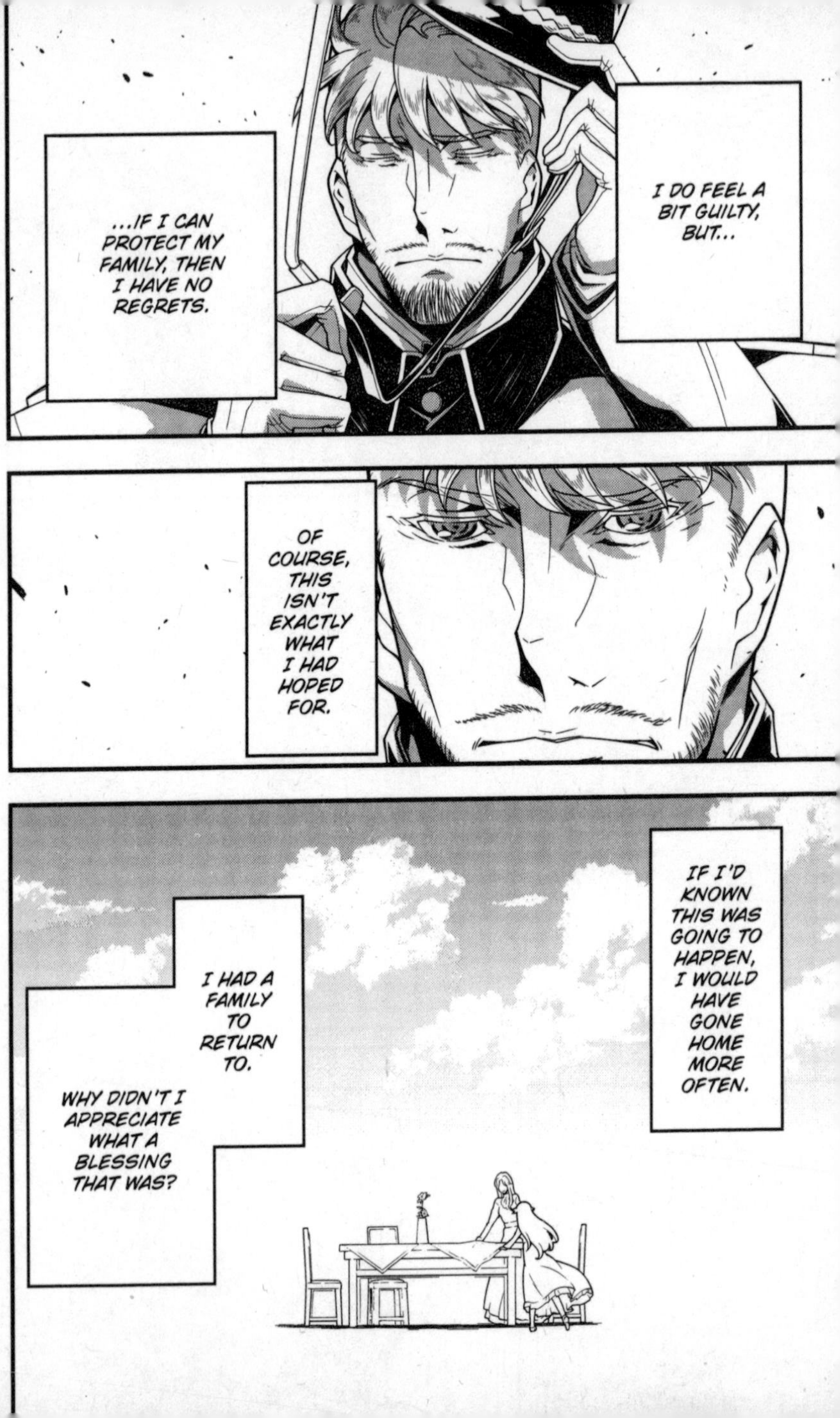
I DO FEEL A BIT GUILTY, BUT...
...IF I CAN PROTECT MY FAMILY, THEN I HAVE NO REGRETS.
OF COURSE, THIS ISN'T EXACTLY WHAT I HAD HOPED FOR.
IF I'D KNOWN THIS WAS GOING TO HAPPEN, I WOULD HAVE GONE HOME MORE OFTEN.
I HAD A FAMILY TO RETURN TO.
WHY DIDN'T I APPRECIATE WHAT A BLESSING THAT WAS?

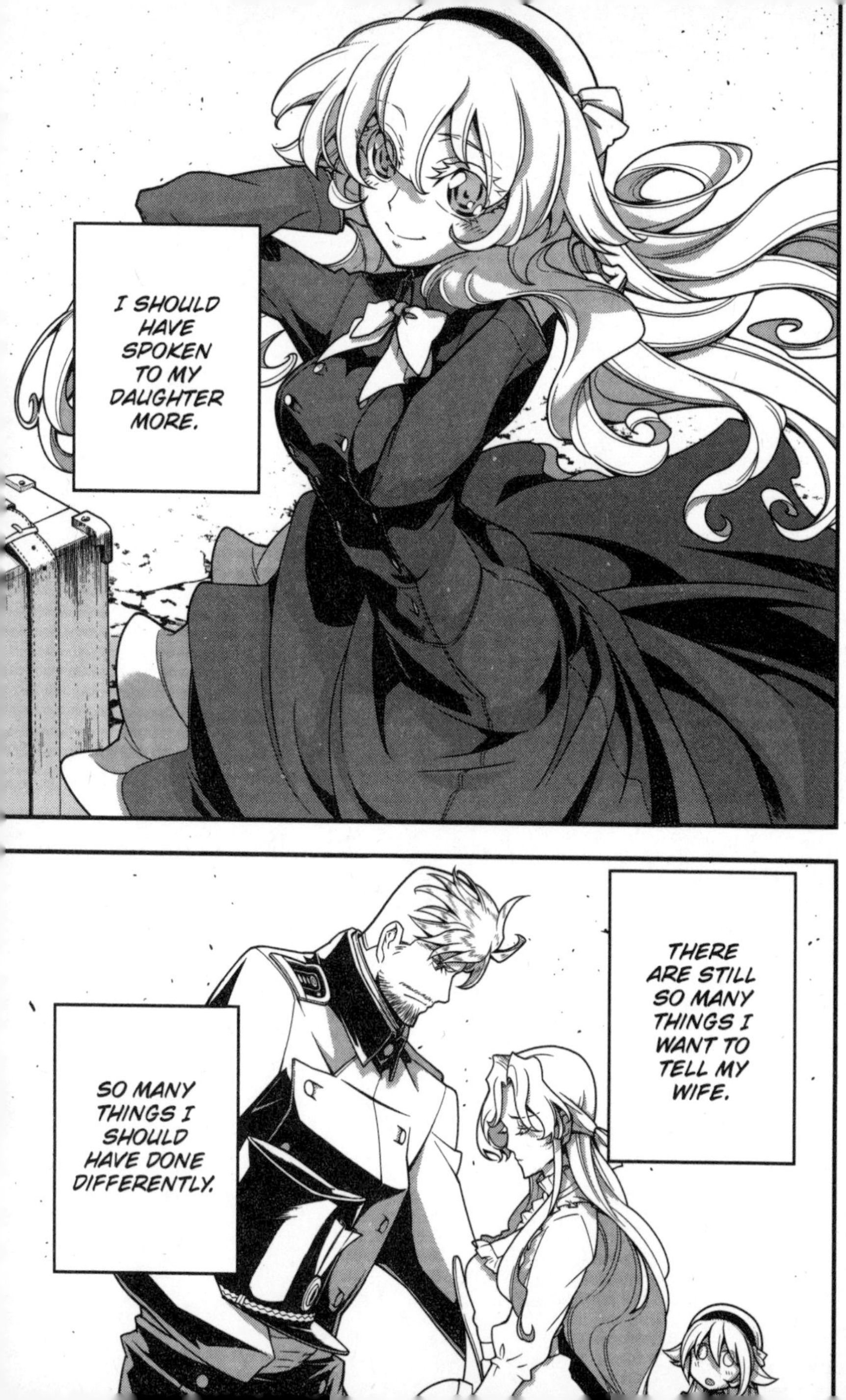
I SHOULD HAVE SPOKEN TO MY DAUGHTER MORE.
THERE ARE STILL SO MANY THINGS I WANT TO TELL MY WIFE.
SO MANY THINGS I SHOULD HAVE DONE DIFFERENTLY.

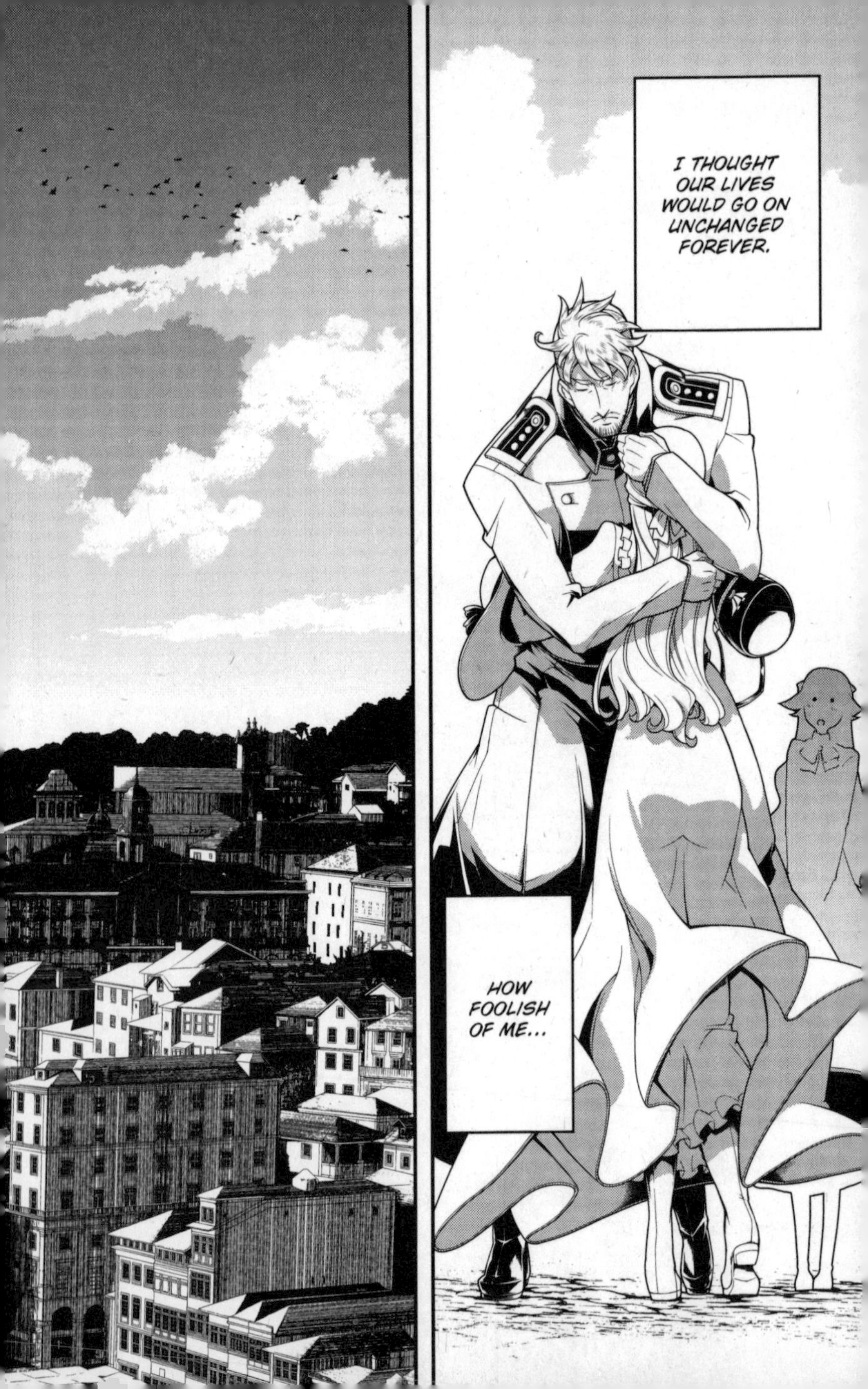
I THOUGHT OUR LIVES WOULD GO ON UNCHANGED FOREVER.
HOW FOOLISH OF ME...

Chapter 23
Devil of the Norden Coast I

The Saga of Tanya the Evil
Chapter: 23

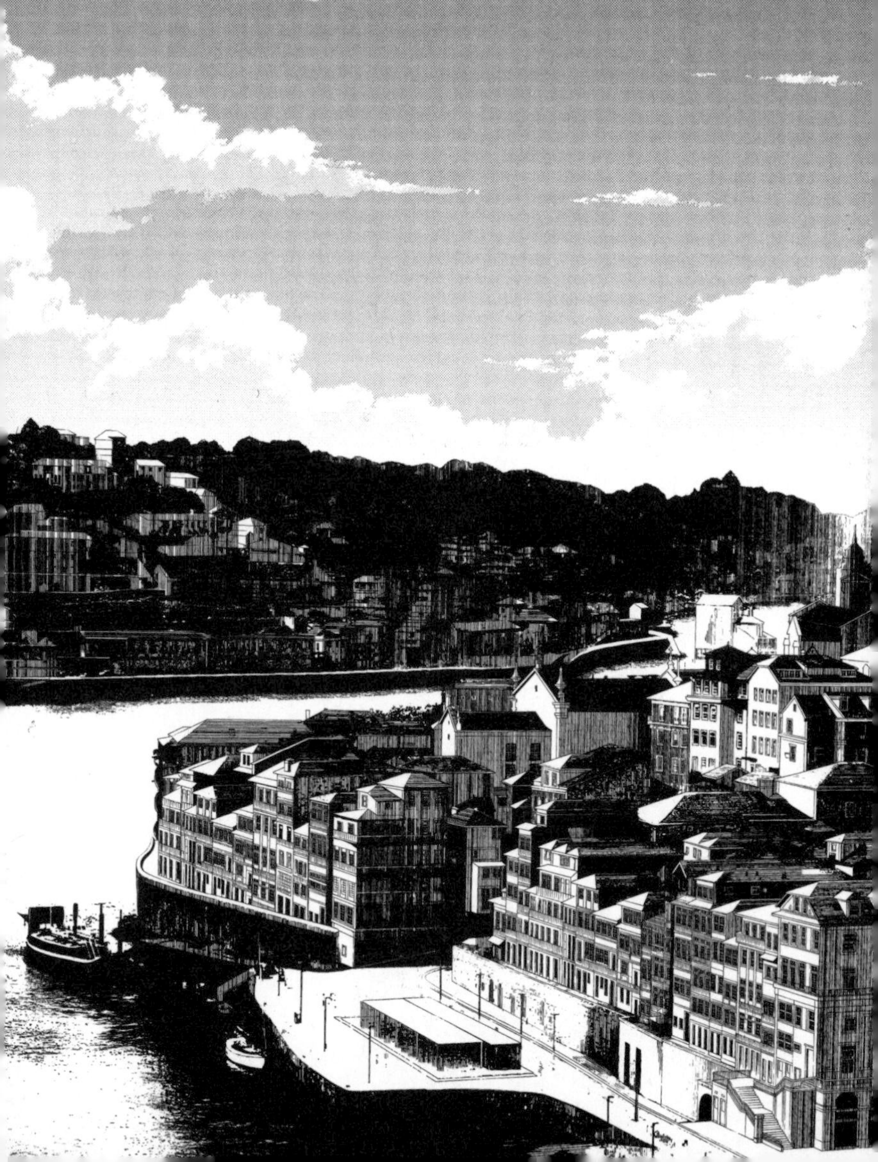

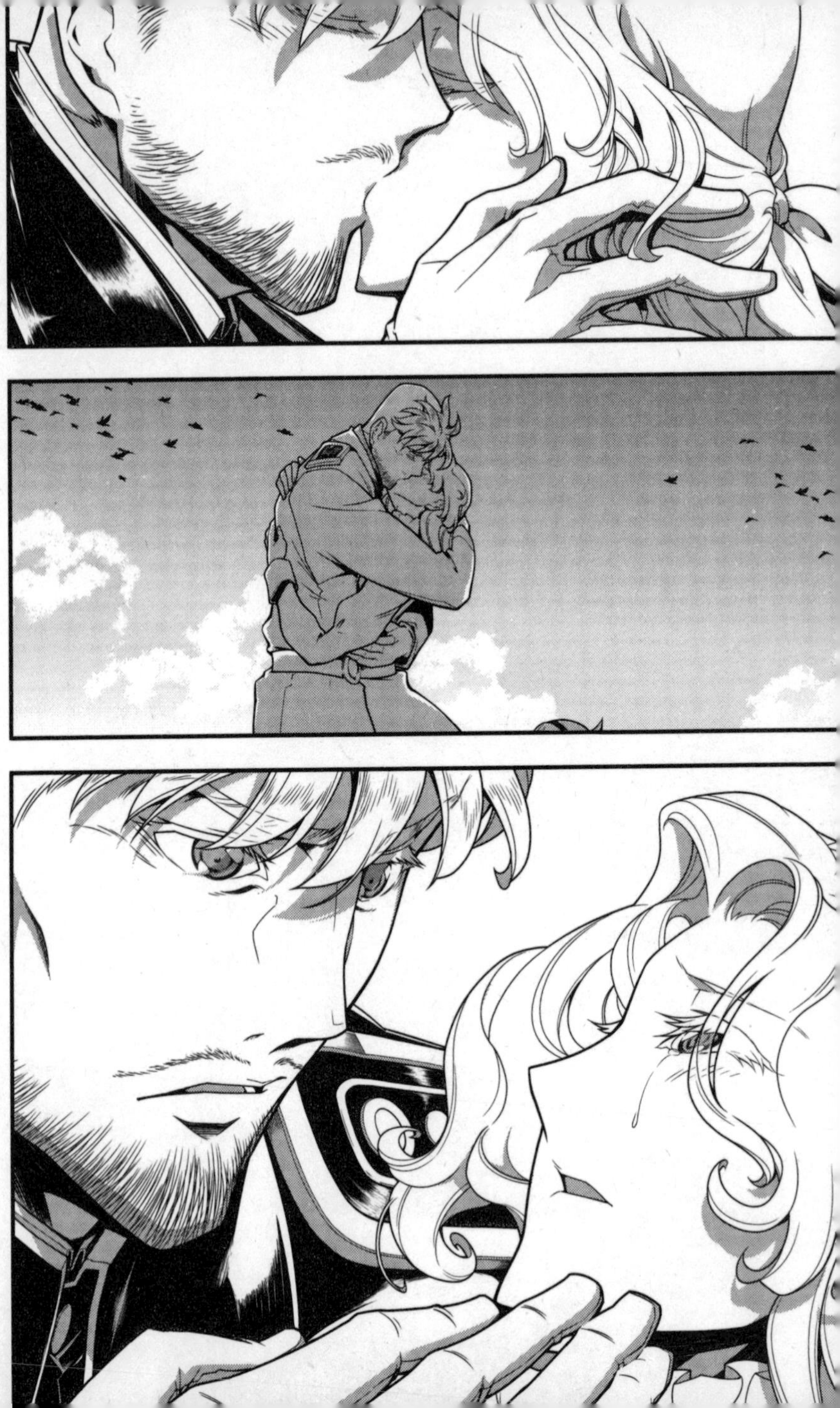

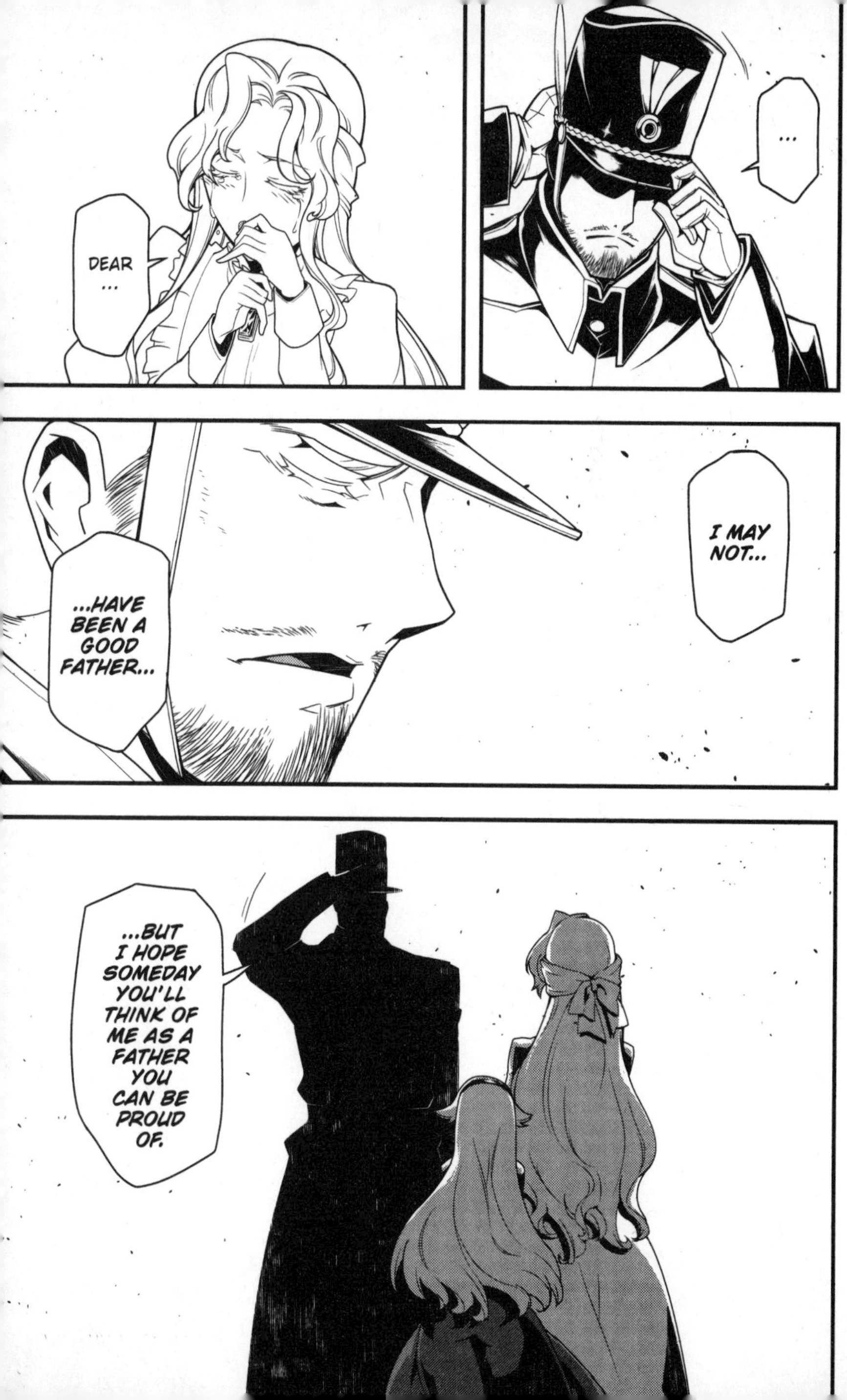
...
DEAR ...
I MAY NOT...
...HAVE BEEN A GOOD FATHER...
...BUT I HOPE SOMEDAY YOU'LL THINK OF ME AS A FATHER YOU CAN BE PROUD OF.

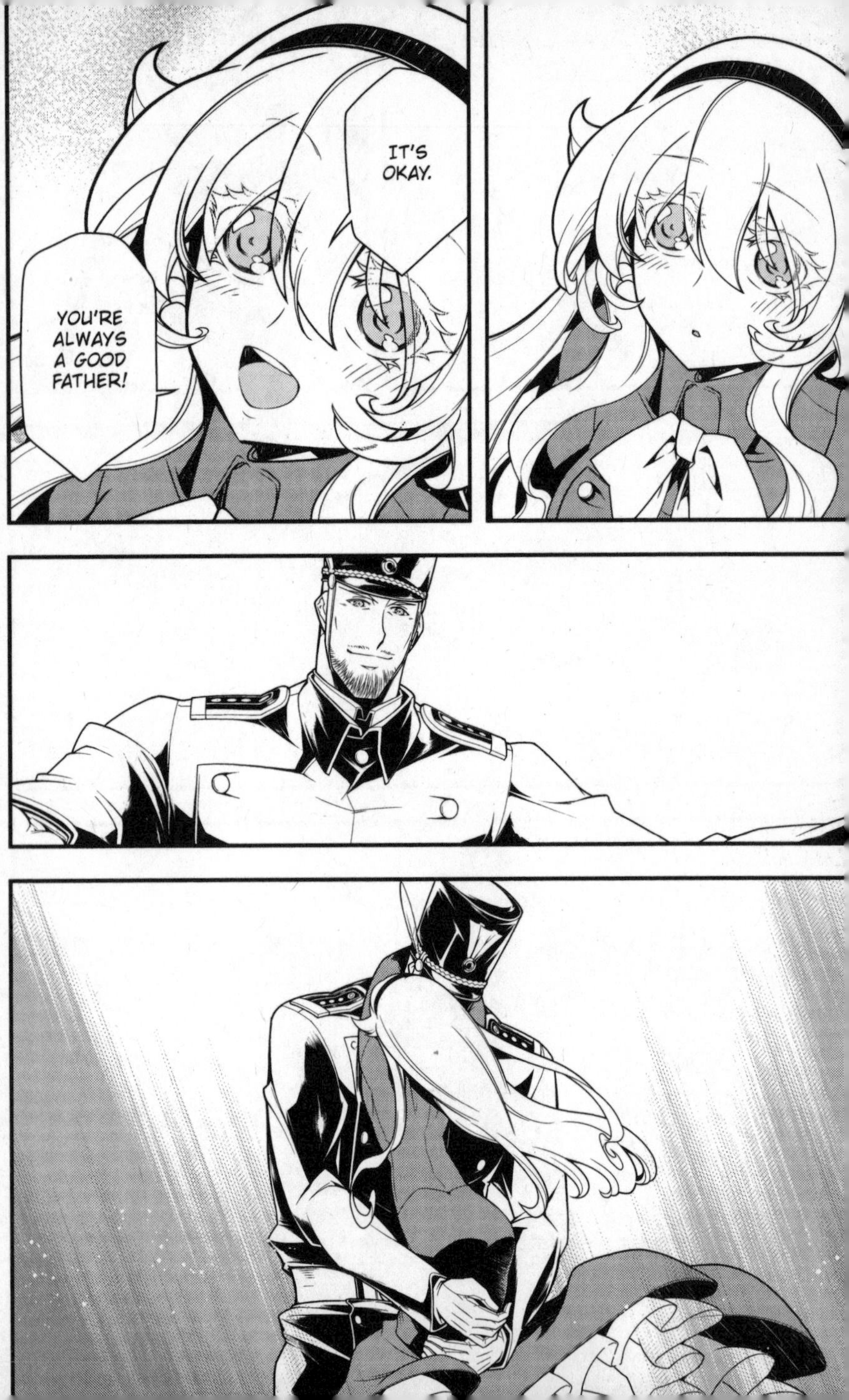
IT'S OKAY.
YOU'RE ALWAYS A GOOD FATHER!

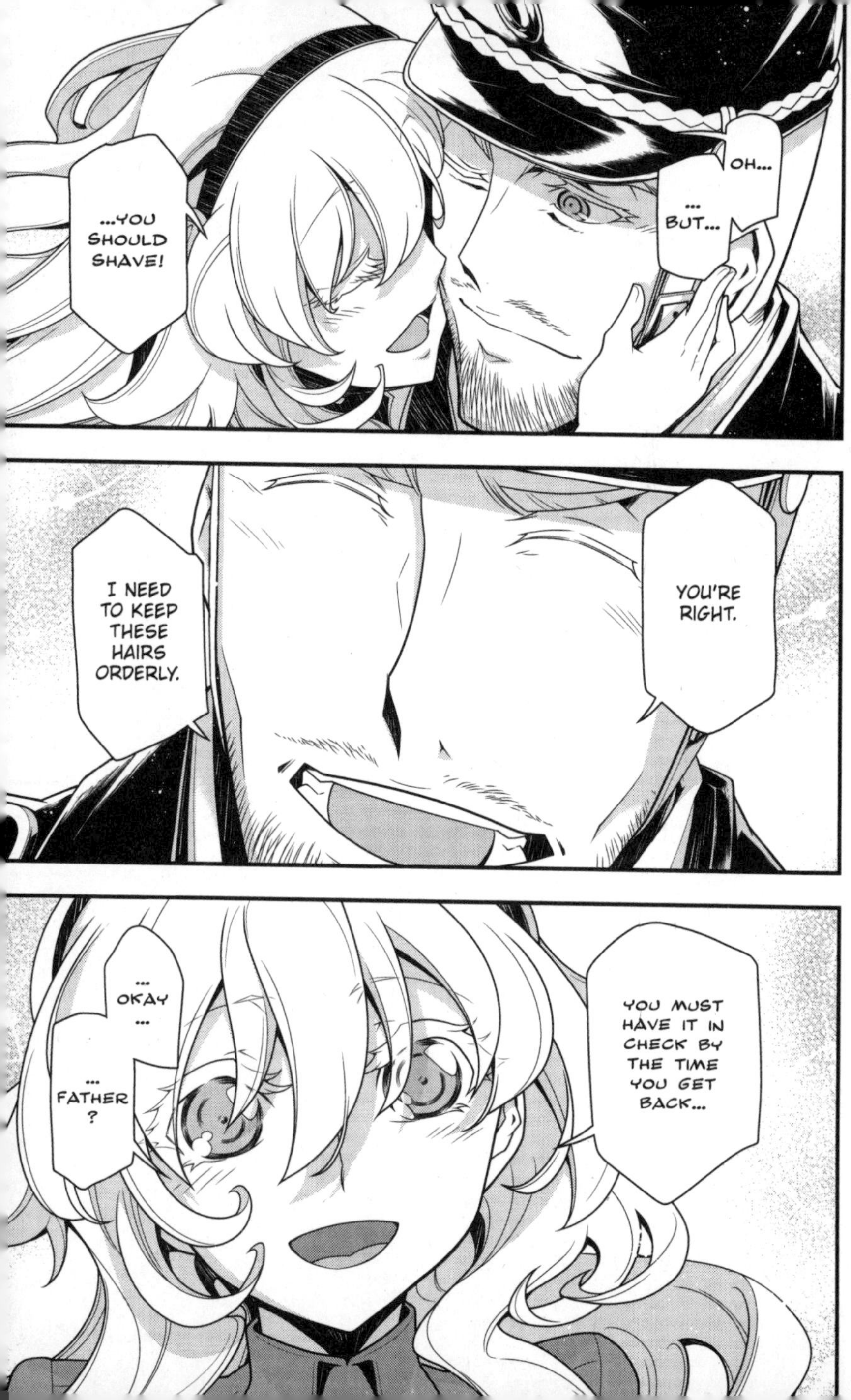
OH... ... BUT...
...YOU SHOULD SHAVE!
YOU'RE RIGHT.
I NEED TO KEEP THESE HAIRS ORDERLY.
YOU MUST HAVE IT IN CHECK BY THE TIME YOU GET BACK...
... OKAY ...
... FATHER ?

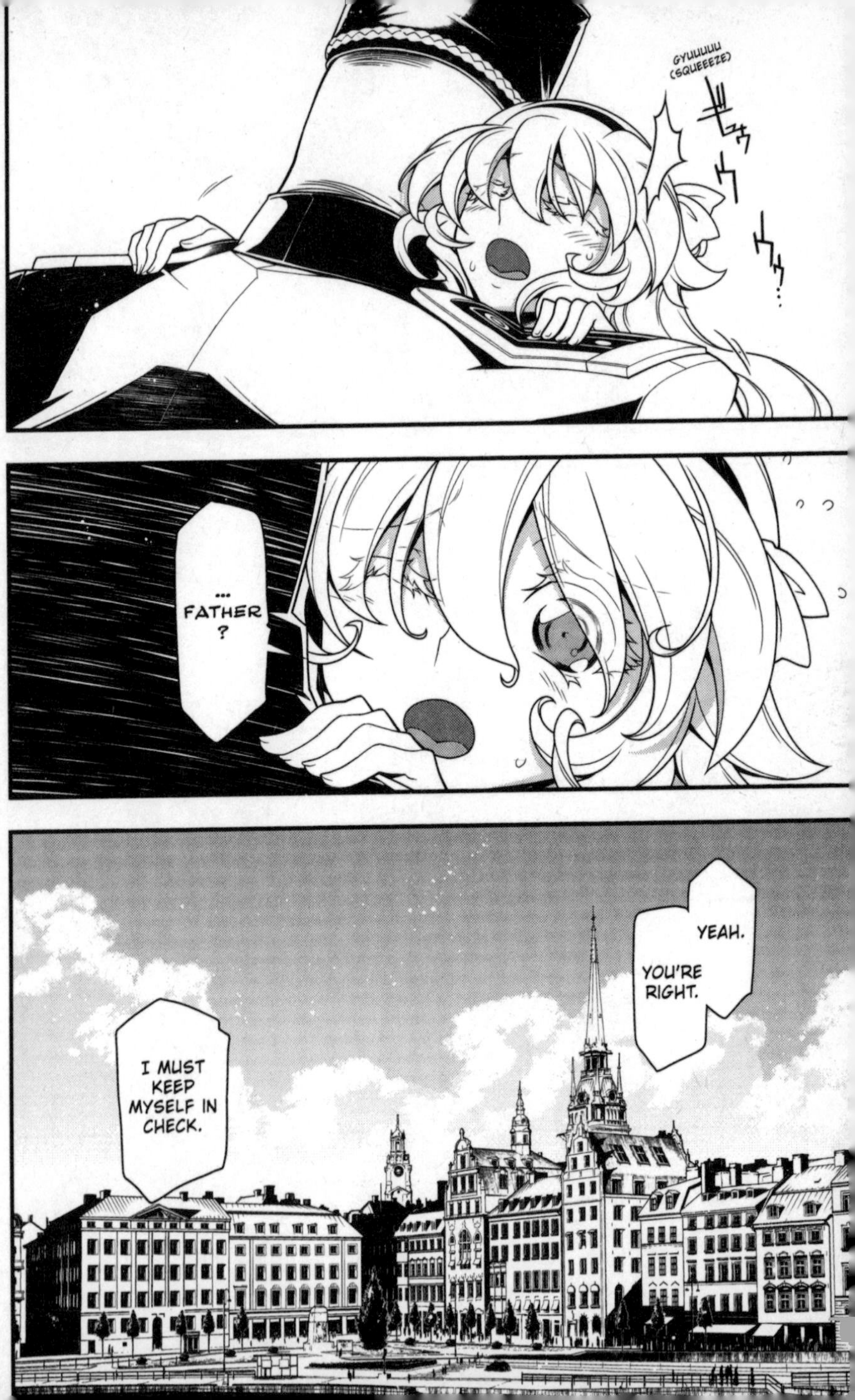
GYUUUUU (SQUEEEZE)
...FATHER?
YEAH.
YOU'RE RIGHT.
I MUST KEEP MYSELF IN CHECK.

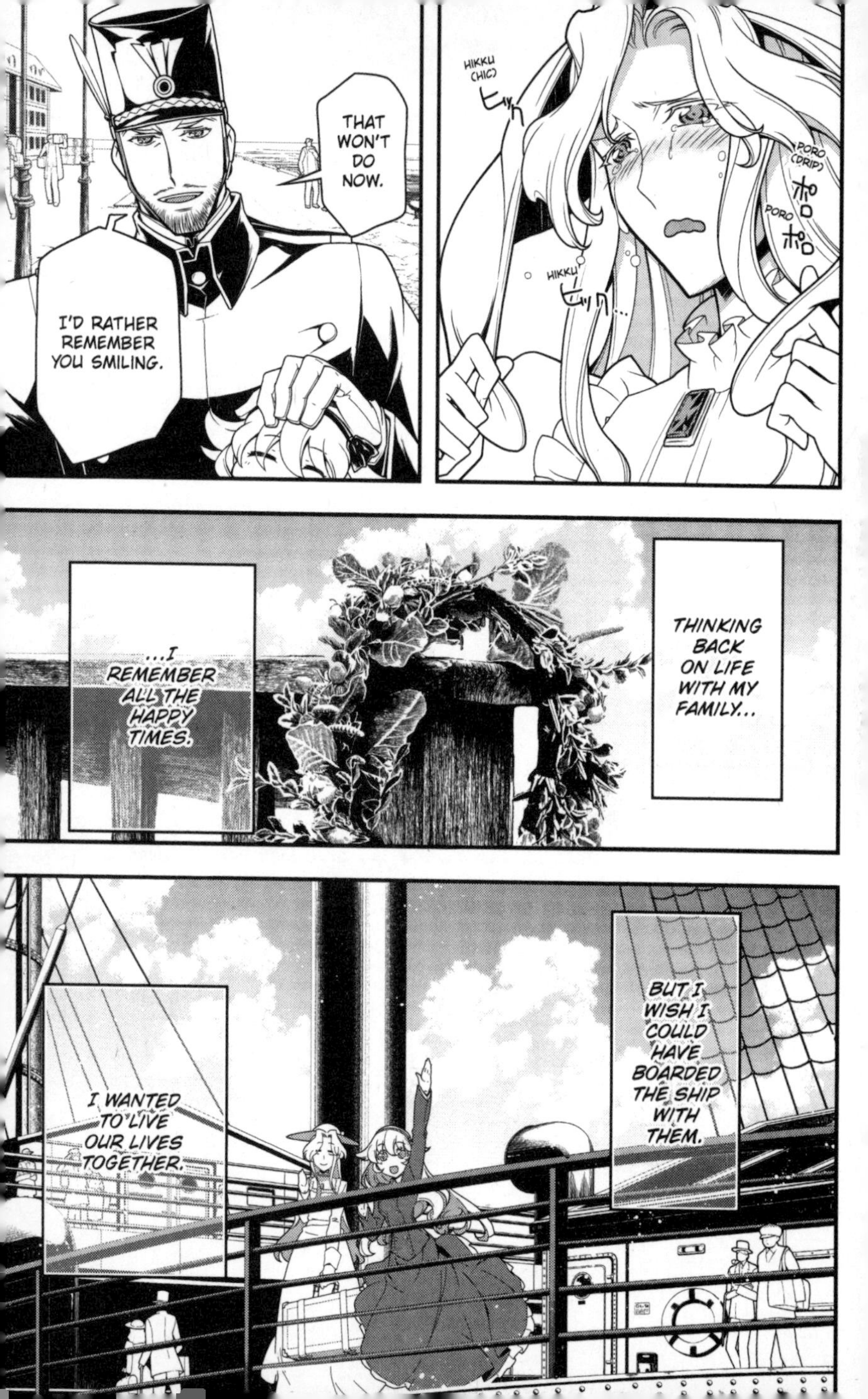
HIKKU (HIC)
ヒック
PORO (DRIP)
ポロ
PORO
ポロ
HIKKU
ヒック…
THAT WON'T DO NOW.
I'D RATHER REMEMBER YOU SMILING.
THINKING BACK ON LIFE WITH MY FAMILY...
...I REMEMBER ALL THE HAPPY TIMES.
BUT I WISH I COULD HAVE BOARDED THE SHIP WITH THEM.
I WANTED TO LIVE OUR LIVES TOGETHER.

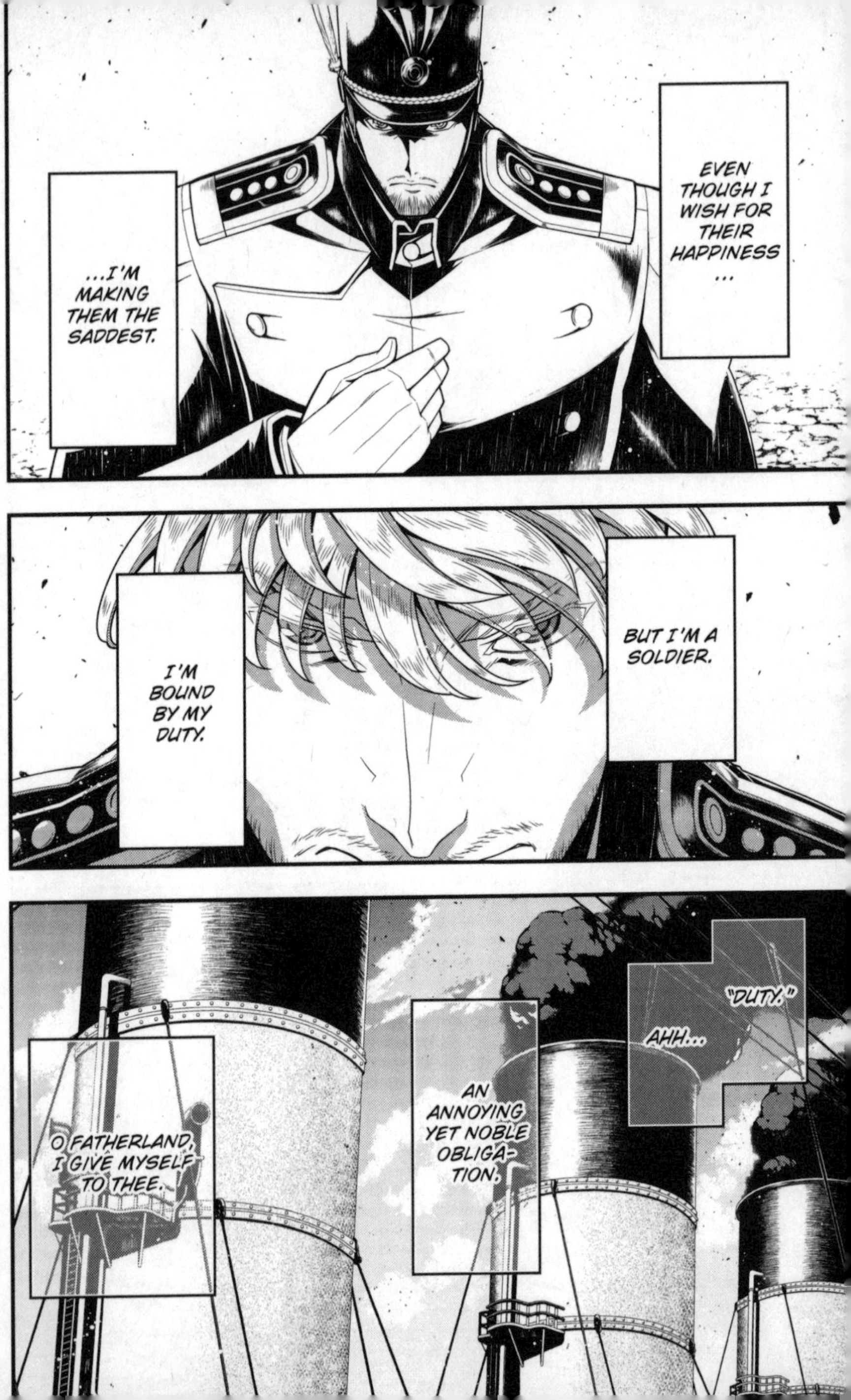
EVEN THOUGH I WISH FOR THEIR HAPPINESS...
...I'M MAKING THEM THE SADDEST.
BUT I'M A SOLDIER.
I'M BOUND BY MY DUTY.
"DUTY."
AHH...
AN ANNOYING YET NOBLE OBLIGATION.
O FATHERLAND, I GIVE MYSELF TO THEE.

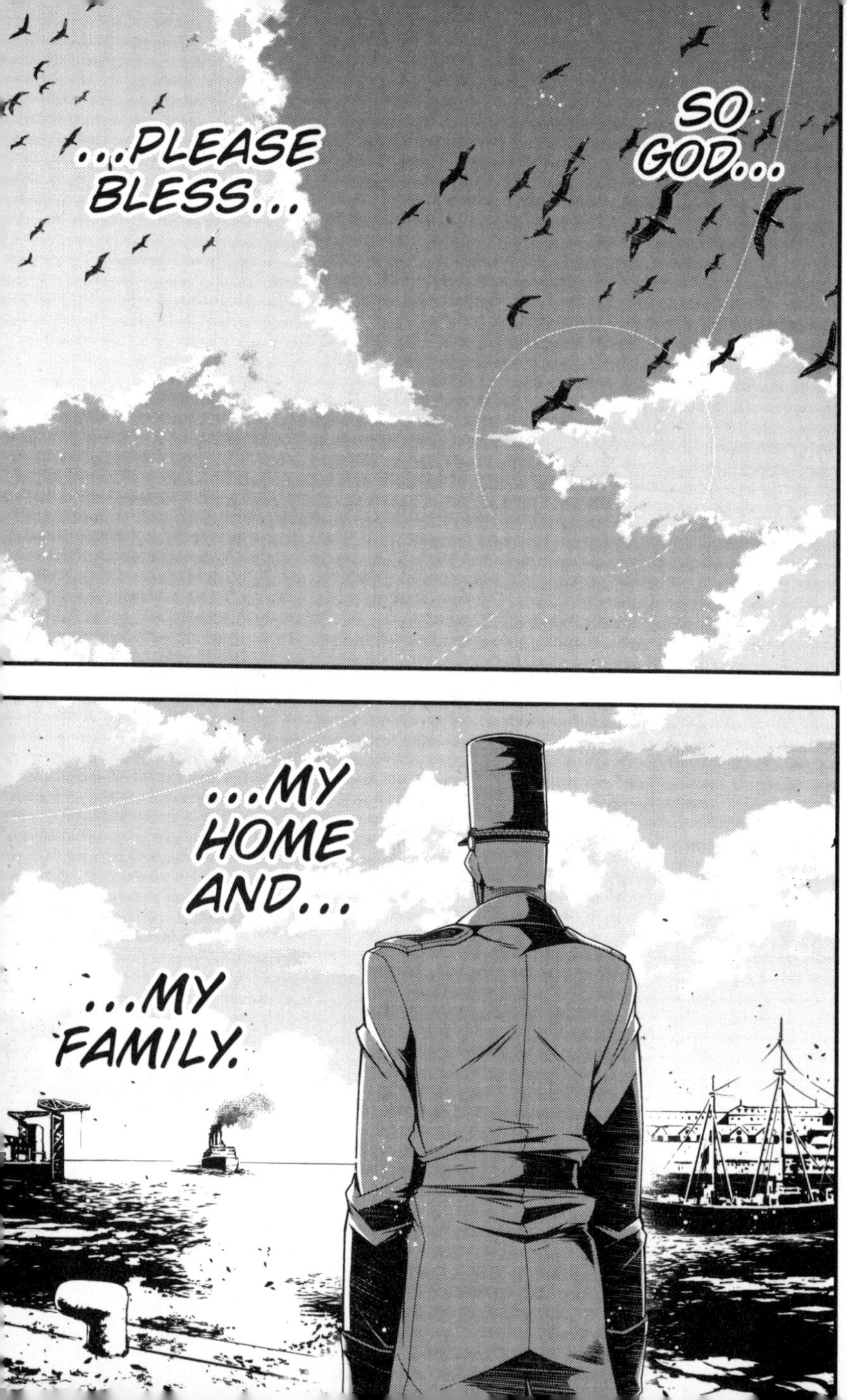
SO GOD...
...PLEASE BLESS...
...MY HOME AND...
...MY FAMILY.

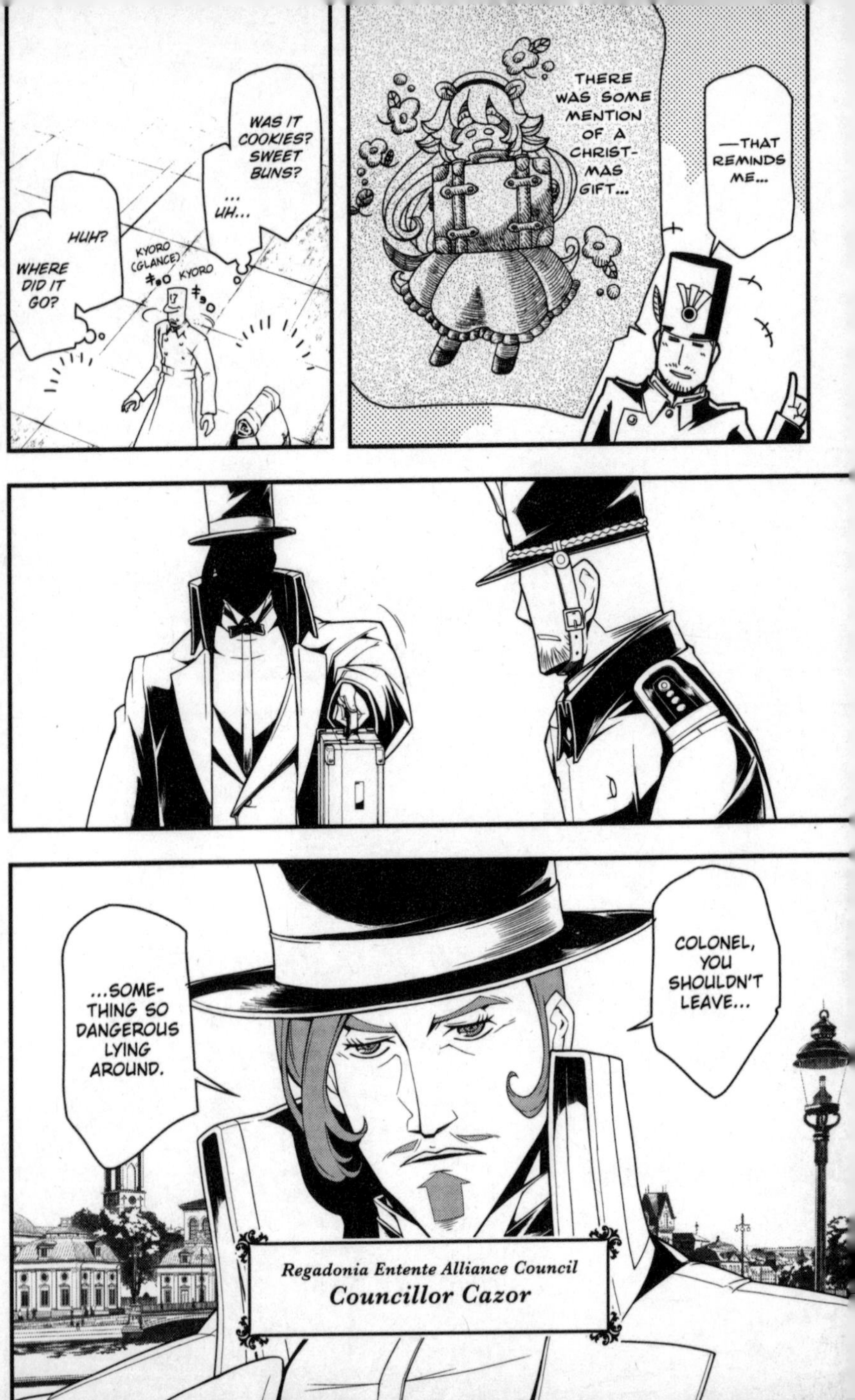
—THAT REMINDS ME...
THERE WAS SOME MENTION OF A CHRIST-MAS GIFT...
WAS IT COOKIES? SWEET BUNS?
...UH...
KYORO (GLANCE)
KYORO
HUH?
WHERE DID IT GO?
COLONEL, YOU SHOULDN'T LEAVE...
...SOME-THING SO DANGEROUS LYING AROUND.
Regadonia Entente Alliance Council
Councillor Cazor

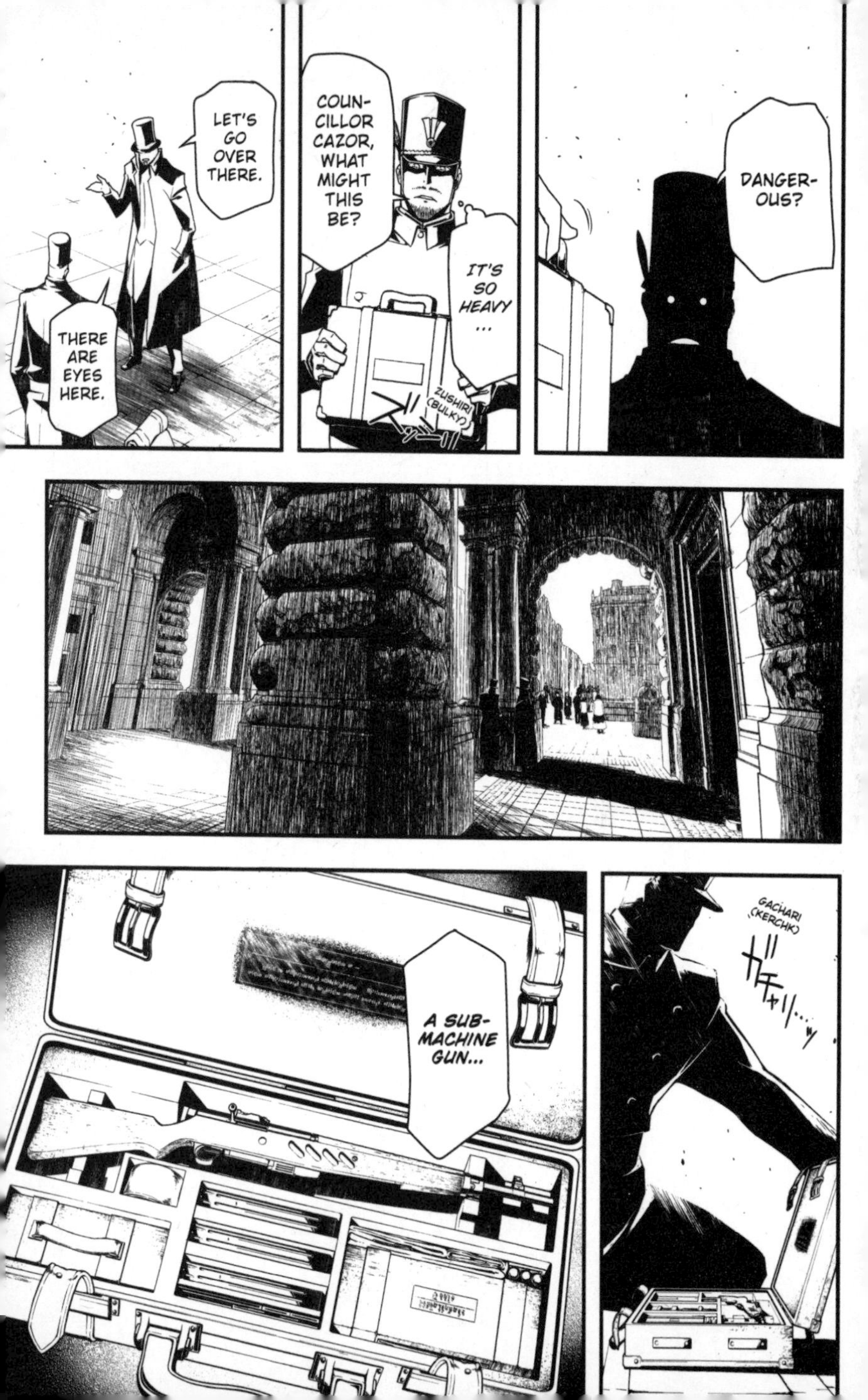
DANGER-OUS?
COUN-CILLOR CAZOR, WHAT MIGHT THIS BE?
IT'S SO HEAVY ...
ZUSHIRI (BULKY)
LET'S GO OVER THERE.
THERE ARE EYES HERE.
GACHARI (KERCHK)
A SUB-MACHINE GUN...

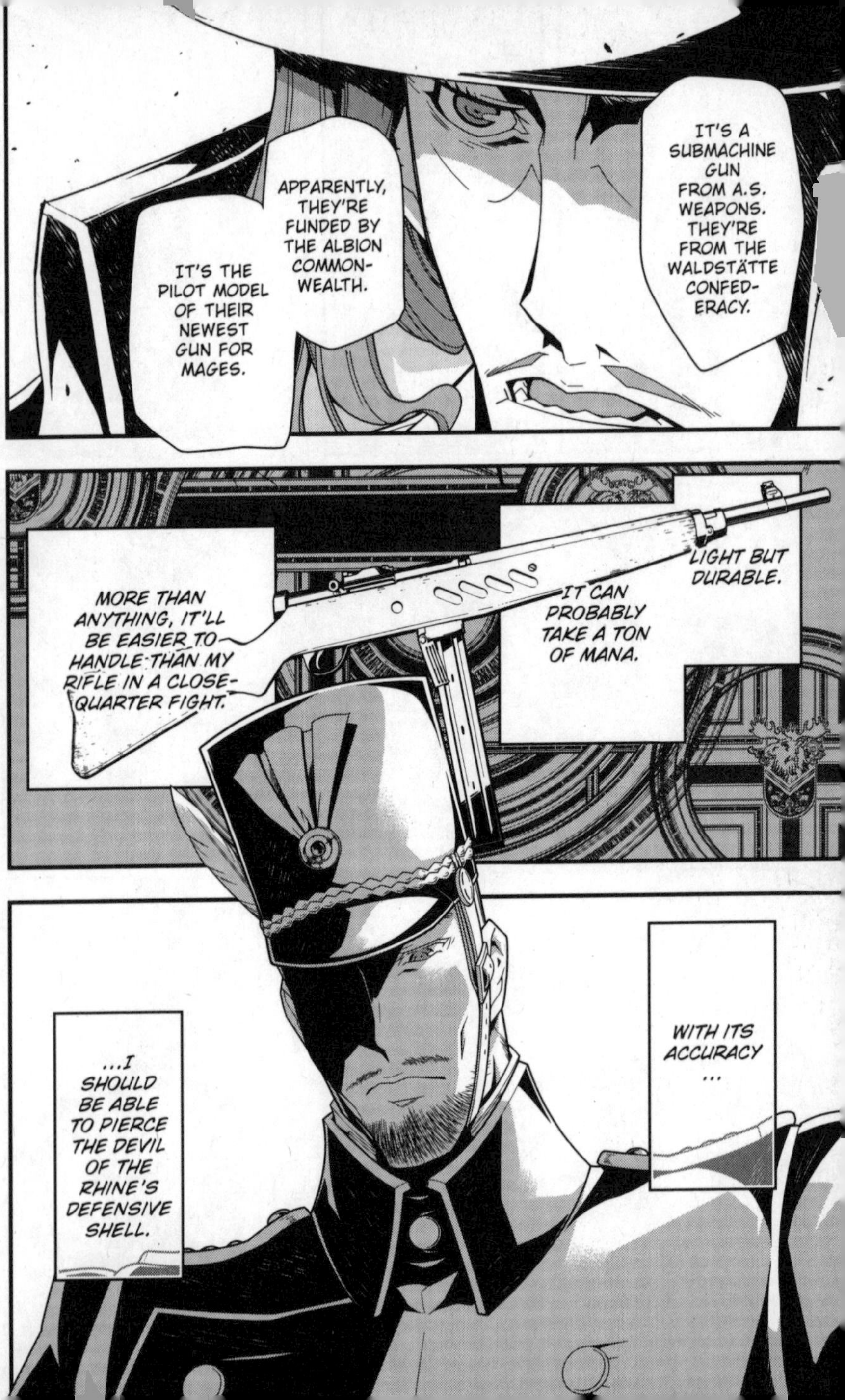
IT'S A SUBMACHINE GUN FROM A.S. WEAPONS. THEY'RE FROM THE WALDSTÄTTE CONFED-ERACY.
APPARENTLY, THEY'RE FUNDED BY THE ALBION COMMON-WEALTH.
IT'S THE PILOT MODEL OF THEIR NEWEST GUN FOR MAGES.
LIGHT BUT DURABLE.
IT CAN PROBABLY TAKE A TON OF MANA.
MORE THAN ANYTHING, IT'LL BE EASIER TO HANDLE THAN MY RIFLE IN A CLOSE-QUARTER FIGHT.
WITH ITS ACCURACY ...
...I SHOULD BE ABLE TO PIERCE THE DEVIL OF THE RHINE'S DEFENSIVE SHELL.

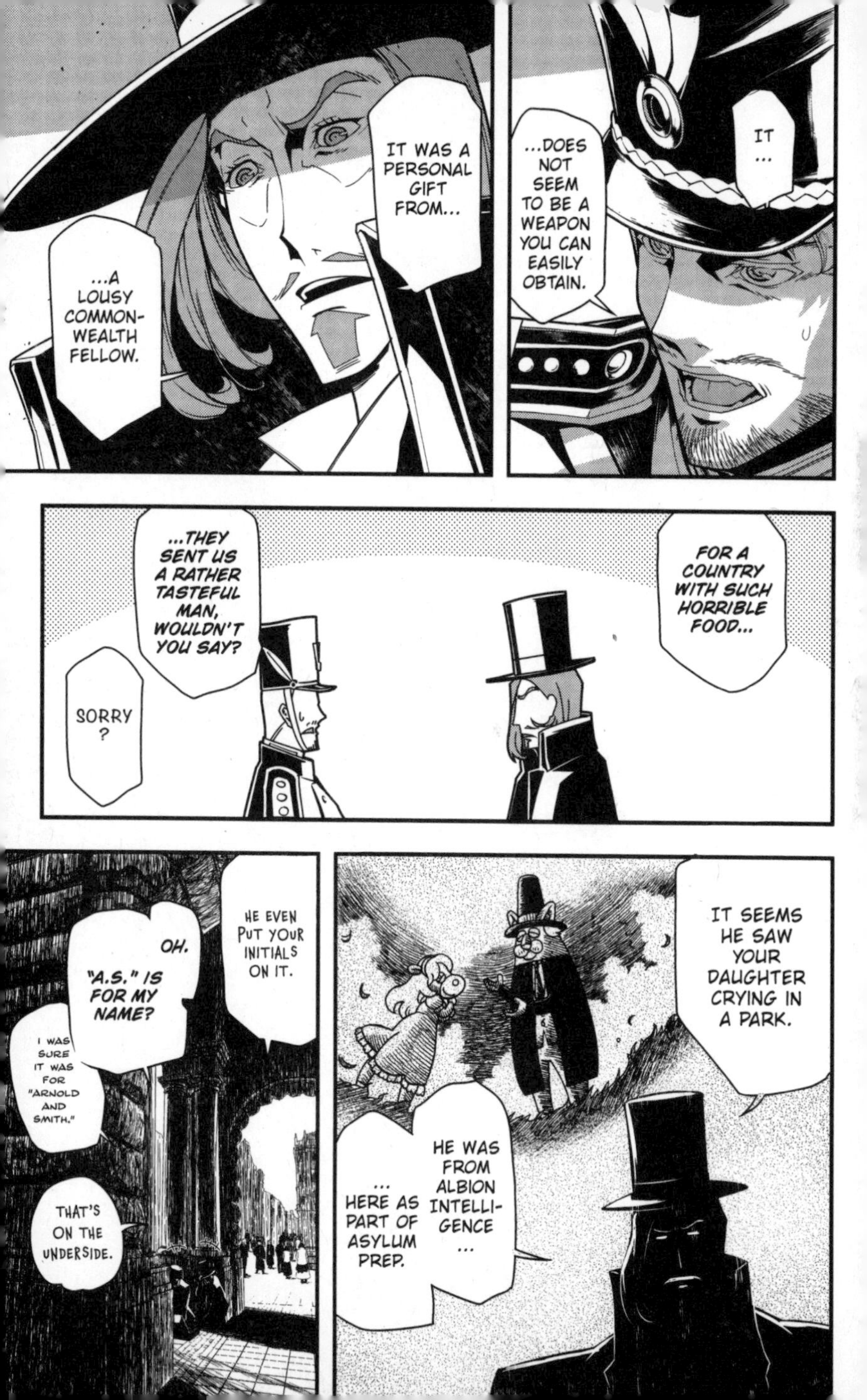
IT ...
...DOES NOT SEEM TO BE A WEAPON YOU CAN EASILY OBTAIN.
IT WAS A PERSONAL GIFT FROM...
...A LOUSY COMMON-WEALTH FELLOW.
FOR A COUNTRY WITH SUCH HORRIBLE FOOD...
...THEY SENT US A RATHER TASTEFUL MAN, WOULDN'T YOU SAY?
SORRY?
IT SEEMS HE SAW YOUR DAUGHTER CRYING IN A PARK.
HE WAS FROM ALBION INTELLI-GENCE ...
... HERE AS PART OF ASYLUM PREP.
HE EVEN PUT YOUR INITIALS ON IT.
OH.
"A.S." IS FOR MY NAME?
I WAS SURE IT WAS FOR "ARNOLD AND SMITH."
THAT'S ON THE UNDERSIDE.

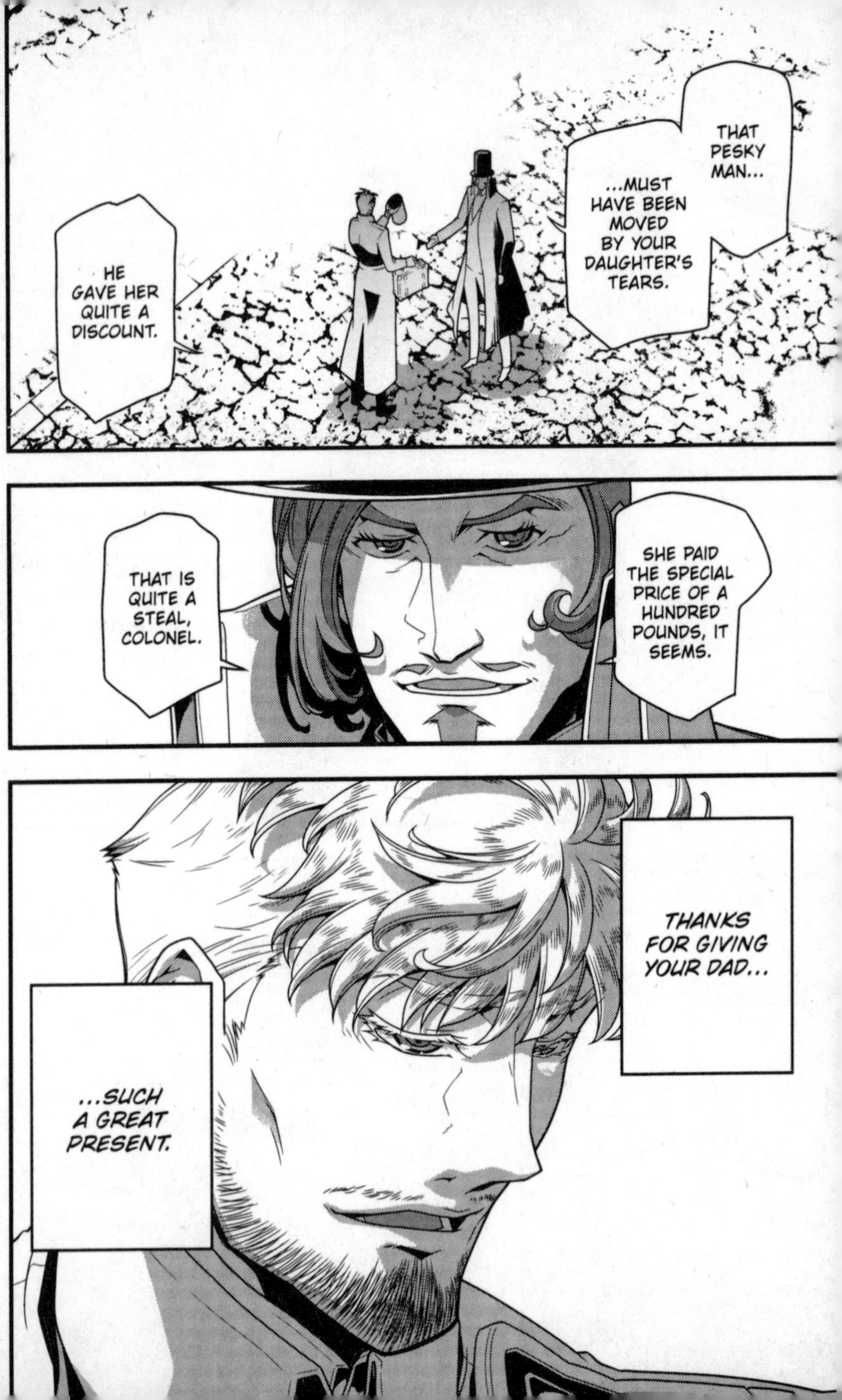
THAT PESKY MAN...
...MUST HAVE BEEN MOVED BY YOUR DAUGHTER'S TEARS.
HE GAVE HER QUITE A DISCOUNT.
SHE PAID THE SPECIAL PRICE OF A HUNDRED POUNDS, IT SEEMS.
THAT IS QUITE A STEAL, COLONEL.
THANKS FOR GIVING YOUR DAD...
...SUCH A GREAT PRESENT.

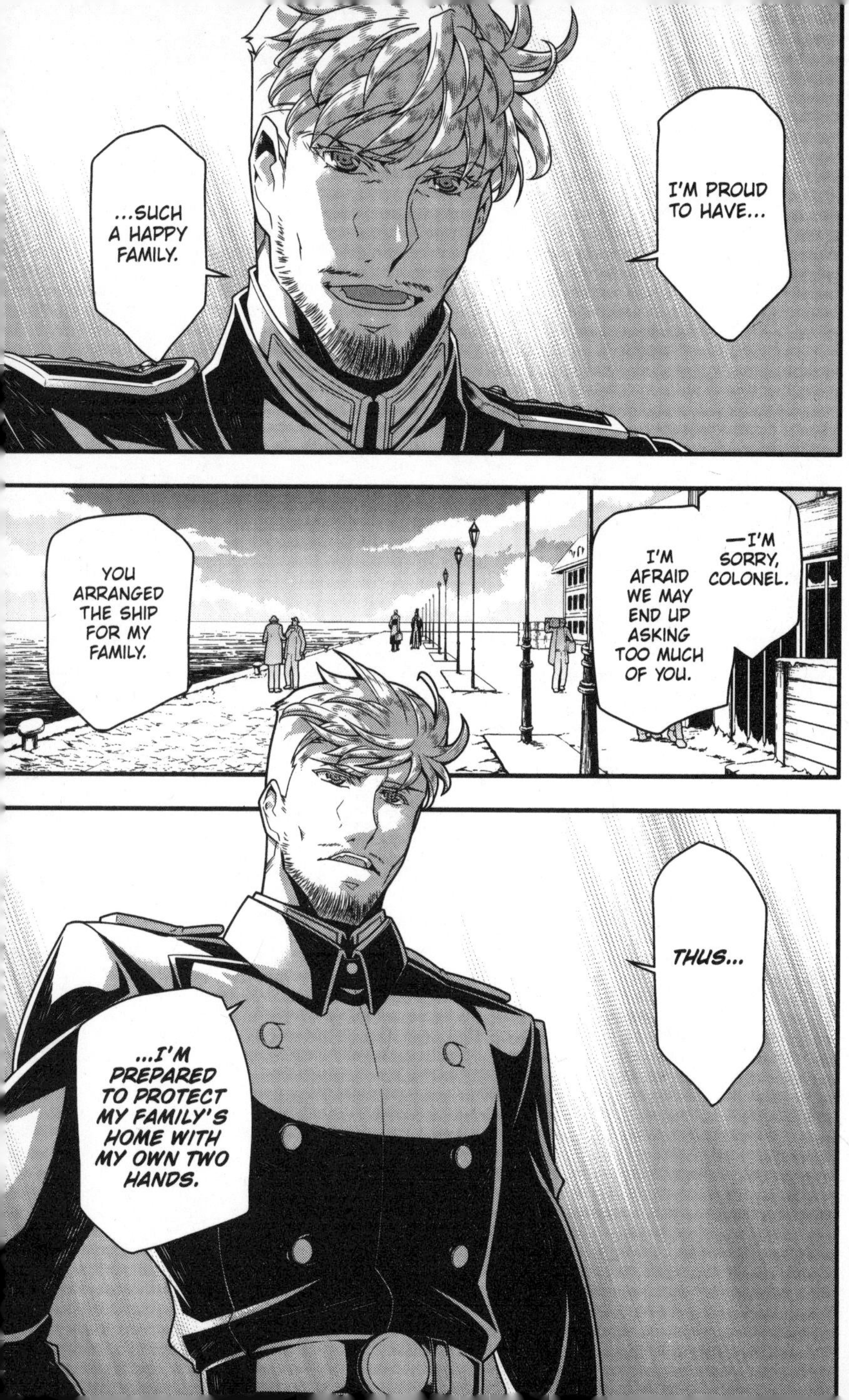
I'M PROUD TO HAVE...
...SUCH A HAPPY FAMILY.
—I'M SORRY, COLONEL.
I'M AFRAID WE MAY END UP ASKING TOO MUCH OF YOU.
YOU ARRANGED THE SHIP FOR MY FAMILY.
THUS...
...I'M PREPARED TO PROTECT MY FAMILY'S HOME WITH MY OWN TWO HANDS.

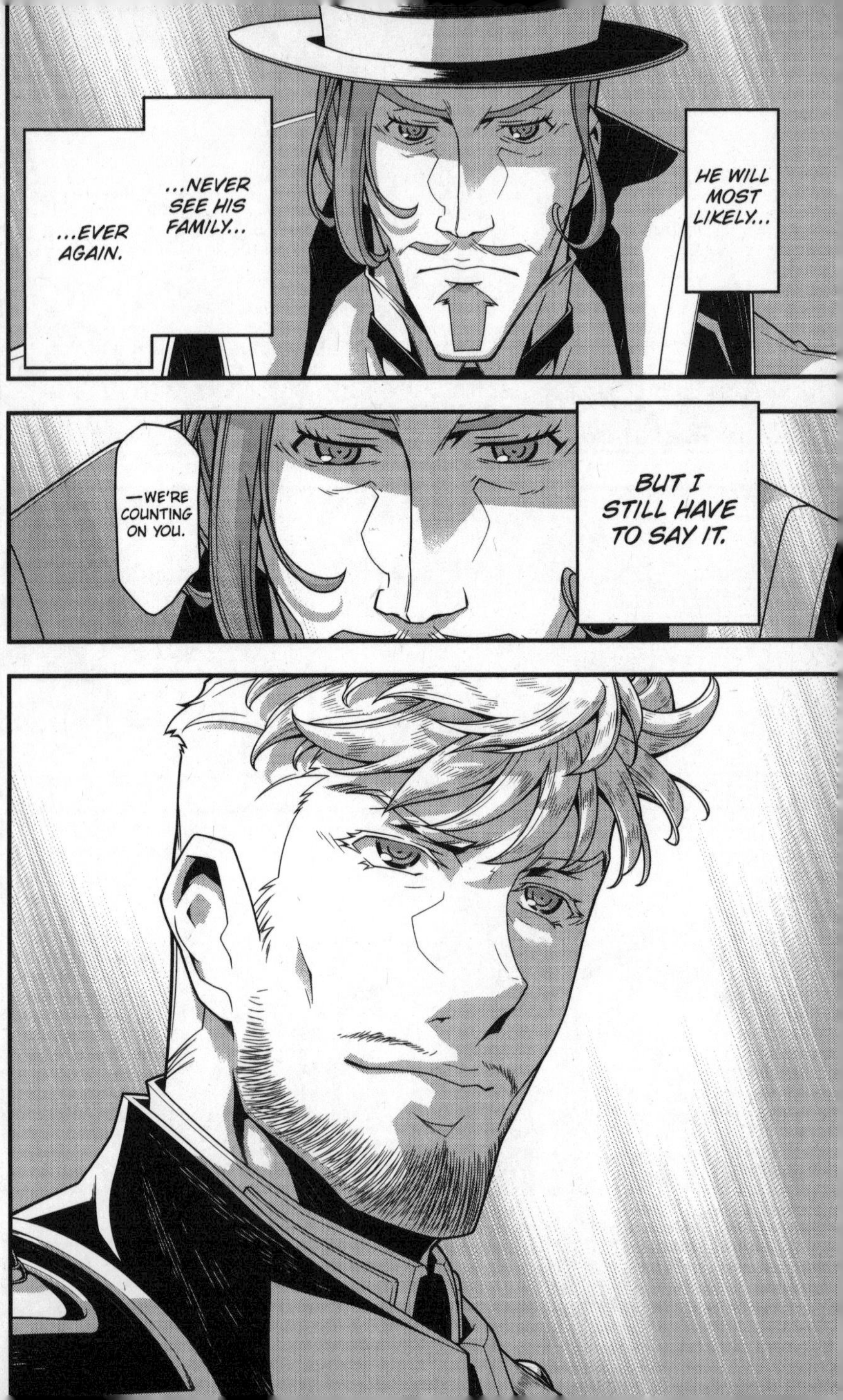
HE WILL MOST LIKELY...
...NEVER SEE HIS FAMILY...
...EVER AGAIN.
BUT I STILL HAVE TO SAY IT.
—WE'RE COUNTING ON YOU.

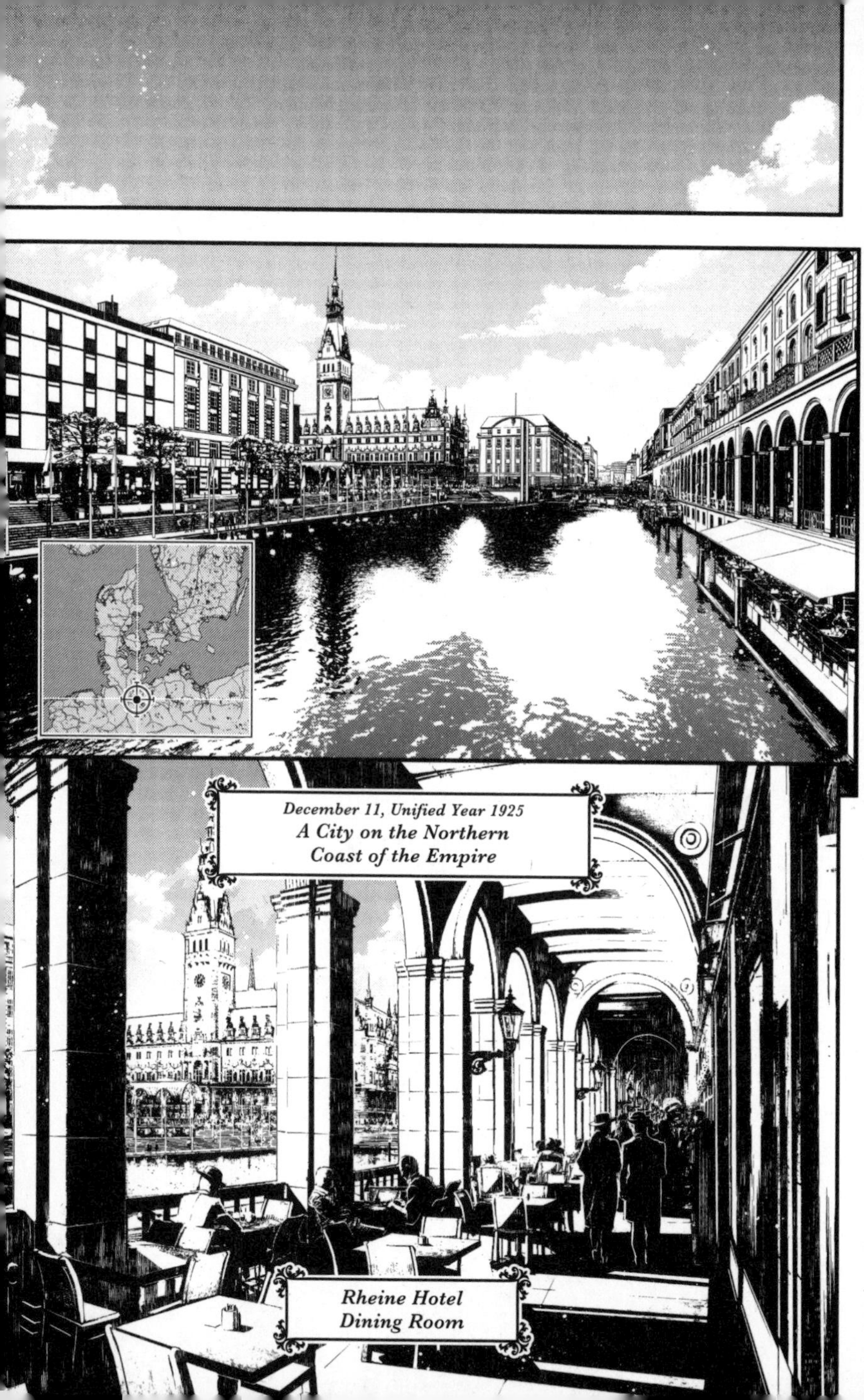
December 11, Unified Year 1925
A City on the Northern Coast of the Empire
Rheine Hotel Dining Room

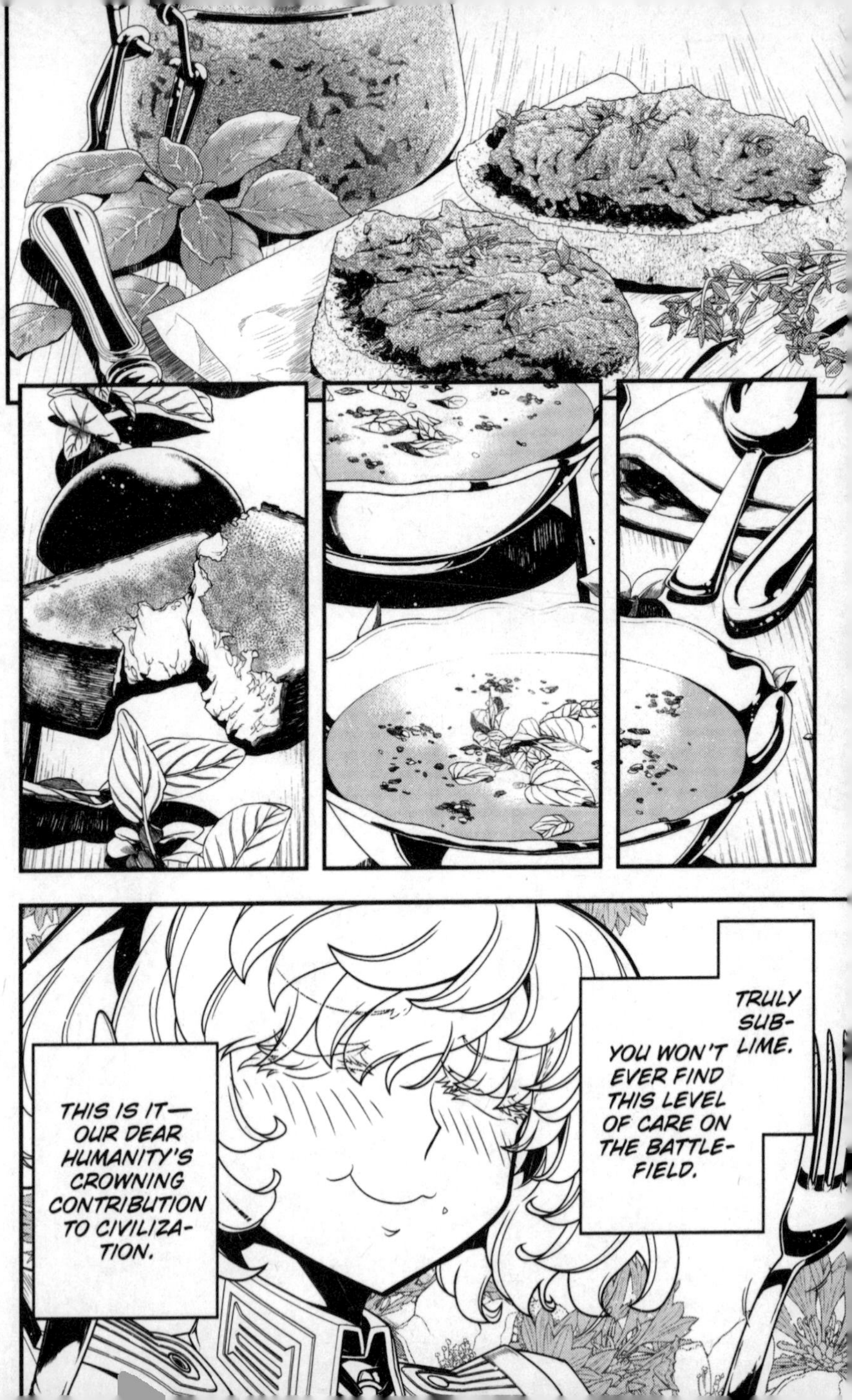
TRULY SUB-LIME.
YOU WON'T EVER FIND THIS LEVEL OF CARE ON THE BATTLE-FIELD.
THIS IS IT—OUR DEAR HUMANITY'S CROWNING CONTRIBUTION TO CIVILIZA-TION.

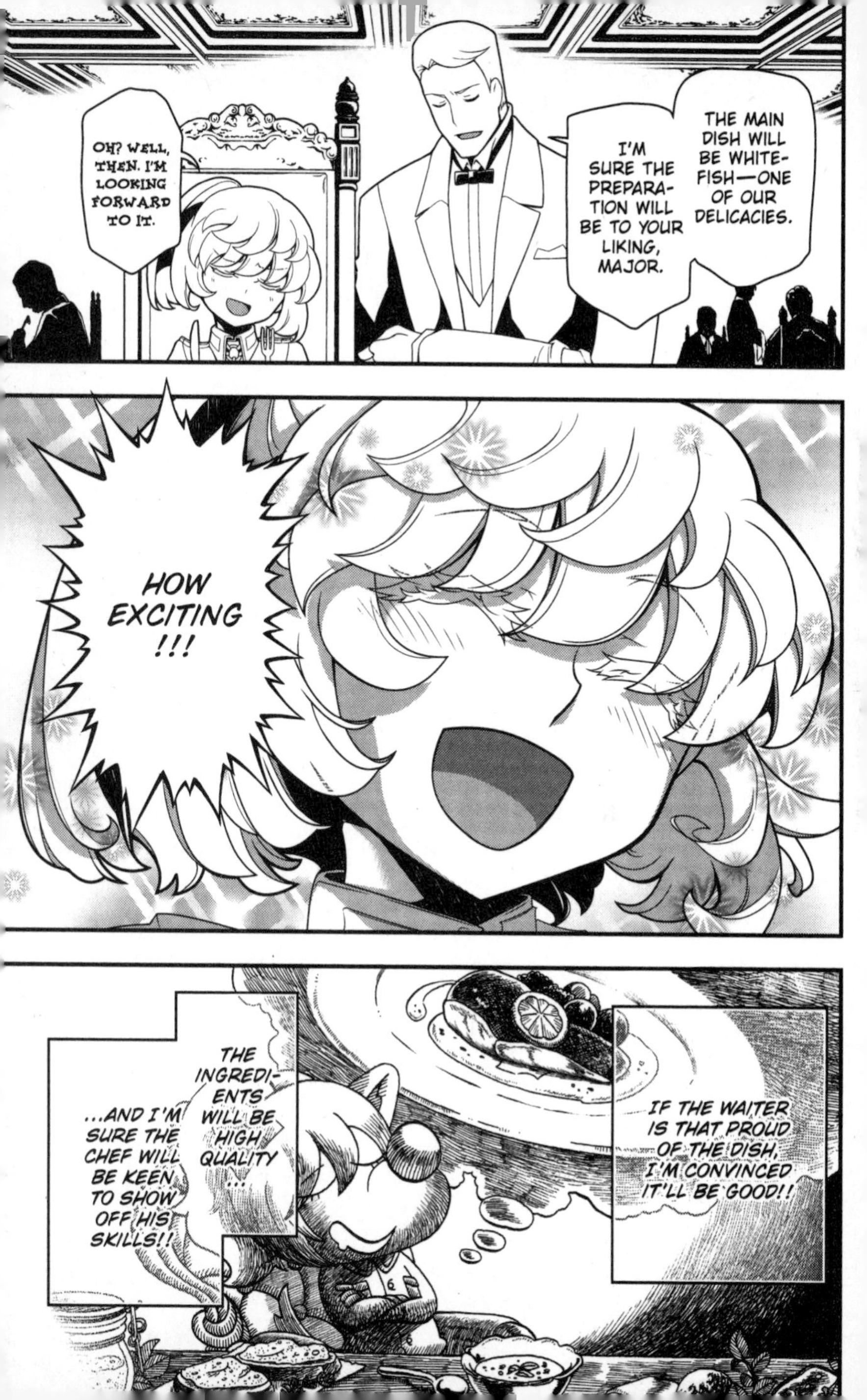
THE MAIN DISH WILL BE WHITE-FISH—ONE OF OUR DELICACIES.
I'M SURE THE PREPARATION WILL BE TO YOUR LIKING, MAJOR.
OH? WELL, THEN. I'M LOOKING FORWARD TO IT.
HOW EXCITING!!!
IF THE WAITER IS THAT PROUD OF THE DISH, I'M CONVINCED IT'LL BE GOOD!!
THE INGREDIENTS WILL BE HIGH QUALITY...
...AND I'M SURE THE CHEF WILL BE KEEN TO SHOW OFF HIS SKILLS!!

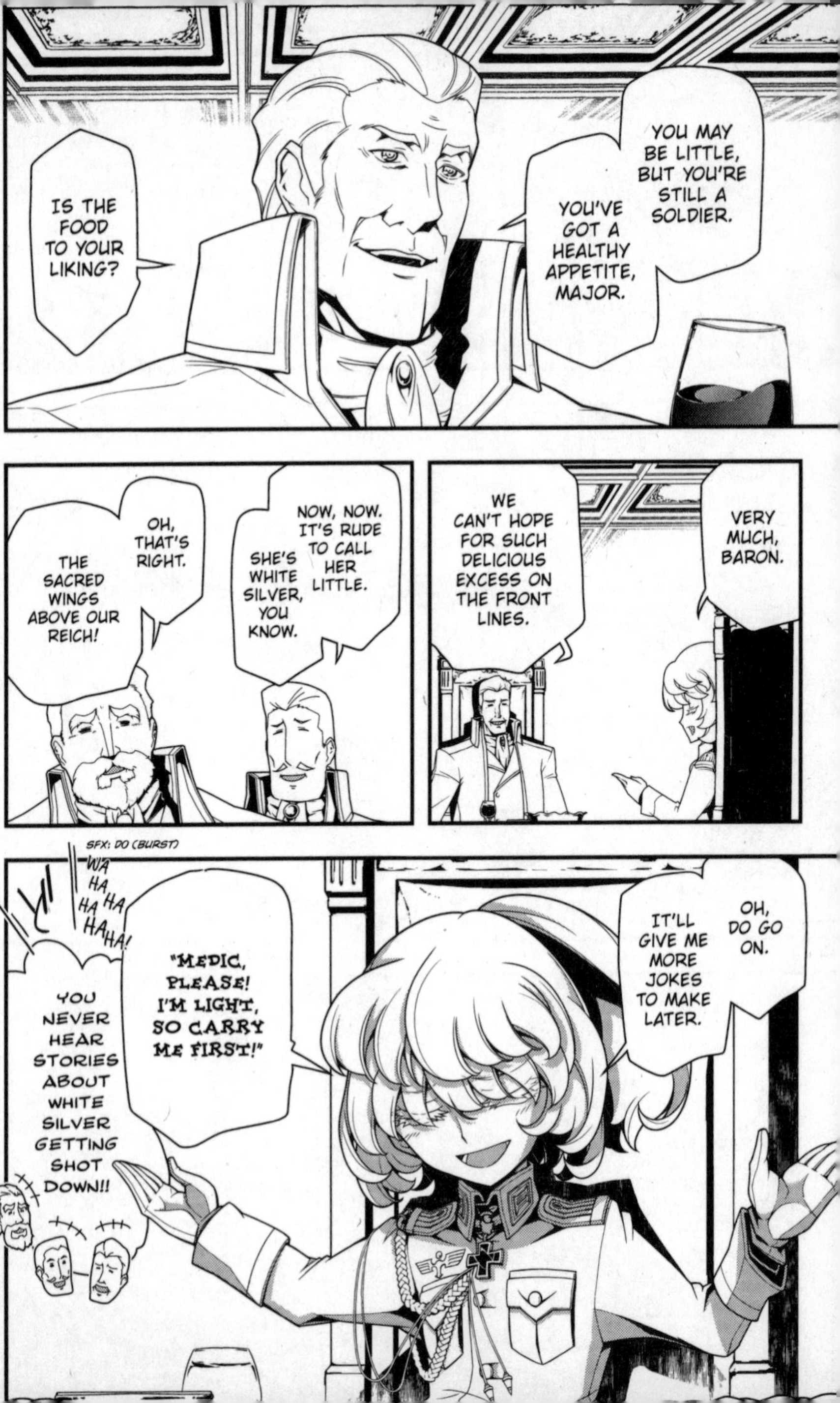
YOU MAY BE LITTLE, BUT YOU'RE STILL A SOLDIER.
YOU'VE GOT A HEALTHY APPETITE, MAJOR.
IS THE FOOD TO YOUR LIKING?
VERY MUCH, BARON.
WE CAN'T HOPE FOR SUCH DELICIOUS EXCESS ON THE FRONT LINES.
NOW, NOW. IT'S RUDE TO CALL HER LITTLE.
SHE'S WHITE SILVER, YOU KNOW.
OH, THAT'S RIGHT.
THE SACRED WINGS ABOVE OUR REICH!
OH, DO GO ON.
IT'LL GIVE ME MORE JOKES TO MAKE LATER.
"MEDIC, PLEASE! I'M LIGHT, SO CARRY ME FIRST!"
YOU NEVER HEAR STORIES ABOUT WHITE SILVER GETTING SHOT DOWN!!
SFX: DO (BURST)
WA HA HA HA HAHA!

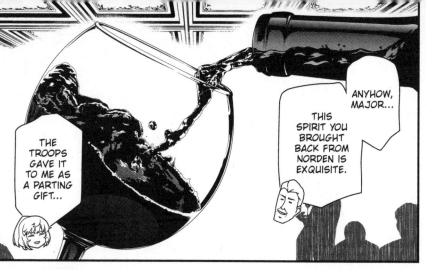

ANYHOW, MAJOR... THIS SPIRIT YOU BROUGHT BACK FROM NORDEN IS EXQUISITE.

THE TROOPS GAVE IT TO ME AS A PARTING GIFT...

...BUT SADLY, I THINK THEY FORGOT IT'S PROHIBITED DUE TO MY AGE.

MY OWN BATTALION...

...OFTEN SEEMS TO FORGET THAT I'M A YOUNG GIRL.

MAJOR. I AM SORRY THAT...

...WE'VE SHOVED THE TROUBLE OUR GENERATION CAUSED...

...UPON YOU YOUNG ONES.

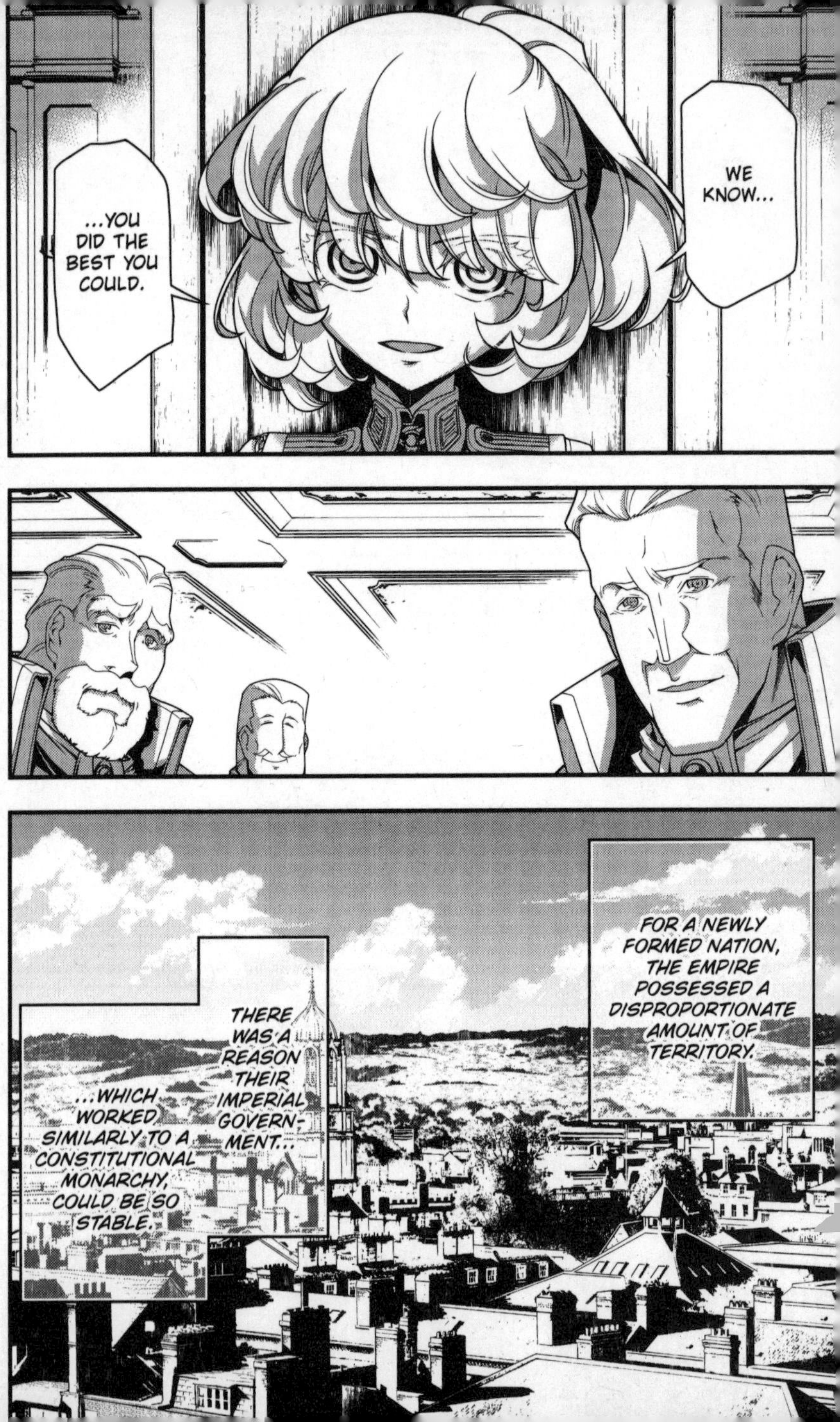
WE KNOW...
...YOU DID THE BEST YOU COULD.
FOR A NEWLY FORMED NATION, THE EMPIRE POSSESSED A DISPROPORTIONATE AMOUNT OF TERRITORY.
THERE WAS A REASON THEIR IMPERIAL GOVERNMENT...
...WHICH WORKED SIMILARLY TO A CONSTITUTIONAL MONARCHY, COULD BE SO STABLE.

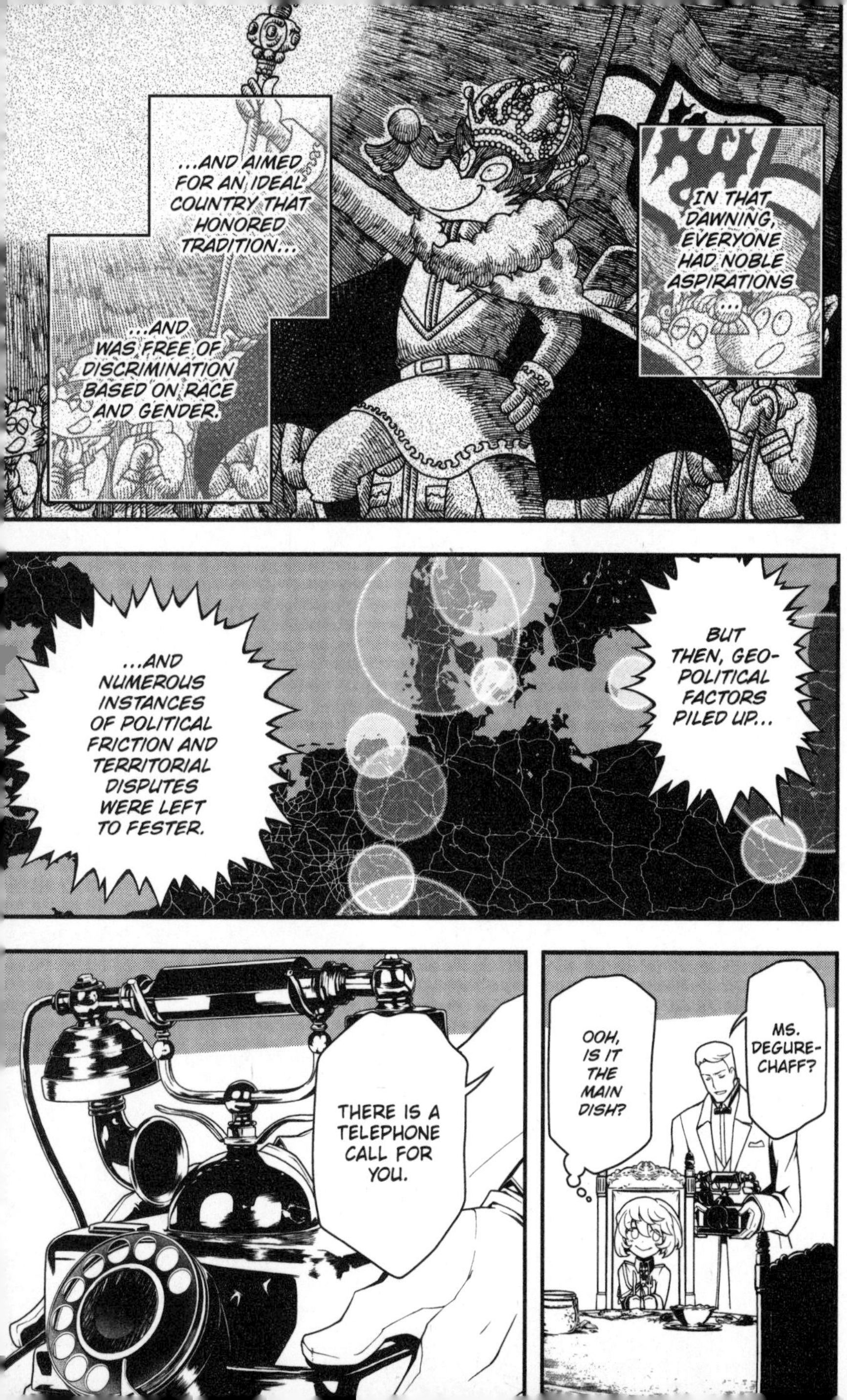
IN THAT DAWNING, EVERYONE HAD NOBLE ASPIRATIONS
...AND AIMED FOR AN IDEAL COUNTRY THAT HONORED TRADITION...
...AND WAS FREE OF DISCRIMINATION BASED ON RACE AND GENDER.
BUT THEN, GEO-POLITICAL FACTORS PILED UP...
...AND NUMEROUS INSTANCES OF POLITICAL FRICTION AND TERRITORIAL DISPUTES WERE LEFT TO FESTER.
MS. DEGURE-CHAFF?
OOH, IS IT THE MAIN DISH?
THERE IS A TELEPHONE CALL FOR YOU.

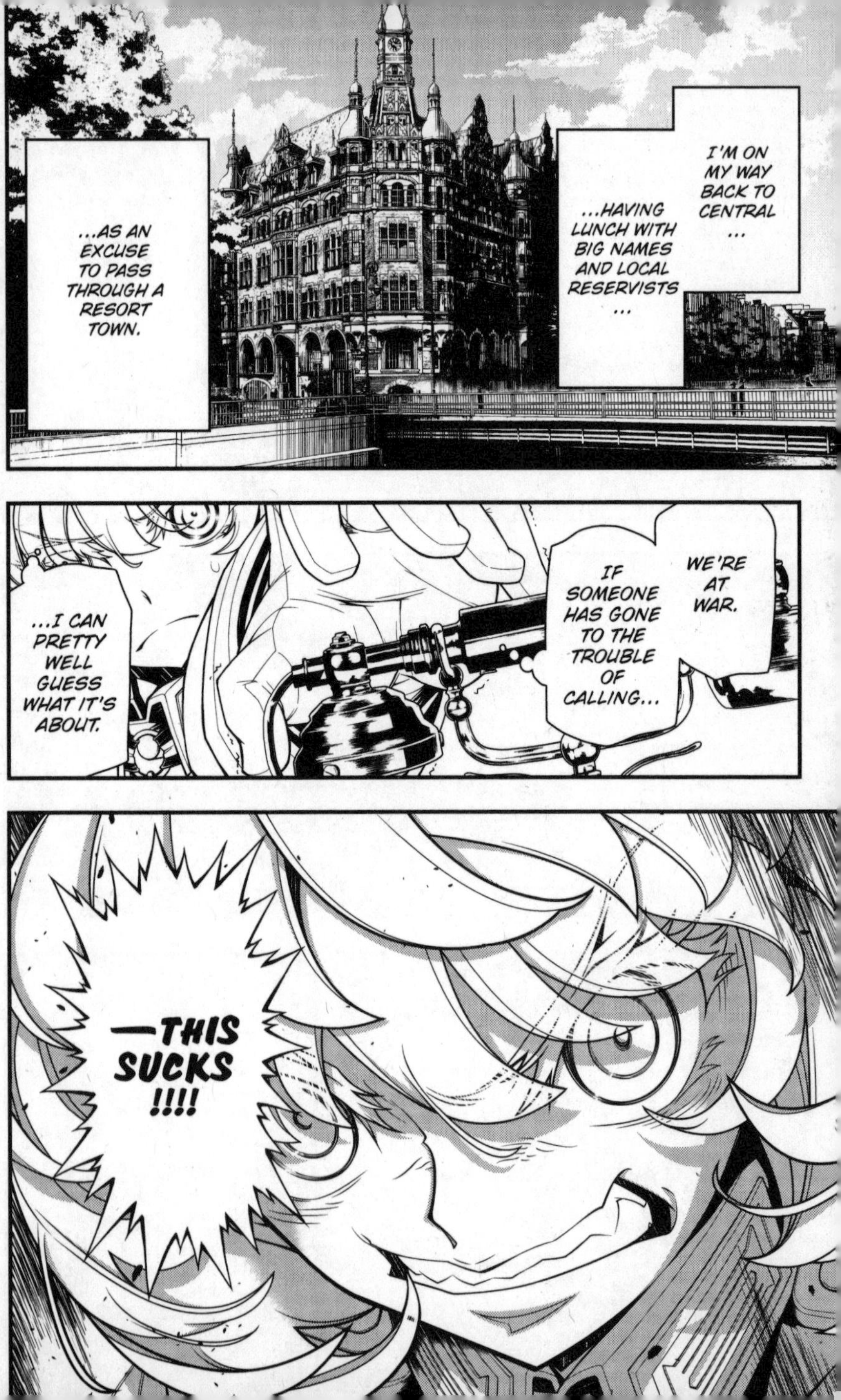
I'M ON MY WAY BACK TO CENTRAL...
...HAVING LUNCH WITH BIG NAMES AND LOCAL RESERVISTS...
...AS AN EXCUSE TO PASS THROUGH A RESORT TOWN.
WE'RE AT WAR.
IF SOMEONE HAS GONE TO THE TROUBLE OF CALLING...
...I CAN PRETTY WELL GUESS WHAT IT'S ABOUT.
—THIS SUCKS!!!!

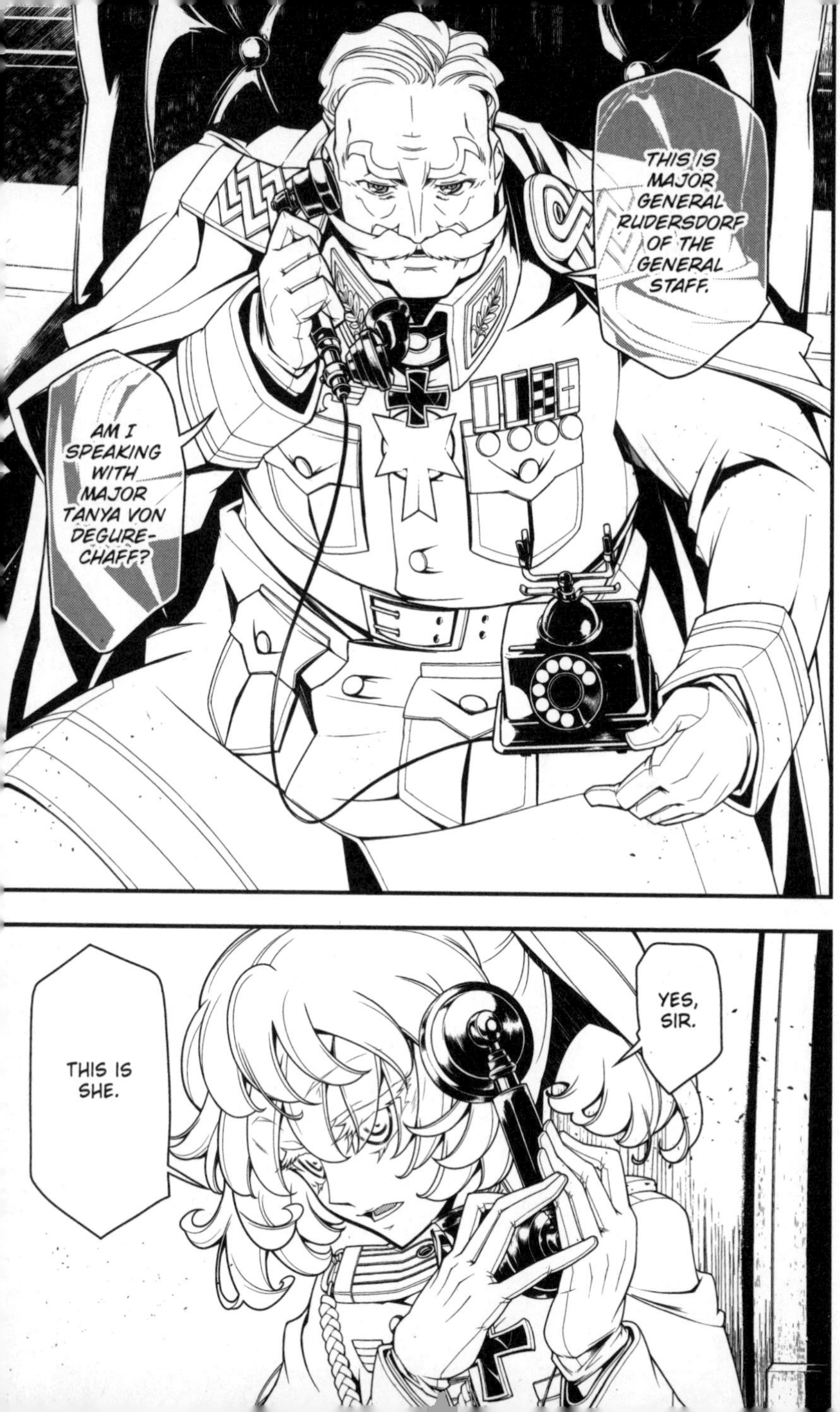
THIS IS MAJOR GENERAL RUDERSDORF OF THE GENERAL STAFF.
AM I SPEAKING WITH MAJOR TANYA VON DEGURE-CHAFF?
YES, SIR.
THIS IS SHE.

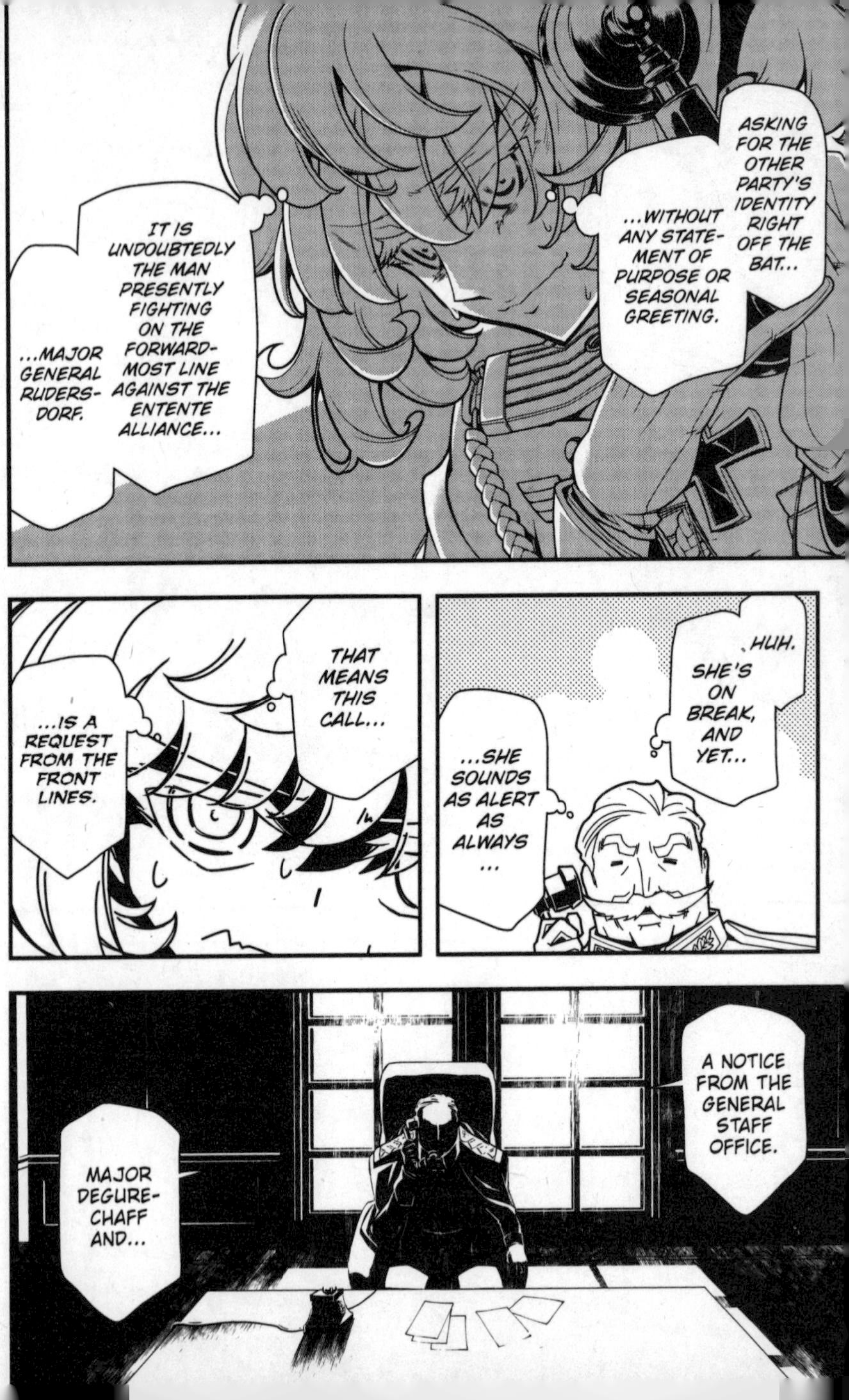
ASKING FOR THE OTHER PARTY'S IDENTITY RIGHT OFF THE BAT...
...WITHOUT ANY STATEMENT OF PURPOSE OR SEASONAL GREETING.
IT IS UNDOUBTEDLY THE MAN PRESENTLY FIGHTING ON THE FORWARD-MOST LINE AGAINST THE ENTENTE ALLIANCE...
...MAJOR GENERAL RUDERSDORF.
HUH. SHE'S ON BREAK, AND YET...
...SHE SOUNDS AS ALERT AS ALWAYS...
THAT MEANS THIS CALL...
...IS A REQUEST FROM THE FRONT LINES.
A NOTICE FROM THE GENERAL STAFF OFFICE.
MAJOR DEGURECHAFF AND...

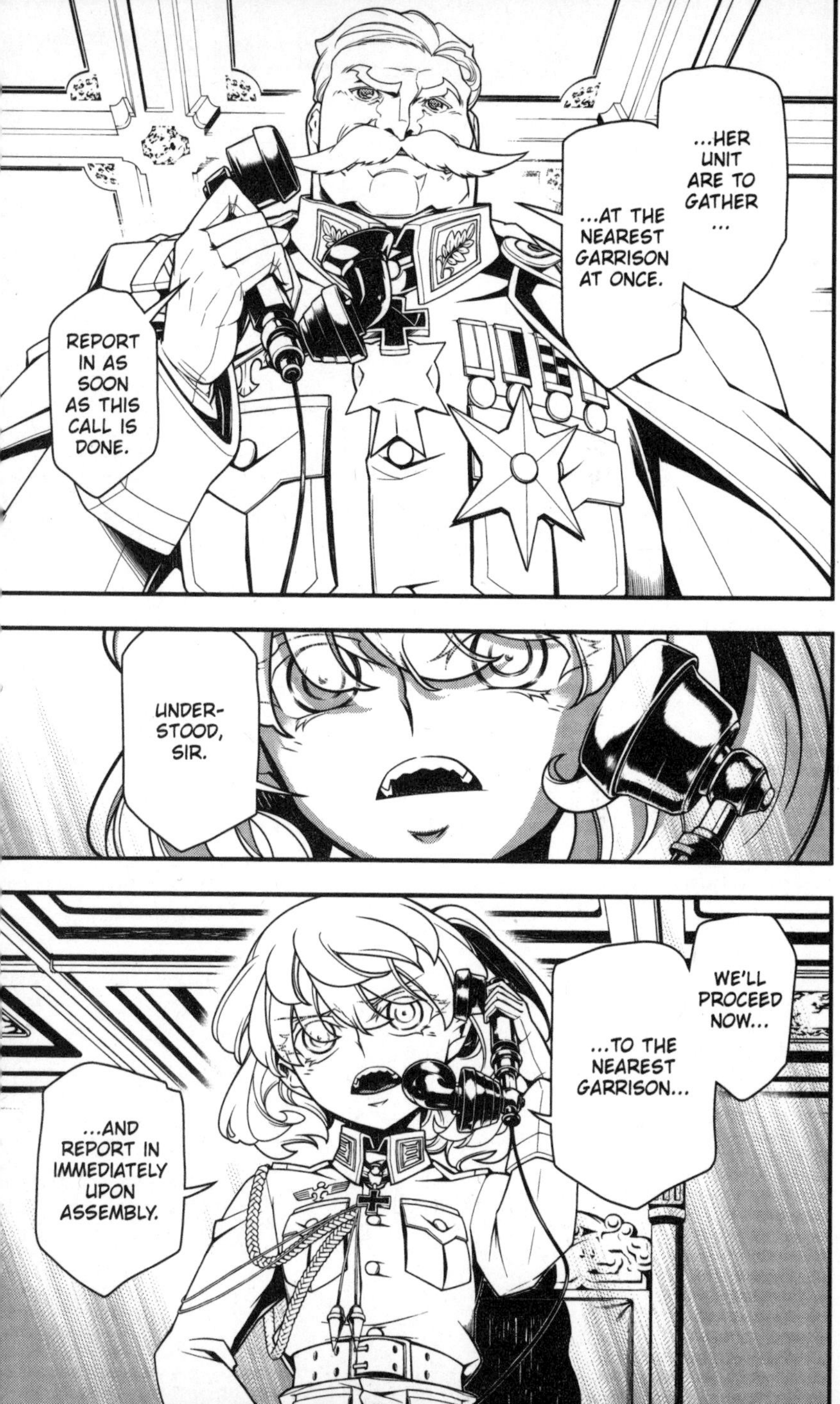
...HER UNIT ARE TO GATHER ...
...AT THE NEAREST GARRISON AT ONCE.
REPORT IN AS SOON AS THIS CALL IS DONE.
UNDER-STOOD, SIR.
WE'LL PROCEED NOW...
...TO THE NEAREST GARRISON...
...AND REPORT IN IMMEDIATELY UPON ASSEMBLY.

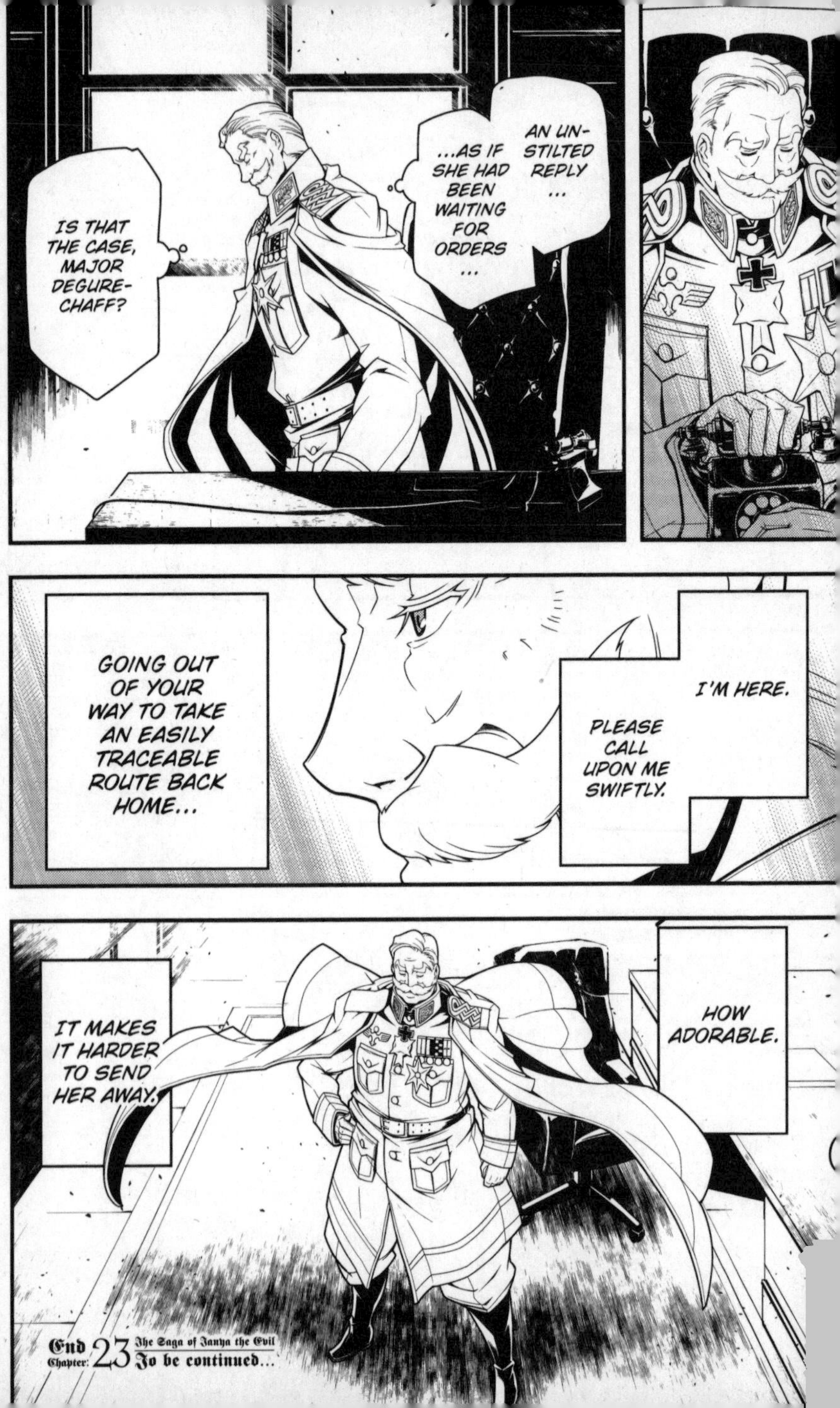
AN UN-STILTED REPLY...
...AS IF SHE HAD BEEN WAITING FOR ORDERS...
IS THAT THE CASE, MAJOR DEGURE-CHAFF?
I'M HERE.
PLEASE CALL UPON ME SWIFTLY.
GOING OUT OF YOUR WAY TO TAKE AN EASILY TRACEABLE ROUTE BACK HOME...
HOW ADORABLE.
IT MAKES IT HARDER TO SEND HER AWAY.
End Chapter: 23 The Saga of Tanya the Evil
To be continued...

Glossary Chapter 29

Asylum

Leaving one's home country and appealing to another nation for protection against political, racial, or religious prosecution. Happens often in cases of war, revolution, and upheaval and includes people who flee from an invading army.

In the law of war, there is no difference between an asylum seeker and a refugee. In Japan, it used to be that one or a handful of expatriates were called nanmin and a larger group of expatriates were called bōmeisha. However, lately it seems bōmeisha is used for politicians and soldiers seeking political asylum while nanmin is used for people evacuating from war or disaster zones.

Government-in-Exile

A provisional administration set up by the heads of a state exiled from their country by invasion or revolution in the country of their refuge. It must be recognized by the host country and other nearby nations. The purpose of a government-in-exile is to deny the administration that was established through invasion or revolution in their home country and to move back once the situation becomes more favorable.

Throughout history, there have been many examples of governments-in-exile as well as many different outcomes. While one may manage to retake a country and govern once more, another may back their own head of state for generations before accepting the government of their home country and disappearing. Longtime governments-in-exile, especially, tend to lean toward anti-government terrorism, so for that reason and others, whether or not a country will host a government-in-exile is a high-level political decision.

Resistance

A movement in opposition to an occupying army or other authority. Here we are talking about the former type.

Resistance can take many forms: passing out anti-occupation flyers or pamphlets, stockpiling weapons, destroying facilities, forming ideological groups, putting together debates, etc.... Among them, units that use direct force are called partisans. Sometimes they expand to include multiple units and take over an area that they designate a holy land.

The interests involved in partisan activities are varied. At times, they take on a nationalist hue or are there for an ideological cause. Due to communication issues or clashing interests, they don't always work with the government-in-exile. There have been examples where each actor gets in touch with the occupying army in order to eliminate the activities of people who think differently from themselves, and balancing between these actors is an extremely difficult problem in the unique environment of war.

Glossary Chapter 30

Submachine Gun

A small machine gun that fires pistol ammunition and was designed to be carried by an individual. They are particularly useful in close-quarter combat, and thanks to the hail of bullets they can create with their rapid rate of fire, they boast great suppression capabilities.

In history, they appeared near the end of World War I after trench warfare had developed. Up until then, bayonets had been used for close combat, but they were difficult to wield in the narrow trenches and thus ineffective. Though SMGs don't have the range of small arms, they rampaged with their rapid rate of fire in place of bayonets, and by World War II, each country was mass-producing them. Since they are cheap and don't require special training to use, they eventually trickled into the cities for self-defense and riot suppression or as weapons used by criminal organizations.

Accuracy

The ability to hit the same point with multiple shots. In other words, minimal error is ideal and indicates good accuracy. A gun with poor accuracy has a loose grouping and is less capable of hitting a target with precision, while a gun with good accuracy has a tight grouping and is more capable of hitting a target with precision.

While accuracy tends to be prioritized in sniper rifles, arms for close-quarter encounters like submachine guns don't emphasize it as much.

Rifle

Broadly defined, any firearm with a rifled barrel. Here, we're specifying the small arm that soldiers carry.

Different types tend to be used depending on the anticipated fighting distance. For long distances, bolt-action types are often employed for their aim since each shot is quite accurate. For medium distances, almost any gun becomes a candidate. At close ranges, options include shotguns and submachine guns.

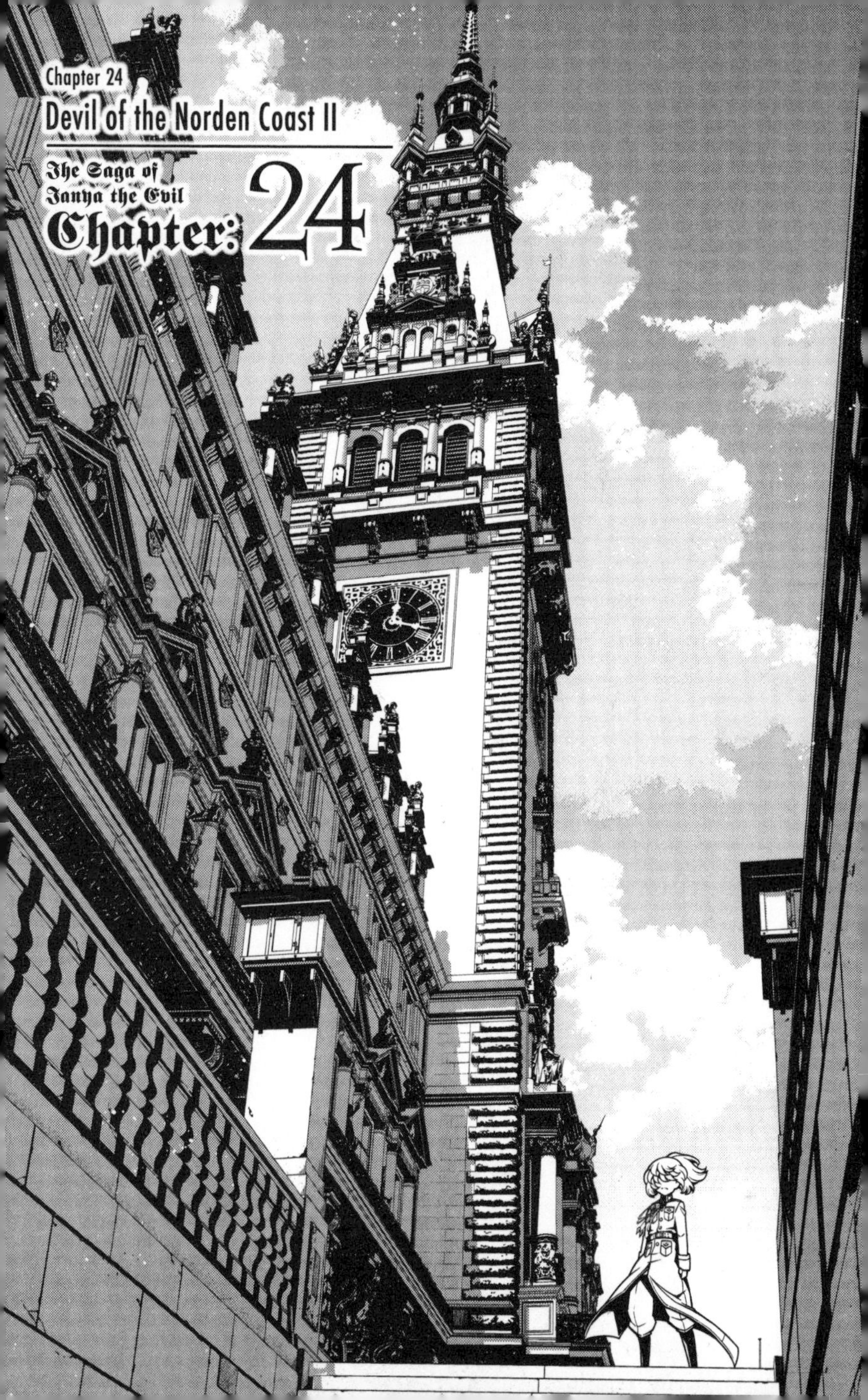
Chapter 24
Devil of the Norden Coast II
The Saga of Tanya the Evil
Chapter: 24

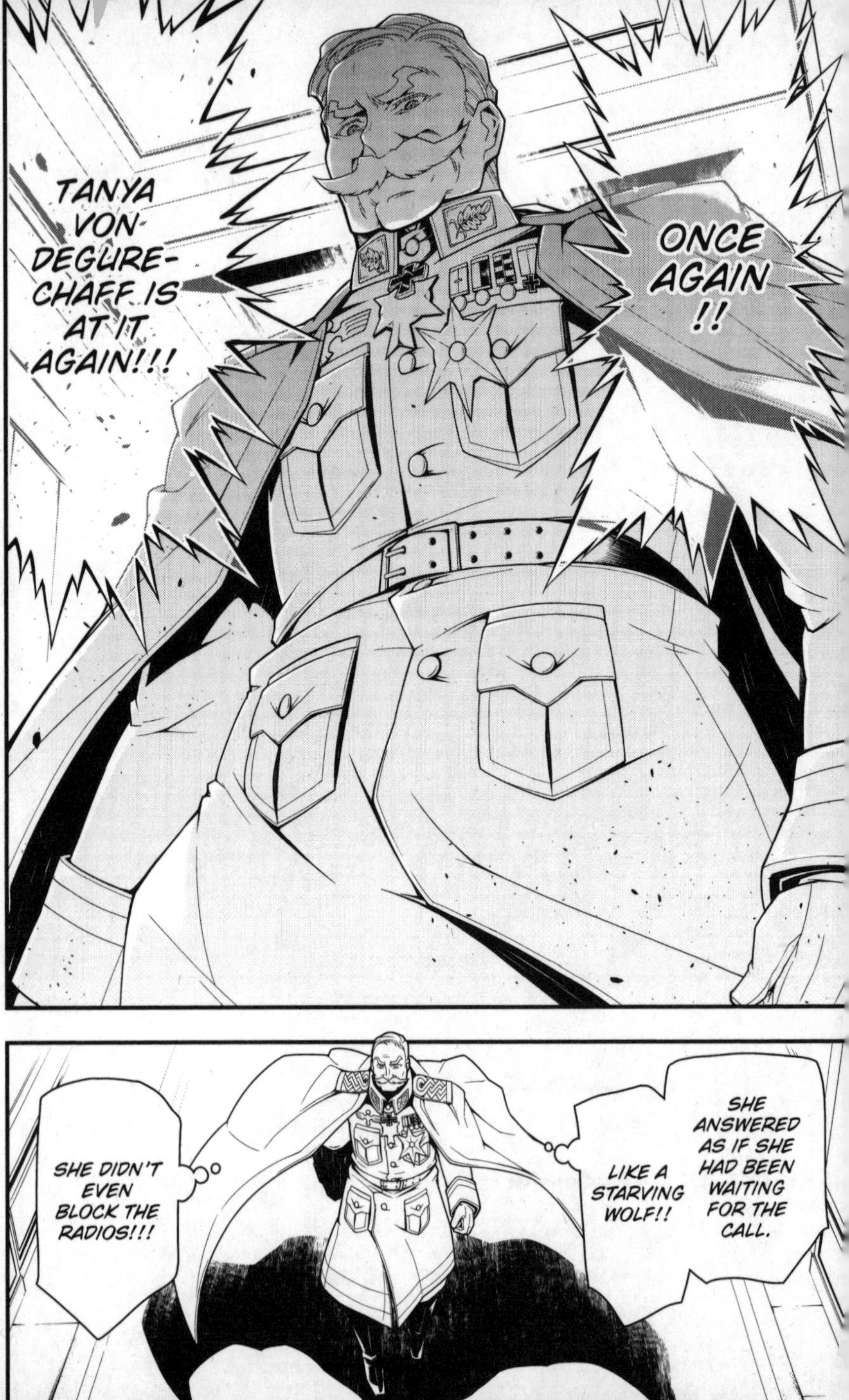
ONCE AGAIN!!
TANYA VON-DEGURE-CHAFF IS AT IT AGAIN!!!
SHE ANSWERED AS IF SHE HAD BEEN WAITING FOR THE CALL.
LIKE A STARVING WOLF!!
SHE DIDN'T EVEN BLOCK THE RADIOS!!!

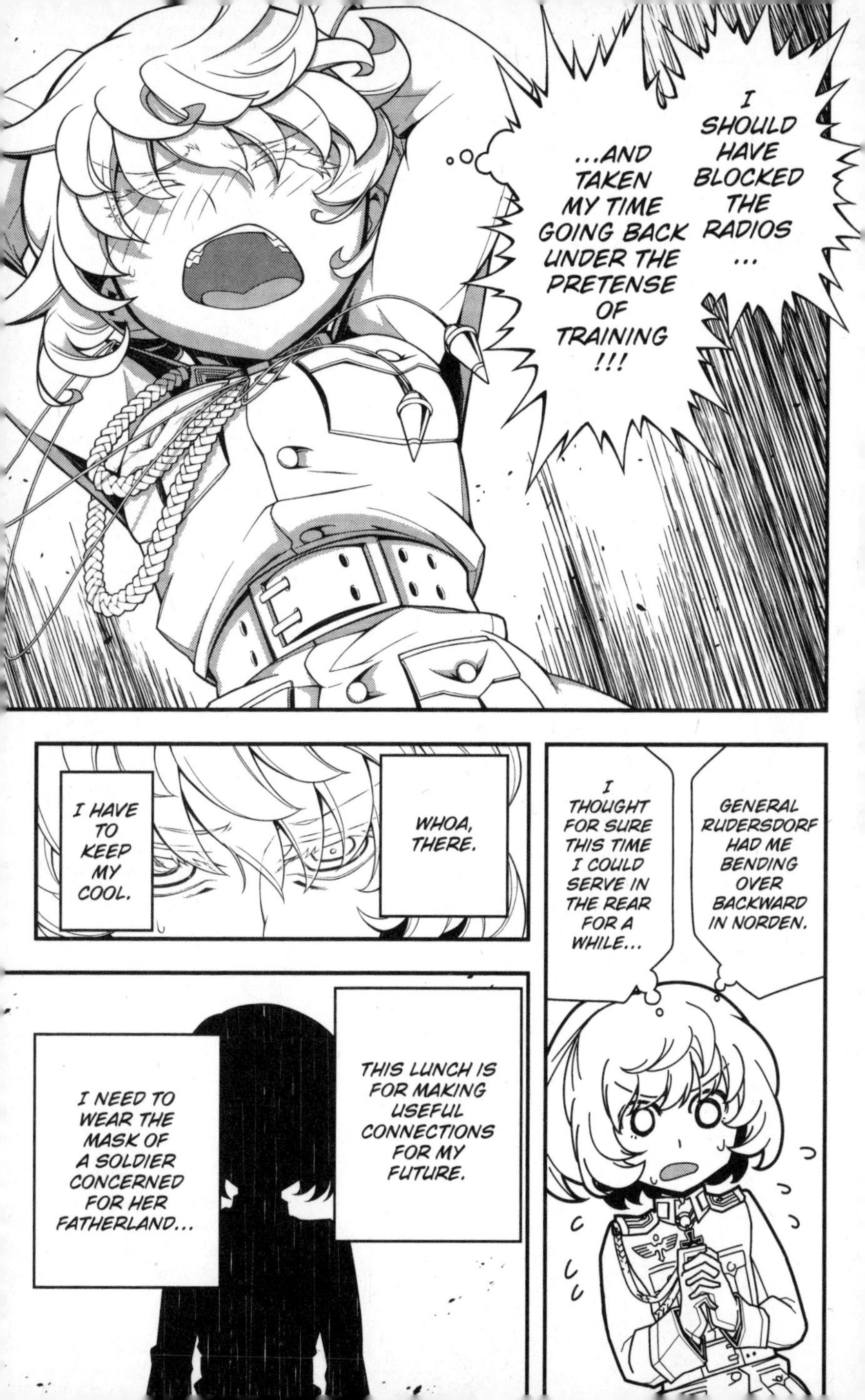
I SHOULD HAVE BLOCKED THE RADIOS...
...AND TAKEN MY TIME GOING BACK UNDER THE PRETENSE OF TRAINING!!!
GENERAL RUDERSDORF HAD ME BENDING OVER BACKWARD IN NORDEN.
I THOUGHT FOR SURE THIS TIME I COULD SERVE IN THE REAR FOR A WHILE...
WHOA, THERE.
I HAVE TO KEEP MY COOL.
THIS LUNCH IS FOR MAKING USEFUL CONNECTIONS FOR MY FUTURE.
I NEED TO WEAR THE MASK OF A SOLDIER CONCERNED FOR HER FATHERLAND...

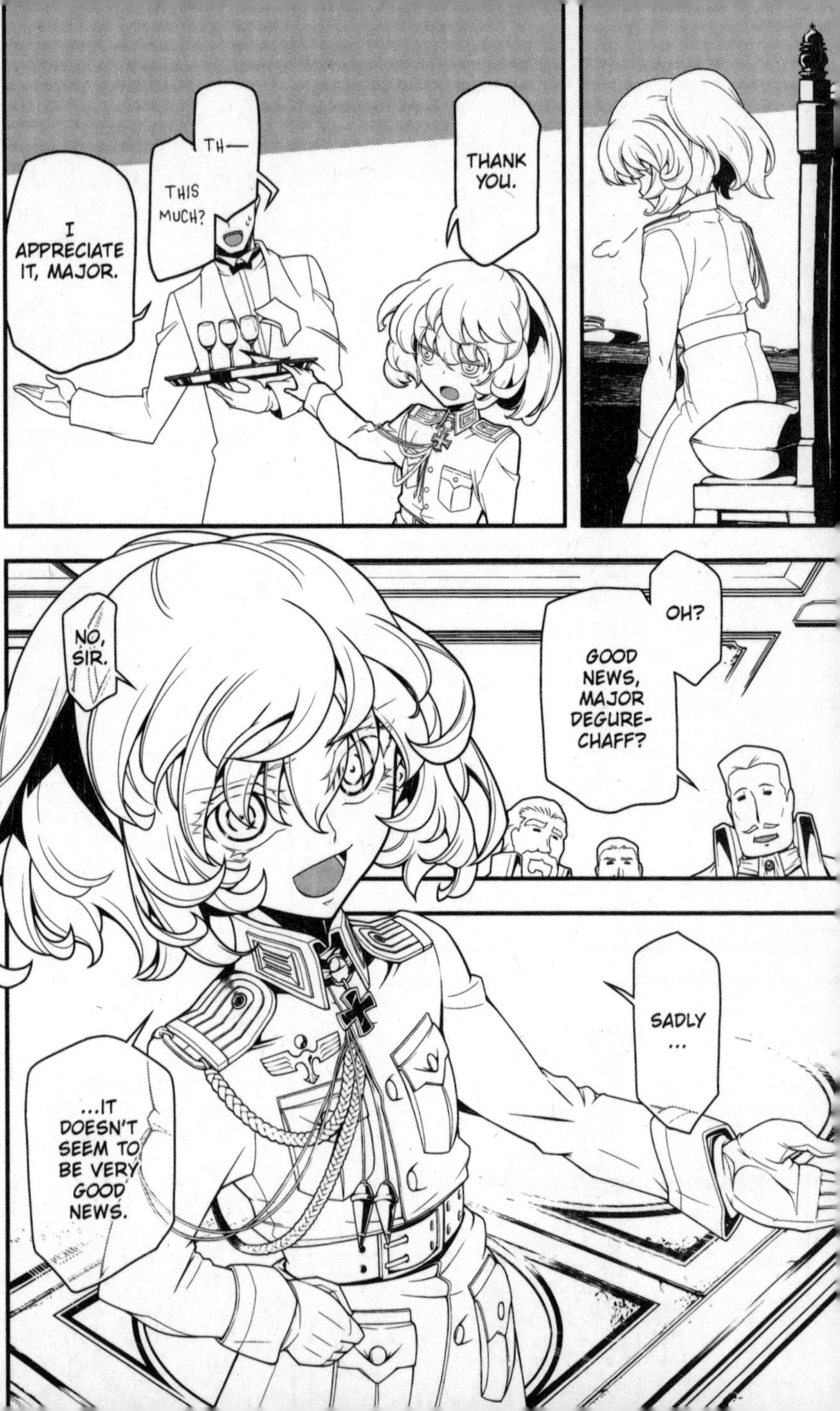
THANK YOU.
TH— THIS MUCH?
I APPRECIATE IT, MAJOR.
OH? GOOD NEWS, MAJOR DEGURE-CHAFF?
NO, SIR.
SADLY...
...IT DOESN'T SEEM TO BE VERY GOOD NEWS.

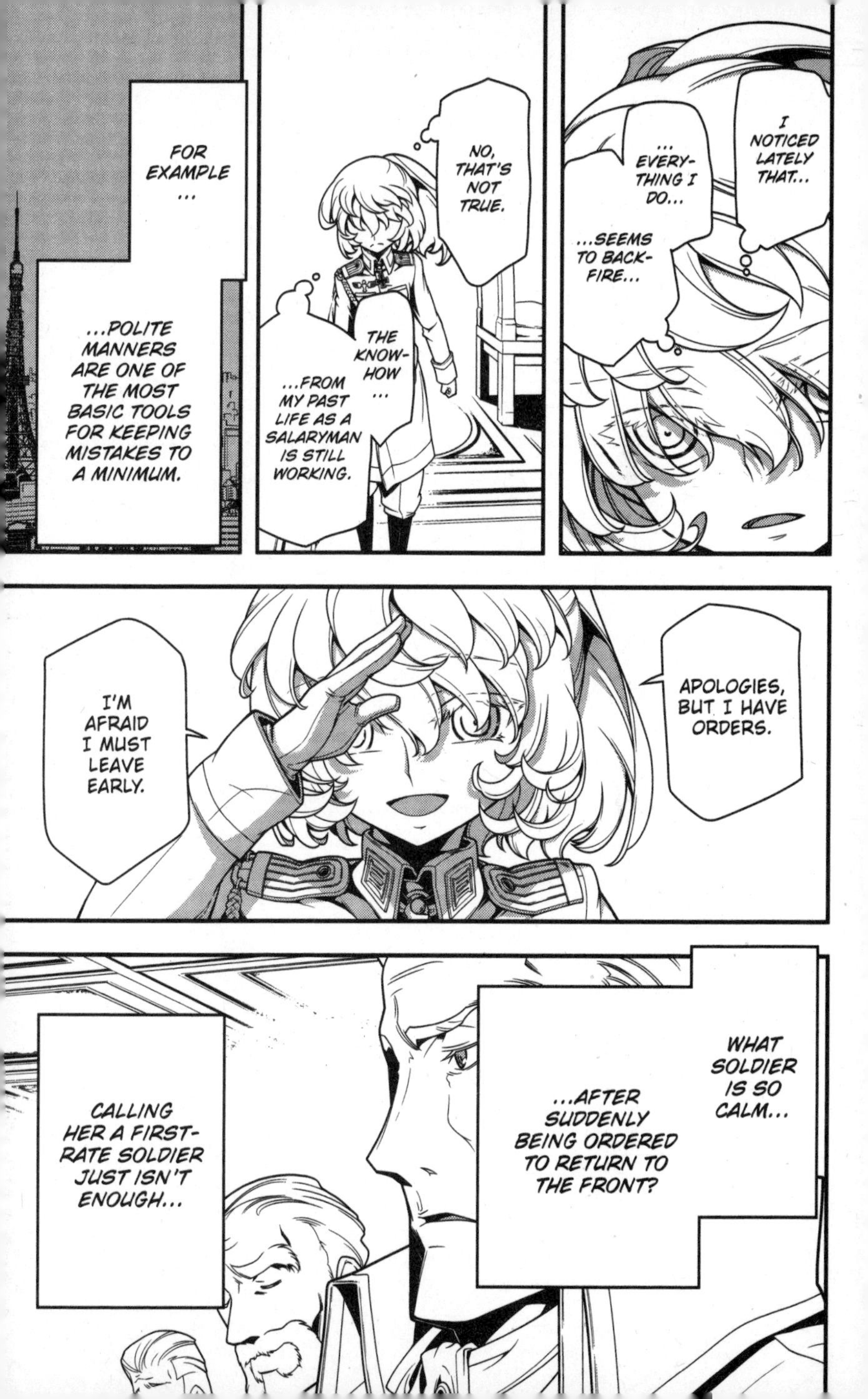
I NOTICED LATELY THAT...
...EVERYTHING I DO...
...SEEMS TO BACKFIRE...
NO, THAT'S NOT TRUE.
THE KNOW-HOW...
...FROM MY PAST LIFE AS A SALARYMAN IS STILL WORKING.
FOR EXAMPLE...
...POLITE MANNERS ARE ONE OF THE MOST BASIC TOOLS FOR KEEPING MISTAKES TO A MINIMUM.
APOLOGIES, BUT I HAVE ORDERS.
I'M AFRAID I MUST LEAVE EARLY.
WHAT SOLDIER IS SO CALM...
...AFTER SUDDENLY BEING ORDERED TO RETURN TO THE FRONT?
CALLING HER A FIRST-RATE SOLDIER JUST ISN'T ENOUGH...

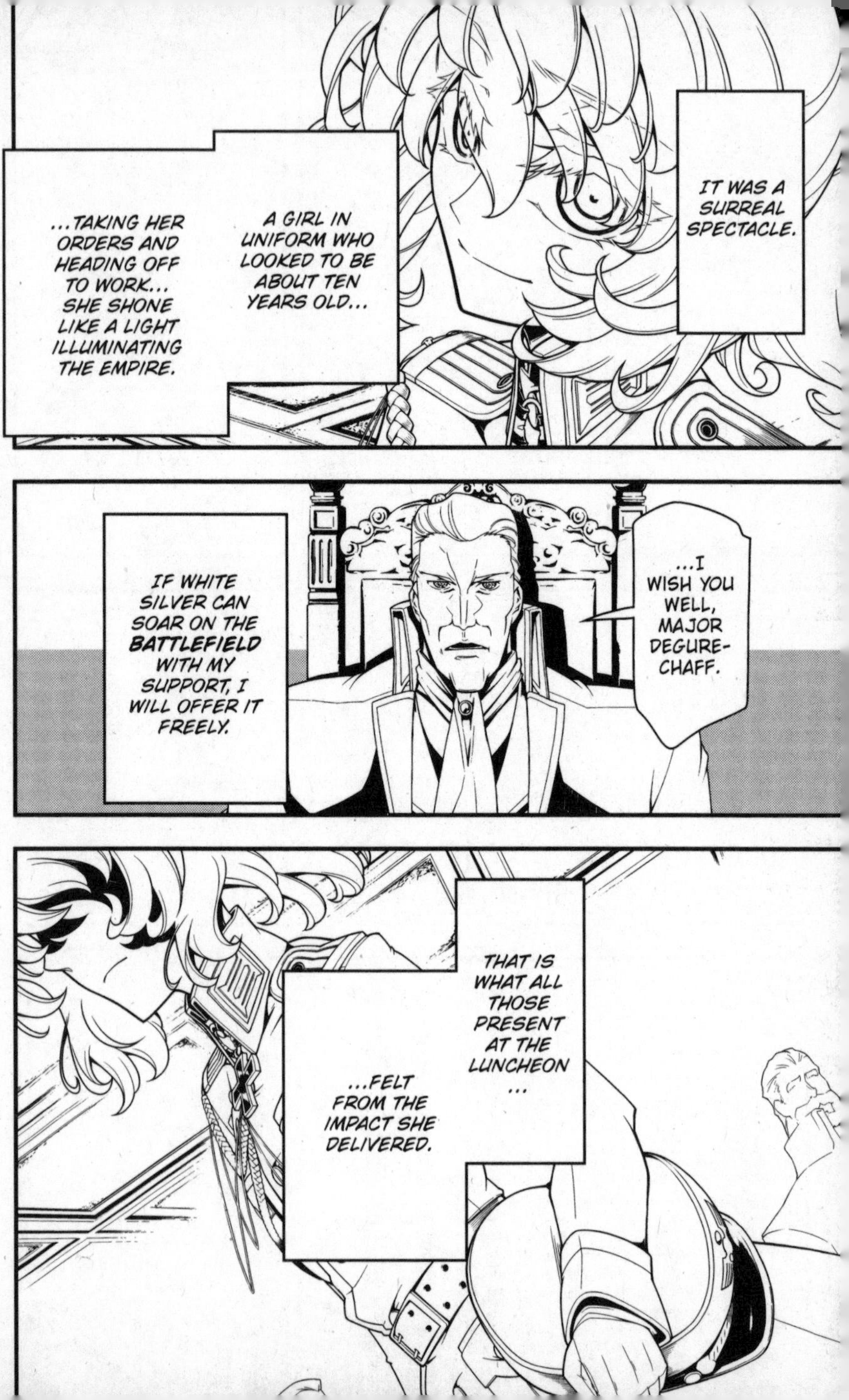
IT WAS A SURREAL SPECTACLE.
A GIRL IN UNIFORM WHO LOOKED TO BE ABOUT TEN YEARS OLD...
...TAKING HER ORDERS AND HEADING OFF TO WORK... SHE SHONE LIKE A LIGHT ILLUMINATING THE EMPIRE.
...I WISH YOU WELL, MAJOR DEGURE-CHAFF.
IF WHITE SILVER CAN SOAR ON THE BATTLEFIELD WITH MY SUPPORT, I WILL OFFER IT FREELY.
THAT IS WHAT ALL THOSE PRESENT AT THE LUNCHEON ...
...FELT FROM THE IMPACT SHE DELIVERED.

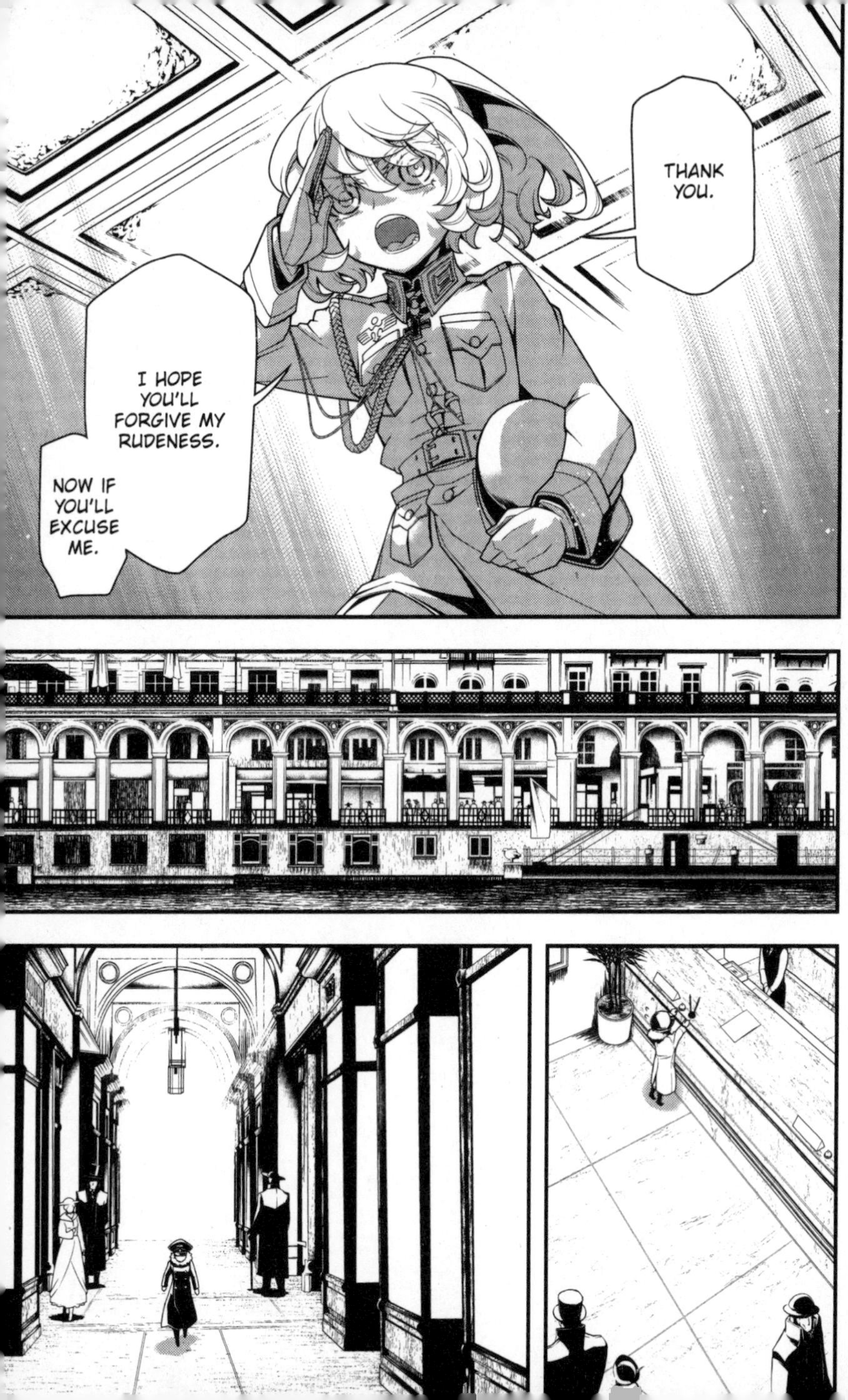
THANK YOU.
I HOPE YOU'LL FORGIVE MY RUDENESS.
NOW IF YOU'LL EXCUSE ME.

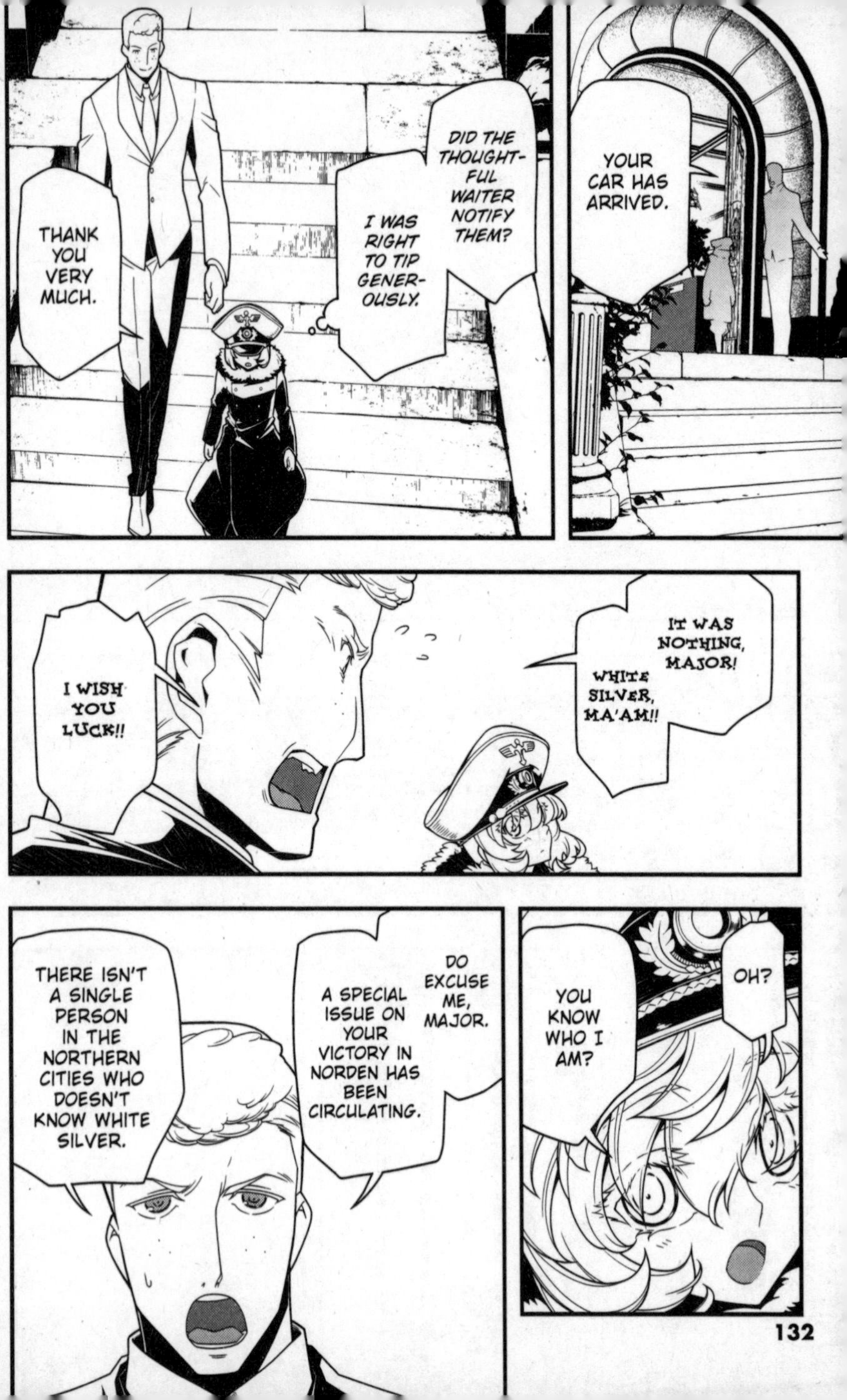
YOUR CAR HAS ARRIVED.
DID THE THOUGHTFUL WAITER NOTIFY THEM?
I WAS RIGHT TO TIP GENEROUSLY.
THANK YOU VERY MUCH.
IT WAS NOTHING, MAJOR!
WHITE SILVER, MA'AM!!
I WISH YOU LUCK!!
OH?
YOU KNOW WHO I AM?
DO EXCUSE ME, MAJOR.
A SPECIAL ISSUE ON YOUR VICTORY IN NORDEN HAS BEEN CIRCULATING.
THERE ISN'T A SINGLE PERSON IN THE NORTHERN CITIES WHO DOESN'T KNOW WHITE SILVER.

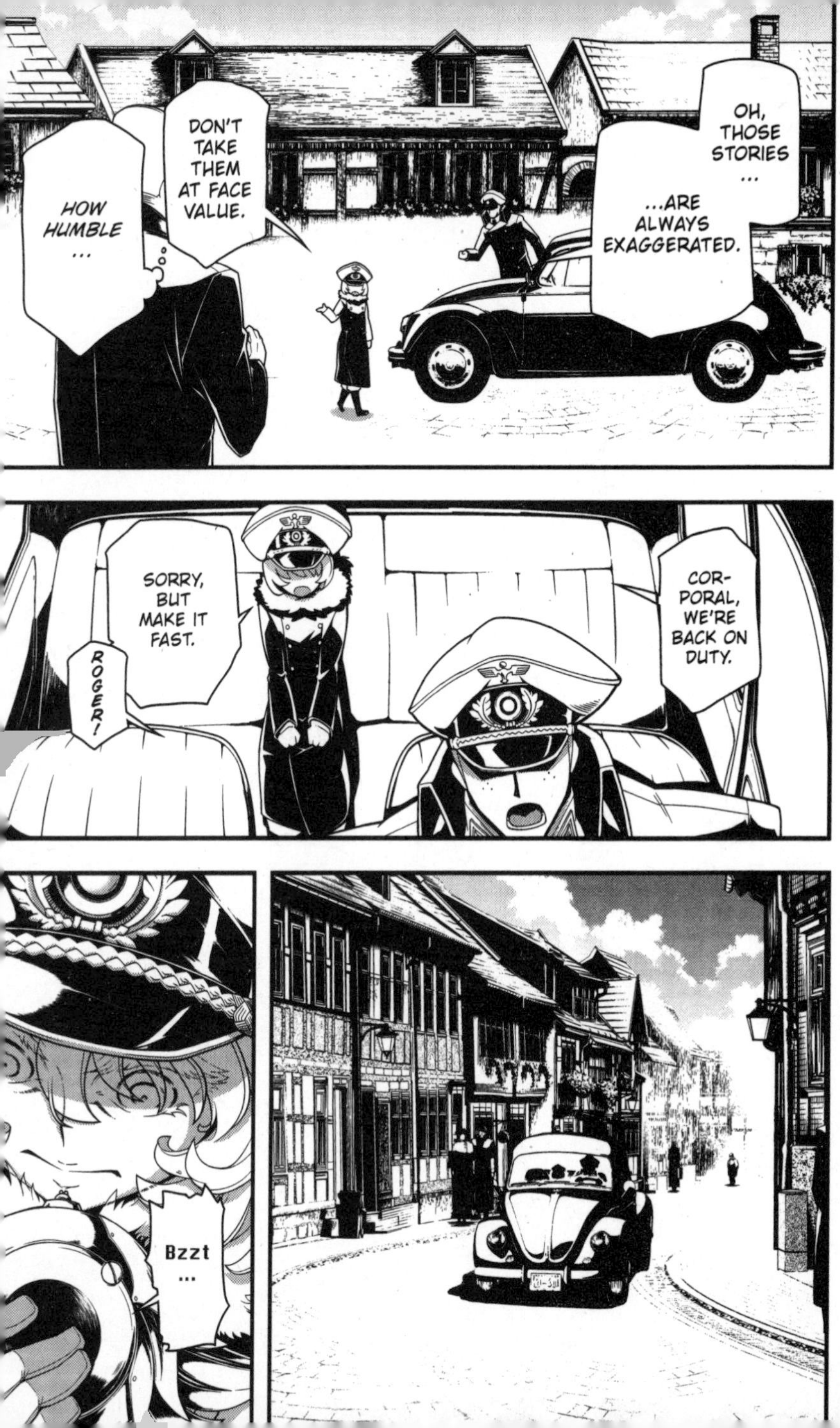
OH, THOSE STORIES...
...ARE ALWAYS EXAGGERATED.
DON'T TAKE THEM AT FACE VALUE.
HOW HUMBLE...
CORPORAL, WE'RE BACK ON DUTY.
SORRY, BUT MAKE IT FAST.
ROGER!
Bzzt...

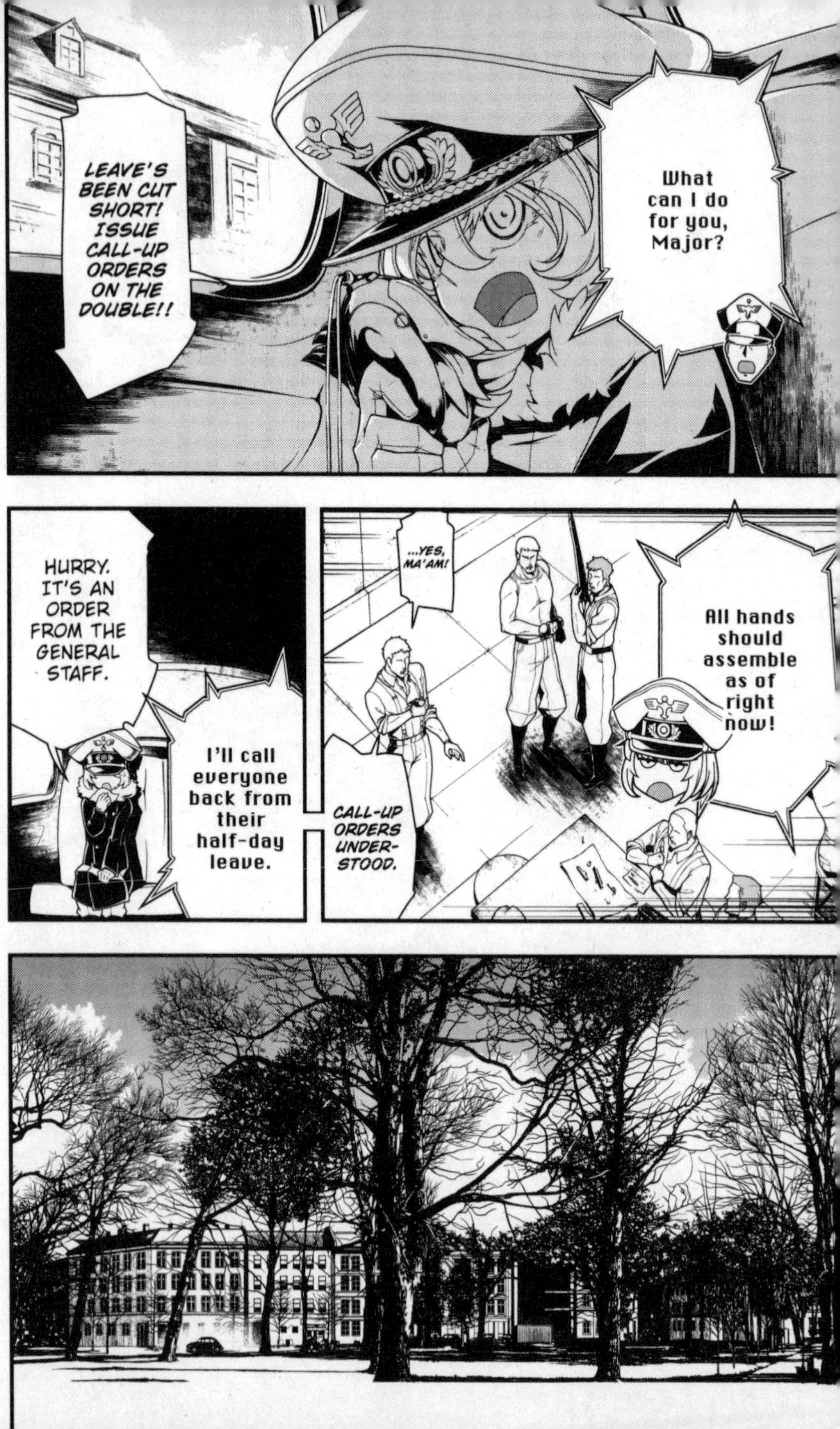
What can I do for you, Major?
LEAVE'S BEEN CUT SHORT! ISSUE CALL-UP ORDERS ON THE DOUBLE!!
All hands should assemble as of right now!
...YES, MA'AM!
CALL-UP ORDERS UNDERSTOOD.
I'll call everyone back from their half-day leave.
HURRY. IT'S AN ORDER FROM THE GENERAL STAFF.

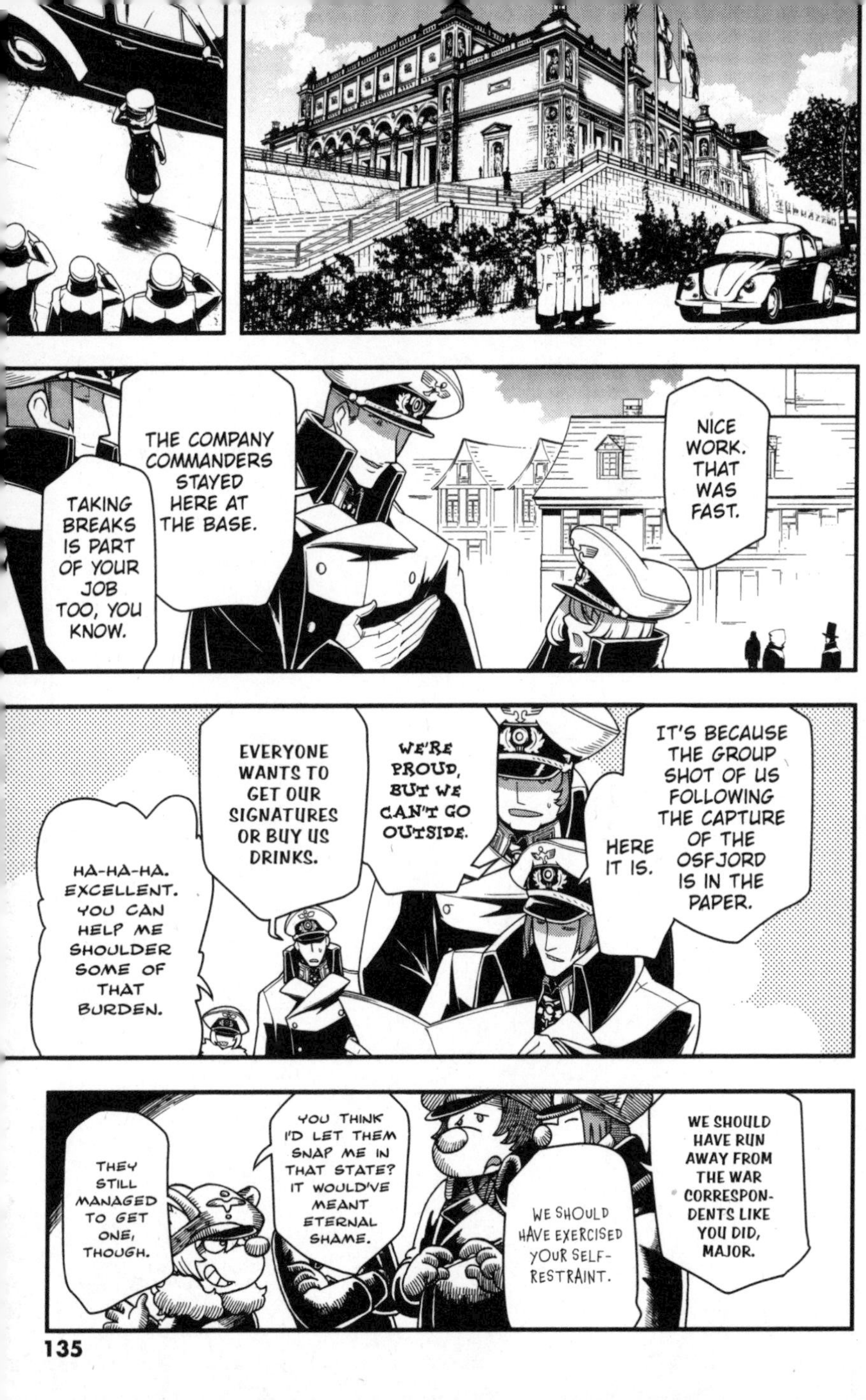
NICE WORK. THAT WAS FAST.
THE COMPANY COMMANDERS STAYED HERE AT THE BASE.
TAKING BREAKS IS PART OF YOUR JOB TOO, YOU KNOW.
IT'S BECAUSE THE GROUP SHOT OF US FOLLOWING THE CAPTURE OF THE OSFJORD IS IN THE PAPER.
HERE IT IS.
WE'RE PROUD, BUT WE CAN'T GO OUTSIDE.
EVERYONE WANTS TO GET OUR SIGNATURES OR BUY US DRINKS.
HA-HA-HA. EXCELLENT. YOU CAN HELP ME SHOULDER SOME OF THAT BURDEN.
WE SHOULD HAVE RUN AWAY FROM THE WAR CORRESPON-DENTS LIKE YOU DID, MAJOR.
WE SHOULD HAVE EXERCISED YOUR SELF-RESTRAINT.
YOU THINK I'D LET THEM SNAP ME IN THAT STATE? IT WOULD'VE MEANT ETERNAL SHAME.
THEY STILL MANAGED TO GET ONE, THOUGH.

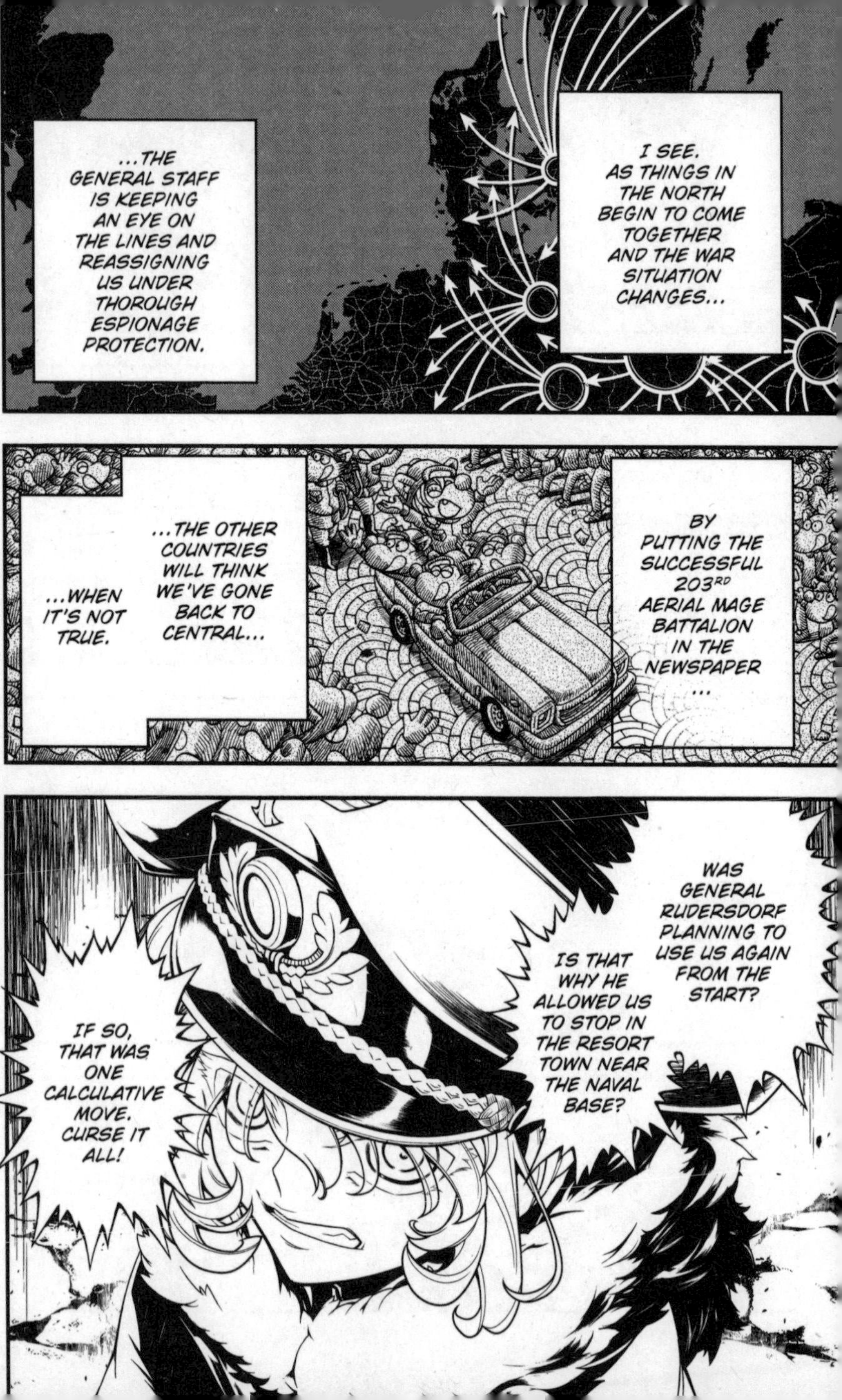
I SEE. AS THINGS IN THE NORTH BEGIN TO COME TOGETHER AND THE WAR SITUATION CHANGES...
...THE GENERAL STAFF IS KEEPING AN EYE ON THE LINES AND REASSIGNING US UNDER THOROUGH ESPIONAGE PROTECTION.
BY PUTTING THE SUCCESSFUL 203RD AERIAL MAGE BATTALION IN THE NEWSPAPER...
...THE OTHER COUNTRIES WILL THINK WE'VE GONE BACK TO CENTRAL...
...WHEN IT'S NOT TRUE.
WAS GENERAL RUDERSDORF PLANNING TO USE US AGAIN FROM THE START?
IS THAT WHY HE ALLOWED US TO STOP IN THE RESORT TOWN NEAR THE NAVAL BASE?
IF SO, THAT WAS ONE CALCULATIVE MOVE. CURSE IT ALL!

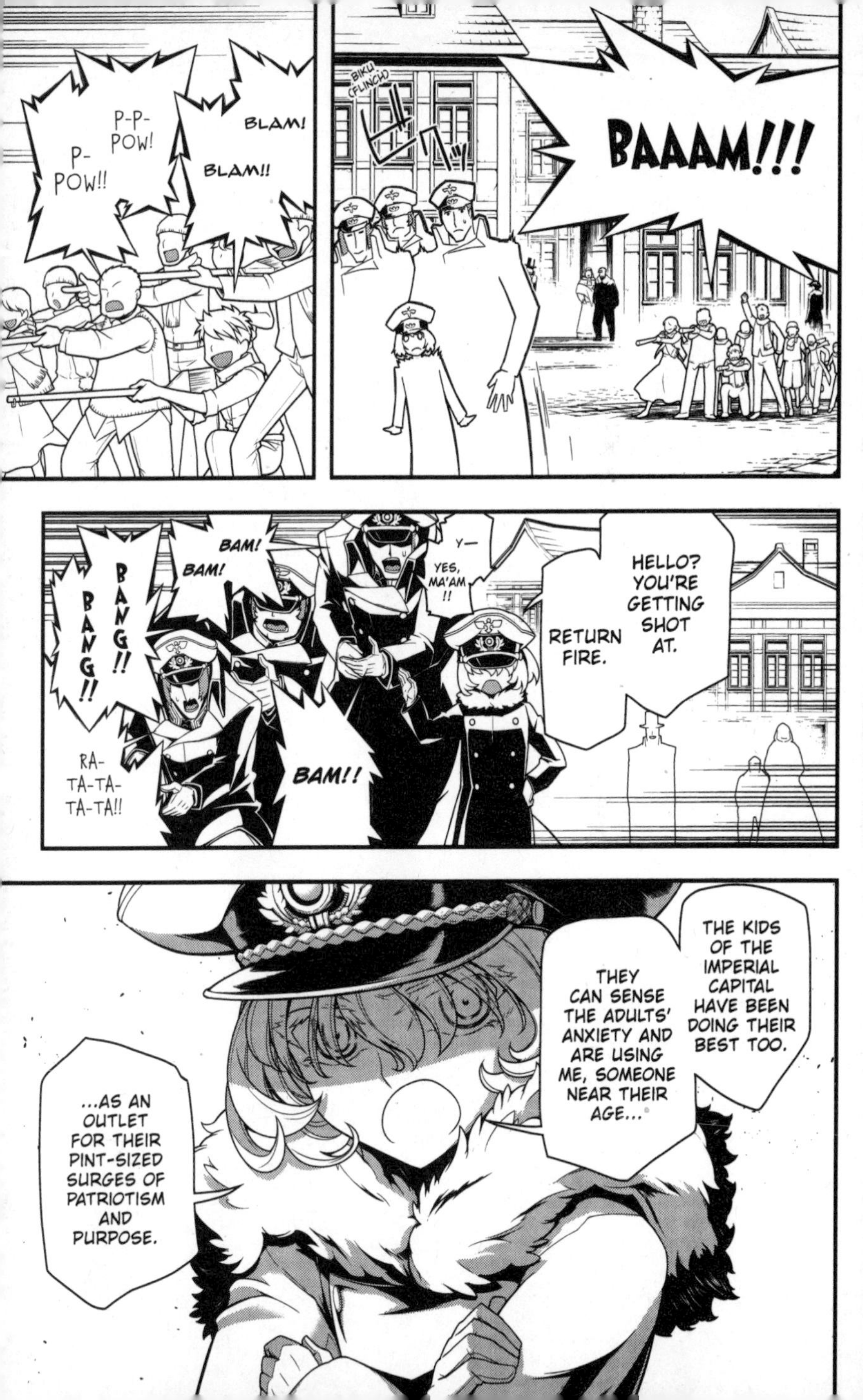
BIKU (FLINCH)
BAAAM!!!
BLAM!
BLAM!!
P-P-POW!
P-POW!!
HELLO? YOU'RE GETTING SHOT AT.
RETURN FIRE.
Y— YES, MA'AM!!
BAM!
BAM!
BANG!!
BANG!!
BAM!!
RA-TA-TA-TA-TA!!
THE KIDS OF THE IMPERIAL CAPITAL HAVE BEEN DOING THEIR BEST TOO.
THEY CAN SENSE THE ADULTS' ANXIETY AND ARE USING ME, SOMEONE NEAR THEIR AGE...
...AS AN OUTLET FOR THEIR PINT-SIZED SURGES OF PATRIOTISM AND PURPOSE.

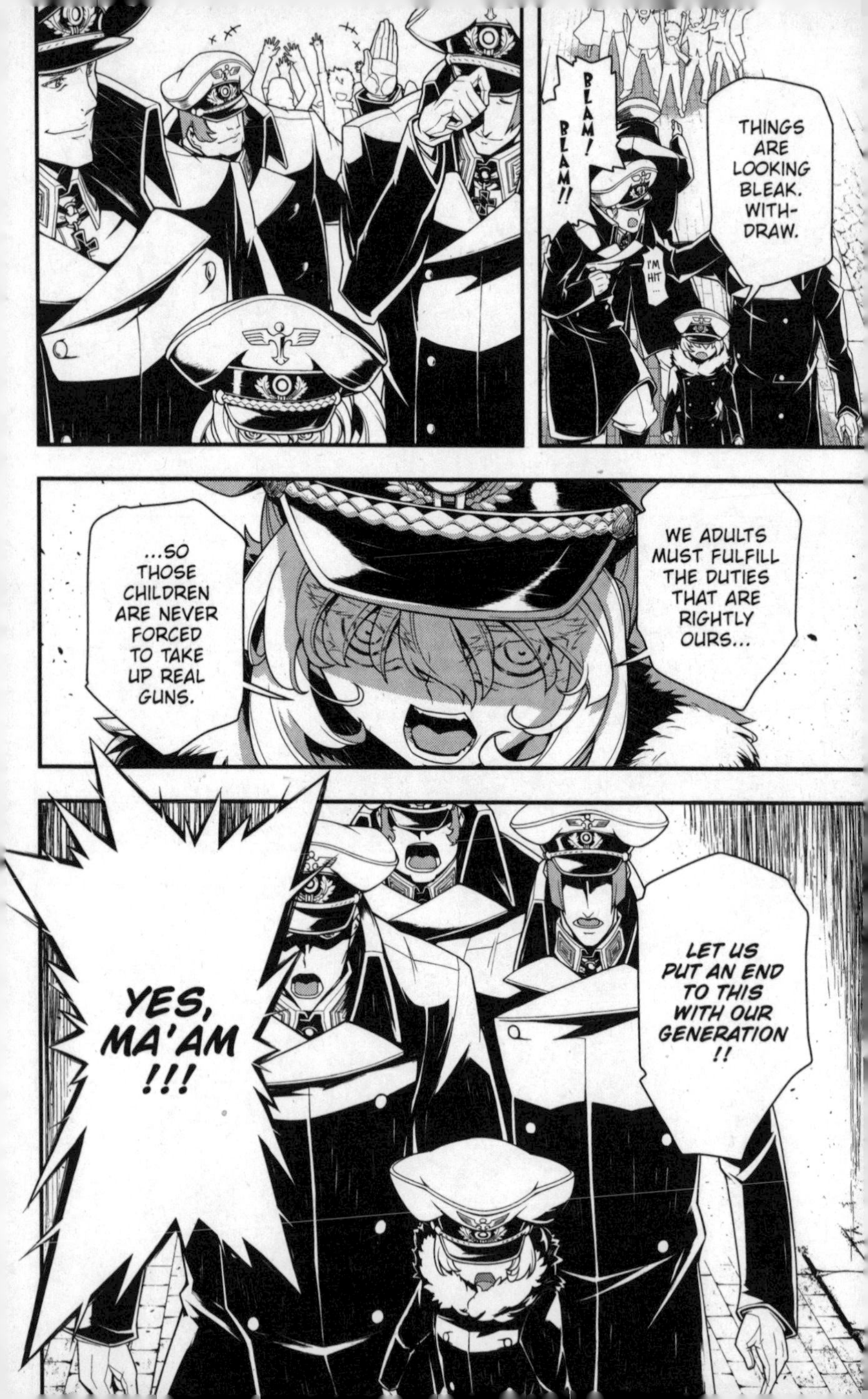
BLAM! BLAM! BLAM!!
THINGS ARE LOOKING BLEAK. WITH-DRAW.
I'M HIT...
WE ADULTS MUST FULFILL THE DUTIES THAT ARE RIGHTLY OURS...
...SO THOSE CHILDREN ARE NEVER FORCED TO TAKE UP REAL GUNS.
LET US PUT AN END TO THIS WITH OUR GENERATION!!
YES, MA'AM!!!

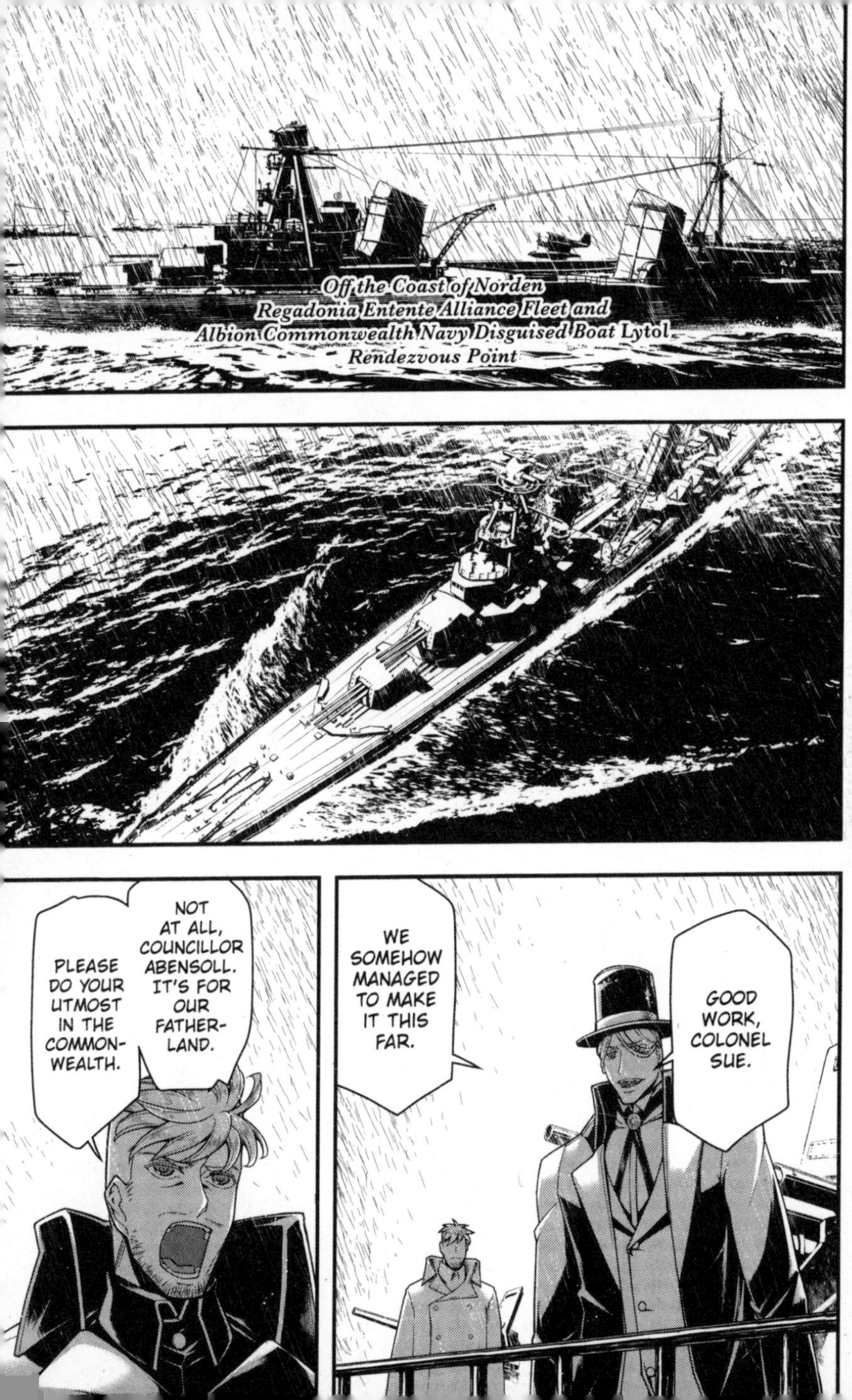
Off the Coast of Norden
Regadonia Entente Alliance Fleet and
Albion Commonwealth Navy Disguised Boat Lytol
Rendezvous Point
GOOD WORK, COLONEL SUE.
WE SOMEHOW MANAGED TO MAKE IT THIS FAR.
NOT AT ALL, COUNCILLOR ABENSOLL. IT'S FOR OUR FATHERLAND.
PLEASE DO YOUR UTMOST IN THE COMMONWEALTH.

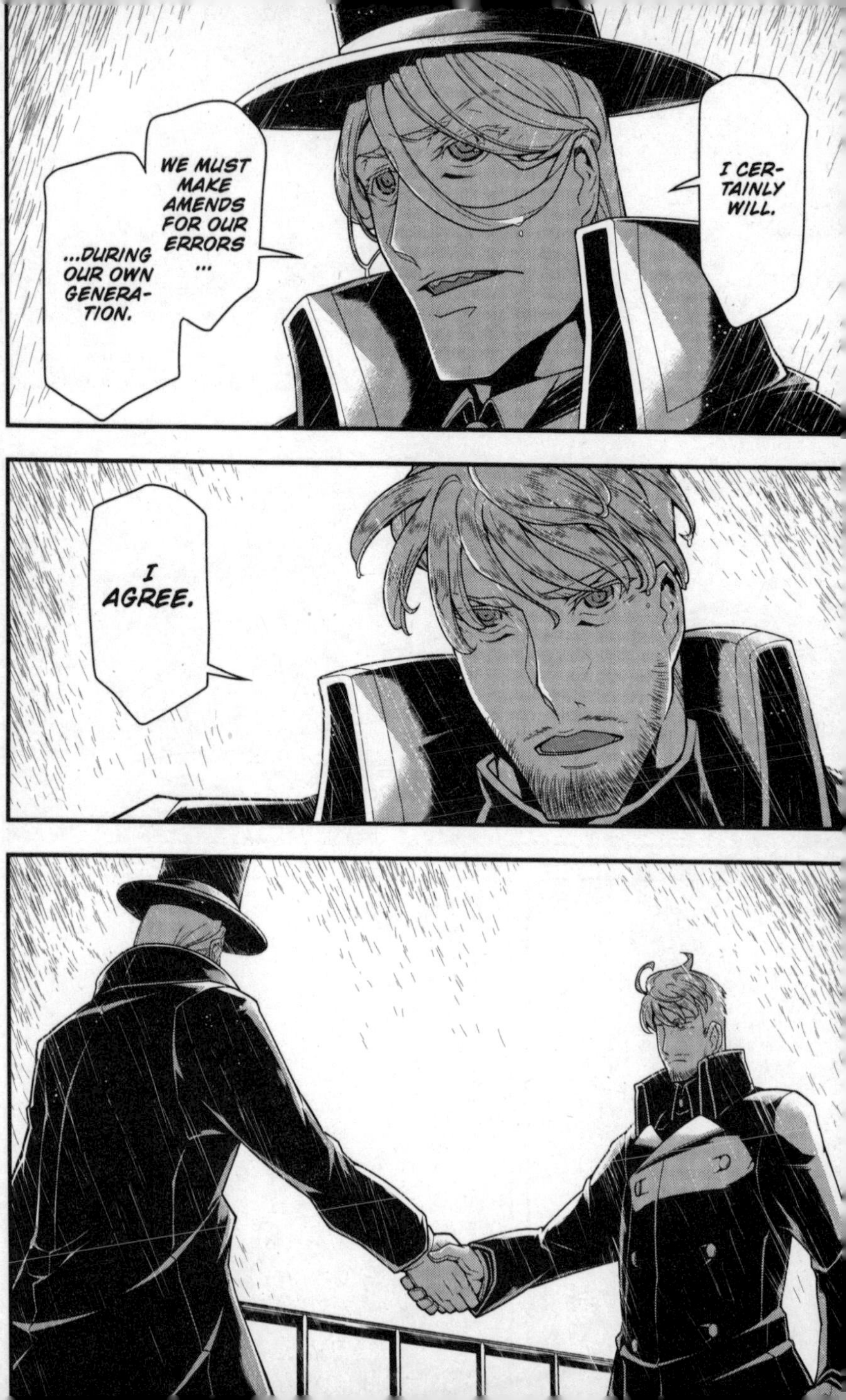
I CER-TAINLY WILL.
WE MUST MAKE AMENDS FOR OUR ERRORS ...
...DURING OUR OWN GENERA-TION.
I AGREE.

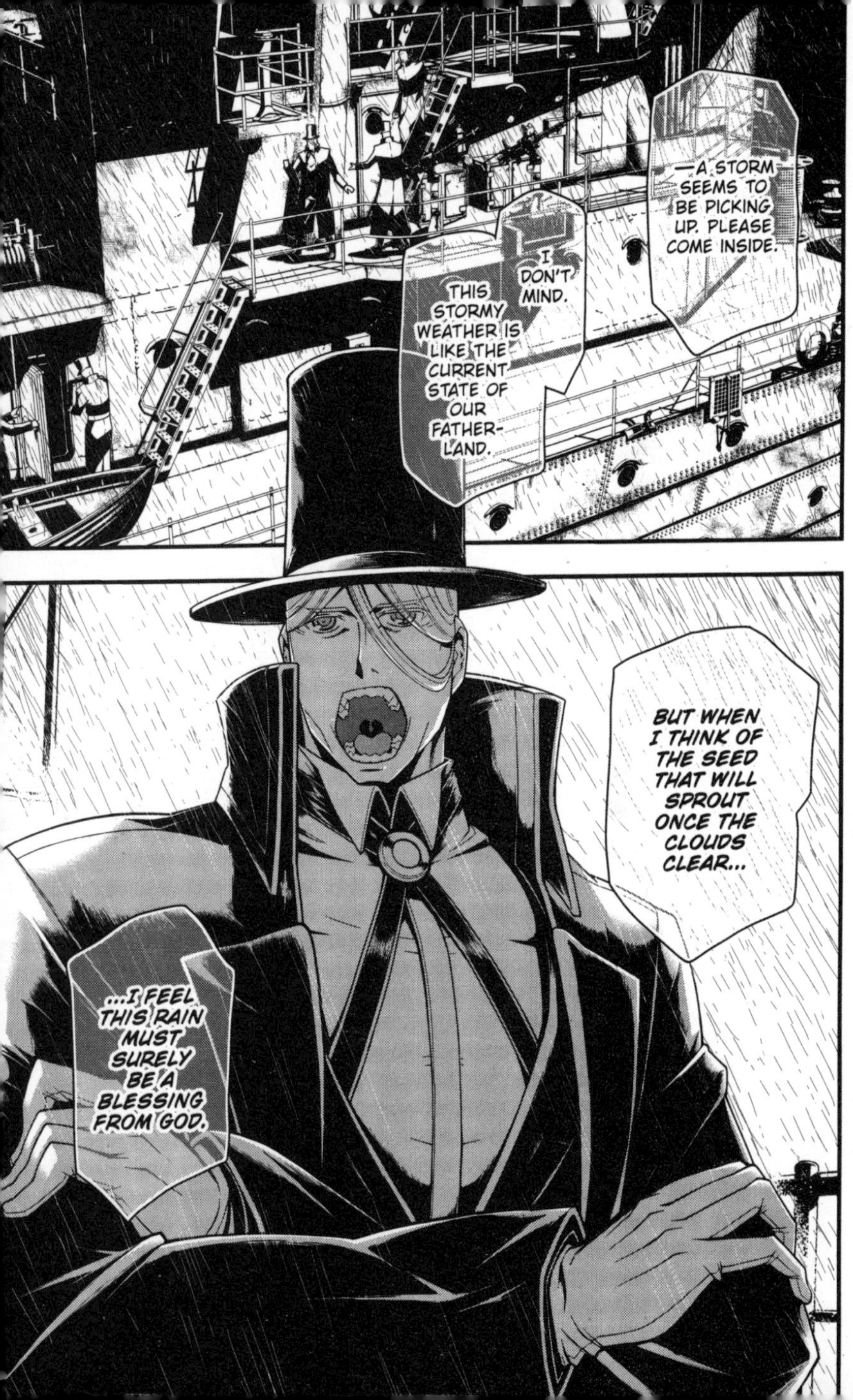
—A STORM SEEMS TO BE PICKING UP. PLEASE COME INSIDE.
I DON'T MIND.
THIS STORMY WEATHER IS LIKE THE CURRENT STATE OF OUR FATHER-LAND.
BUT WHEN I THINK OF THE SEED THAT WILL SPROUT ONCE THE CLOUDS CLEAR...
...I FEEL THIS RAIN MUST SURELY BE A BLESSING FROM GOD.

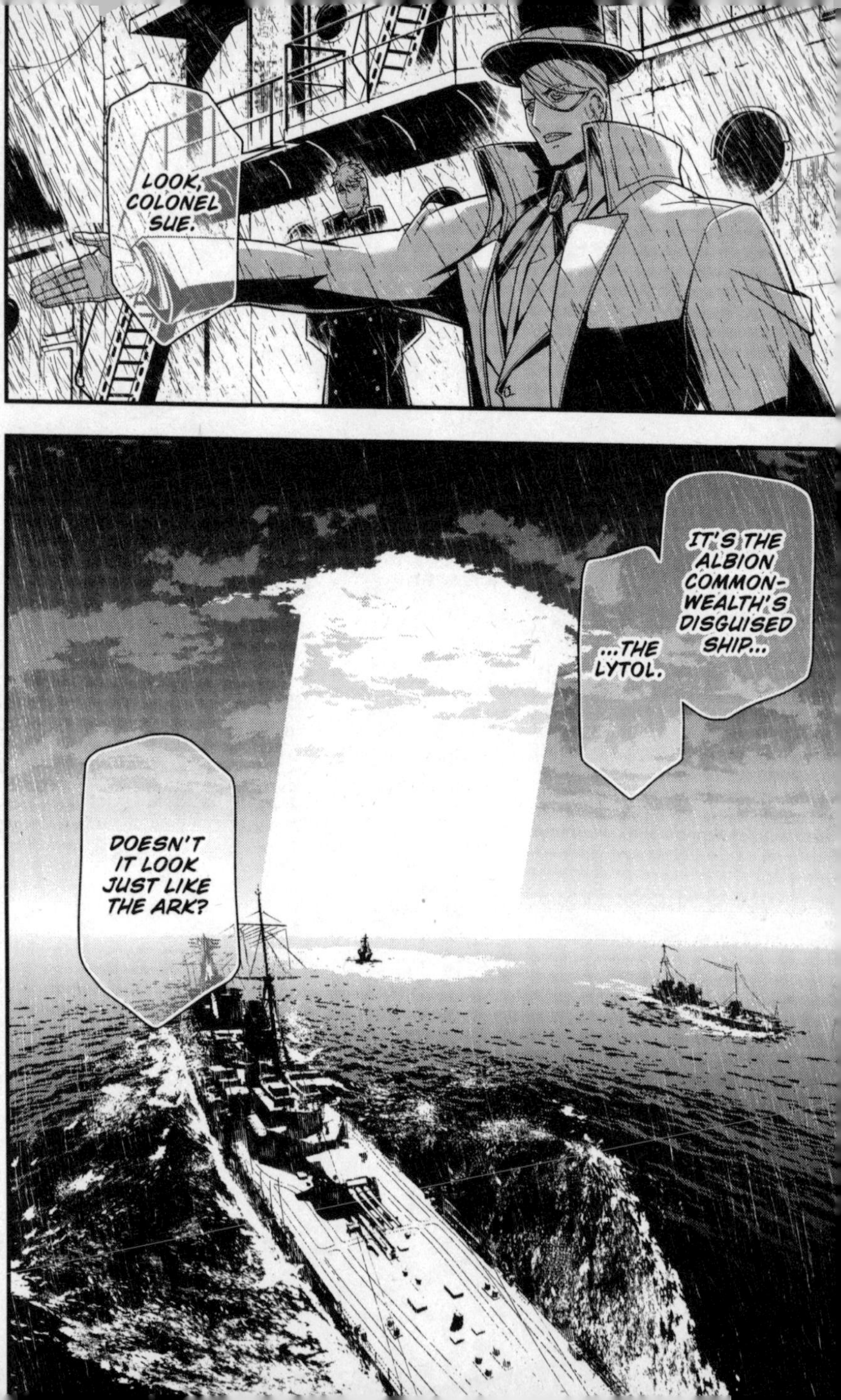
LOOK, COLONEL SUE.
IT'S THE ALBION COMMON-WEALTH'S DISGUISED SHIP...
...THE LYTOL.
DOESN'T IT LOOK JUST LIKE THE ARK?

Glossary Chapter 31

Constitutional Monarchy

A form of state where a monarch rules but their power is limited by an assembly, a constitution, and so on. Also called a limited monarchy.

Unlike in an absolute monarchy where a hereditary monarch rules the nation alone, selected citizens form a parliament and establish laws to restrict the monarch's power. It's more democratic than an absolute monarchy, but you could say it's more of a compromise compared to representative or presidential systems that deny the hereditary title.

Because it's a compromise, the degree of monarchy differs between countries and eras. One country may have a weak assembly that acts mainly as the monarch's advisory council, while another may have an upper house (House of Lords) made up of nobles with inherited status and others appointed by the monarch that counters democracy as the monarch's posse. These types are called constitutional monarchies based on appearances, but internally, they are not much different from absolute monarchies.

Imperial Germany seems to be the model for the Empire here. Both its emperor and chancellor were powerful, so it would seem to have been a classic example of a superficial constitutional monarchy.

Imperial Government

A form of state where an emperor rules.

"Emperor," like "King" and "Pope," is a title of respect for a monarch. Usually it indicates a "King of Kings" who brings together multiple regions, and the word comes from the title of the head of the Roman Empire in Europe.

Most people in history who have called themselves emperors, however, did not bring together multiple regions. Calling oneself an emperor was the equivalent of claiming to be the successor to Rome, so sovereigns often used it to assert their legitimacy. For that reason, it's quite difficult to spot any difference between monarchy and imperial government.

That goes for the historical German Empire as well. In 1871, when Germany was reunified with Prussia, Wilhelm I took the title of emperor to inherit the Holy Roman Empire and established an imperial government. But there was no direct connection between the Holy Roman Empire and the German Empire, and he didn't really have enough territory to call it an empire.

Glossary Chapter 32

Reservist

A former active duty soldier who lives as an ordinary citizen but is a member of the reservist association.

The role of these associations varies depending on the country and era, but they often provide mobilization assistance in emergencies and work on welfare issues for veterans and their families. As a political group, they sometimes publish bulletins or lobby the government.

War Correspondent

Journalists and photographers who accompany the army into war to report from the battlefield.

Their mission is to let the public know what is happening in the war zone and leave records and videos to posterity, but their position varies depending on the country and era.

Usually they go into action with the military and report from the field. That's called embedded reporting, and since the journalist's safety is dependent on the army, the reports tend to come from their own party's perspective. Articles and photos often pass through inspection to prevent intelligence leaks, and there can be limits on what you can cover, like where a unit is deployed and its mission.

Sometimes the army will select a pool of reporters and authorize them to report from a designated location. That makes it easier for the military to regulate what information is going out. However, the method is criticized for severely limiting the freedom of the press.

In our contemporary information society, the impression conveyed via reporting is a pressing issue for the army. A country may require that an embedded photographer belong to the unit they're with, or sometimes the army has its own public affairs unit devoted to propaganda at home and against enemy nations.

Glossary Chapter 33

Espionage Protection

Protecting against espionage means attempting to thwart efforts aiming to steal or destroy your nation's information. Also called counterintelligence.

Although counterintelligence isn't only performed at home, the domestic department in charge of homeland security is often the main thrust, so there is a tendency to keep it separate from the espionage teams that work abroad. Well-known examples include the United Kingdom's MI5 (domestic security) and MI6 (foreign security) and the United States' FBI (a federal bureau and thus domestic) and CIA (Central Intelligence Agency that handles foreign affairs).

The split is often for legal or institutional reasons, but in practice, serious arguments regarding jurisdiction do come up. And in addition to these agencies, the army often has its own units dedicated to counterintelligence.

In the story here, as the Entente Alliance collapses, information about where the troops concentrated in the north will be sent and their numbers is very important in planning its next operation. That's why the Empire makes sure to keep the deployments a secret. We can assume that each country's intelligence agency is following the newspapers on the 203rd's movements. This kind of intelligence collecting from public sources is called OSINT. Surely, the way the 203rd headed back up north after the major coverage of their triumphant return was some advanced counter-OSINT.

Disguised Ship

A military vessel that can perform espionage missions and so on without being targeted by enemy attacks since it's made to look like a civilian ship. Also called armed merchant cruisers or auxiliary cruisers.

Many of them are revamped passenger or cargo merchant vessels, and they almost never have the combat abilities of warships. They perform espionage missions, transport goods or personnel, and carry out commerce raids on unsuspecting enemy merchant vessels. These boats exploit the laws established to protect civilians as their shield, so naturally, if they are exposed, it becomes an international incident. Even a neutral nation's ship can be inspected if there is some doubt regarding the vessel's nationality and cargo, so the fear of being discovered is real.

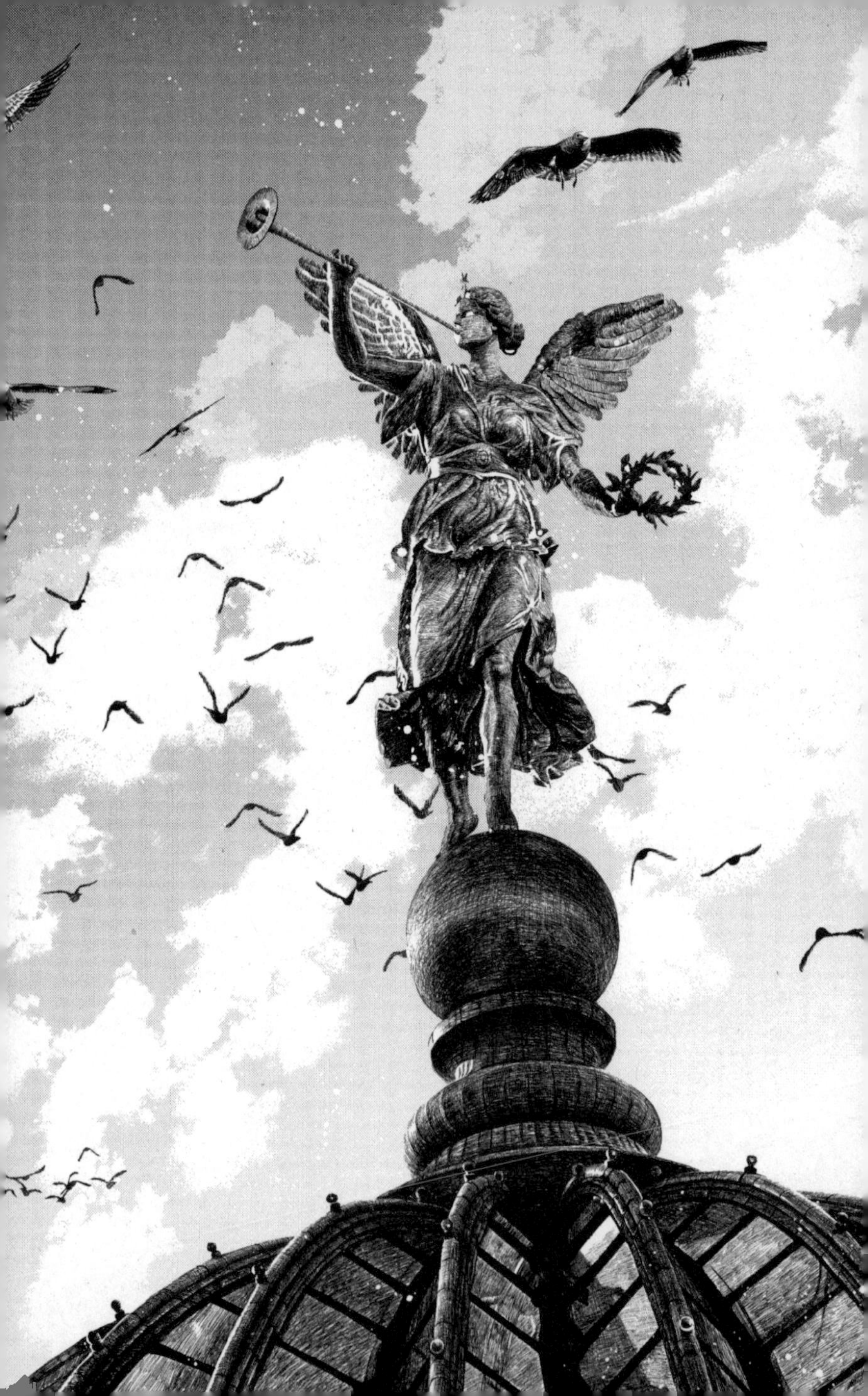

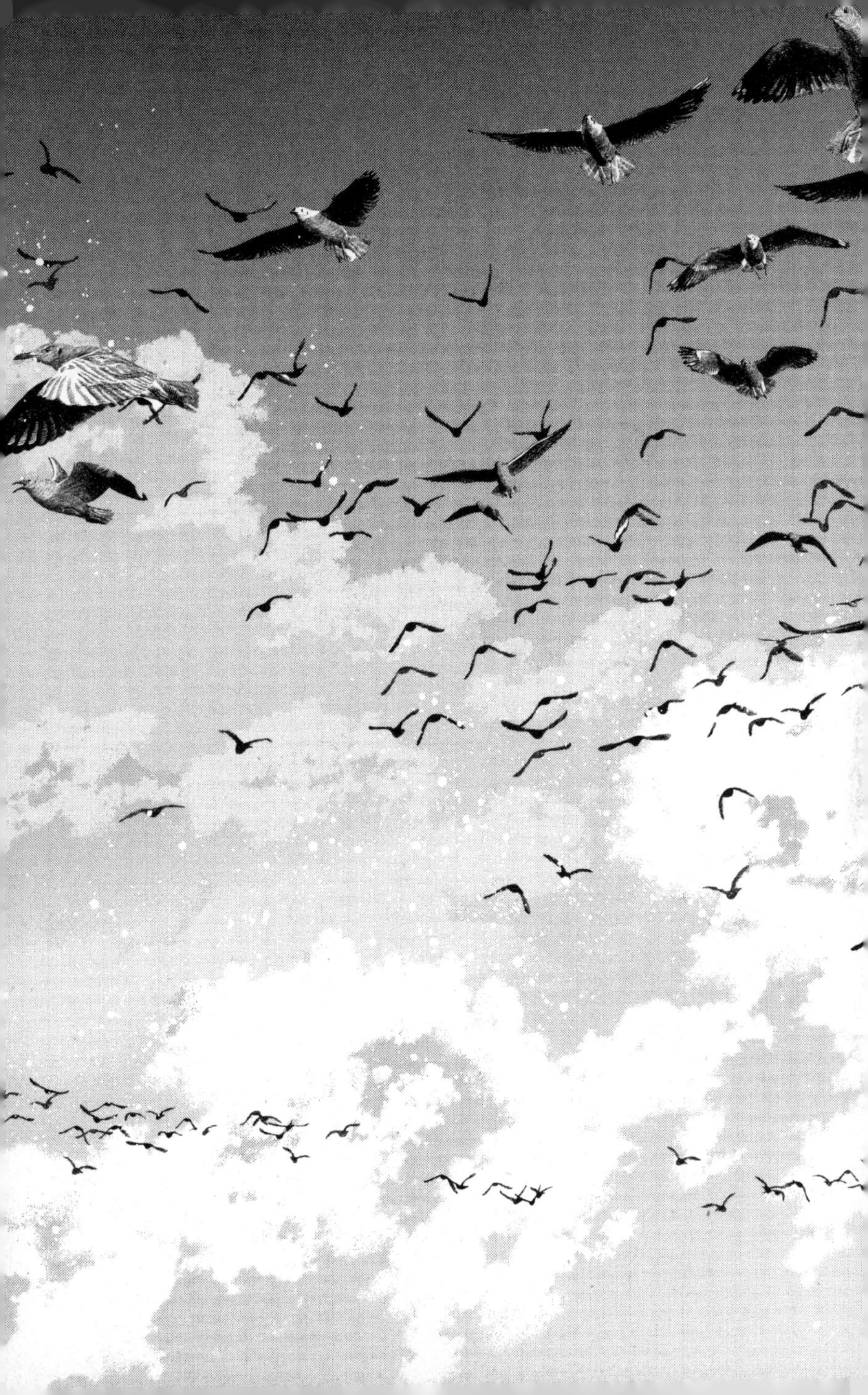

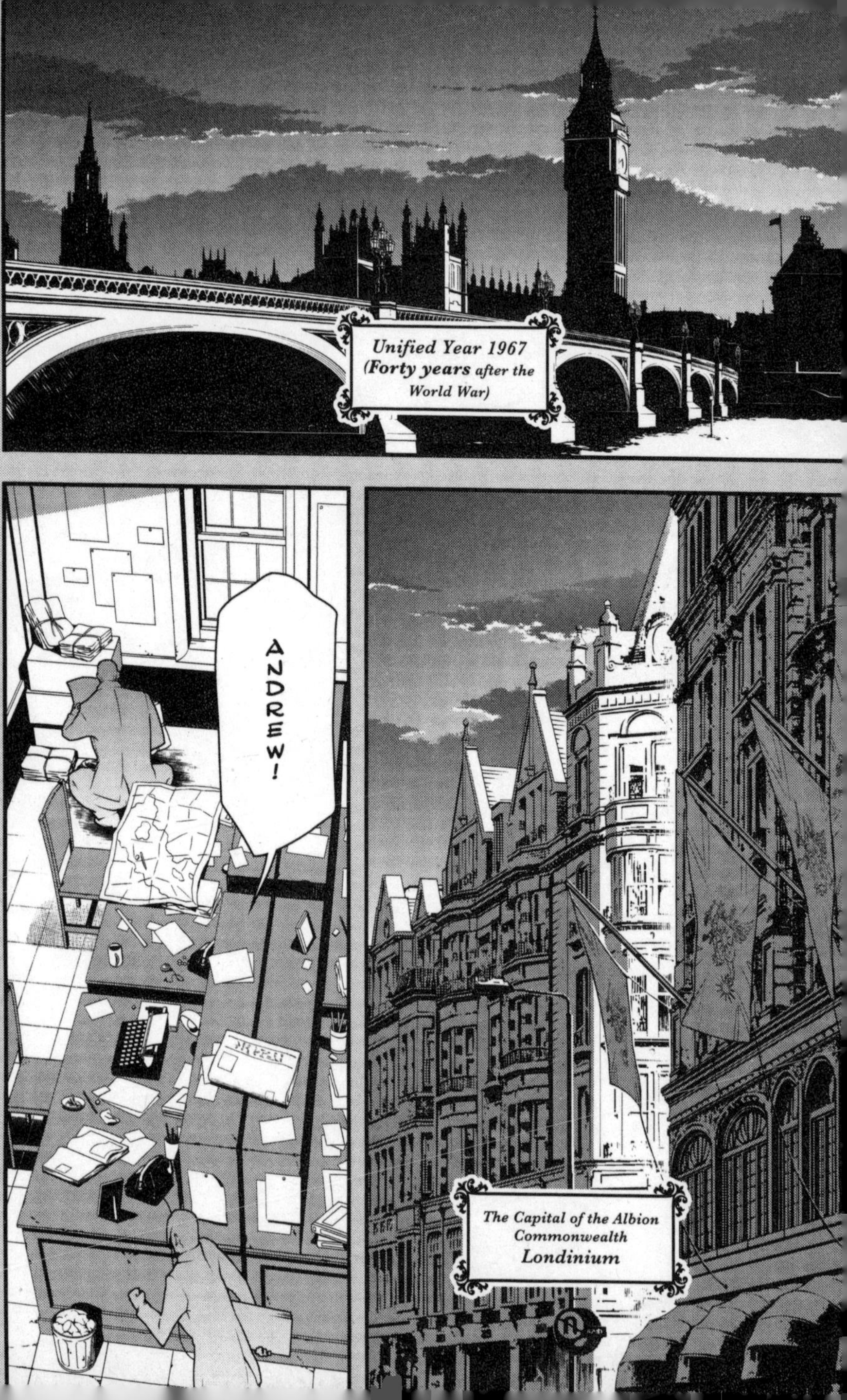
Unified Year 1967 (Forty years after the World War)
The Capital of the Albion Commonwealth Londinium
ANDREW!

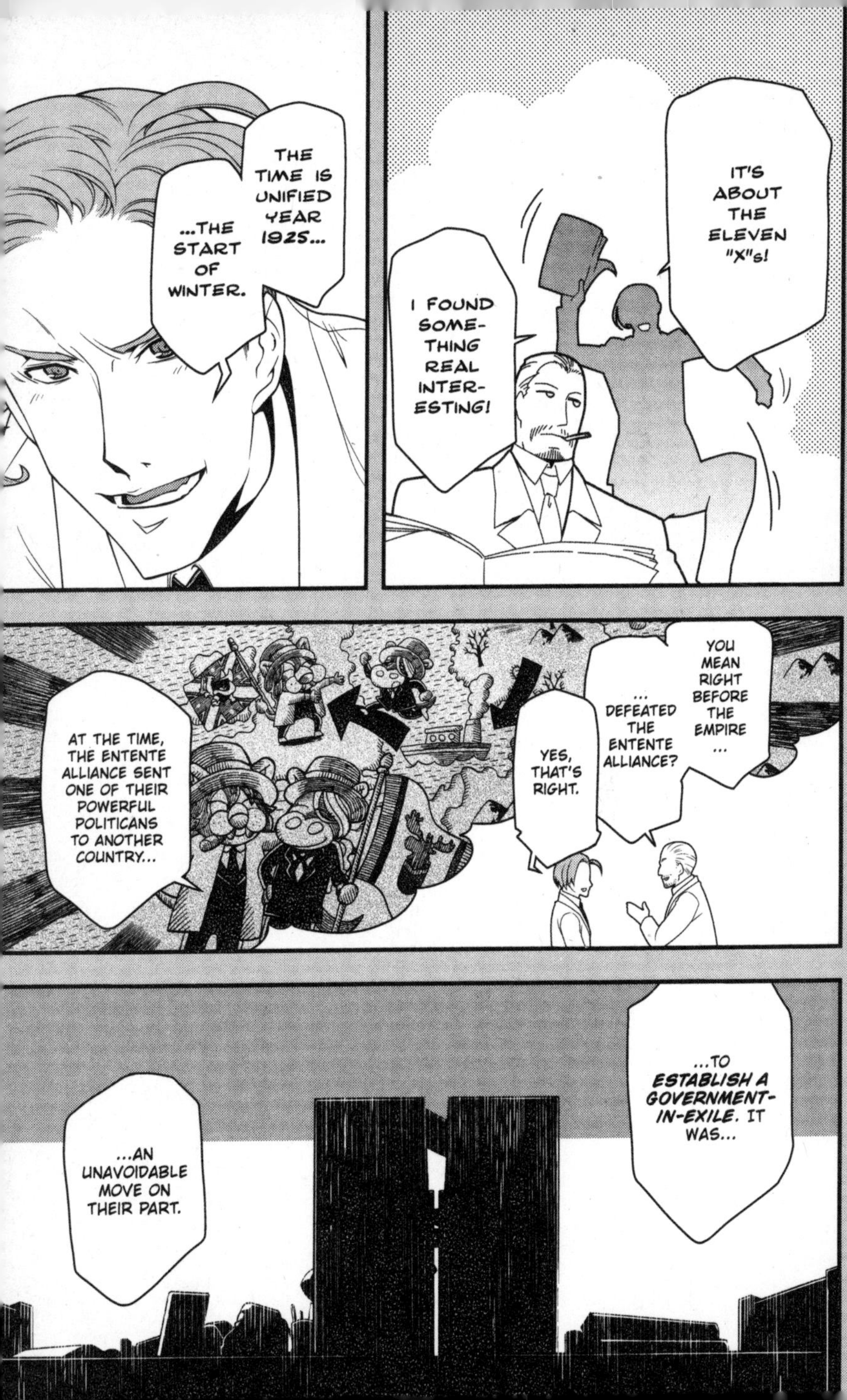
IT'S ABOUT THE ELEVEN "X"s!
I FOUND SOMETHING REAL INTERESTING!
THE TIME IS UNIFIED YEAR 1925...
...THE START OF WINTER.
YOU MEAN RIGHT BEFORE THE EMPIRE...
...DEFEATED THE ENTENTE ALLIANCE?
YES, THAT'S RIGHT.
AT THE TIME, THE ENTENTE ALLIANCE SENT ONE OF THEIR POWERFUL POLITICANS TO ANOTHER COUNTRY...
...TO *ESTABLISH A GOVERNMENT-IN-EXILE*. IT WAS...
...AN UNAVOIDABLE MOVE ON THEIR PART.

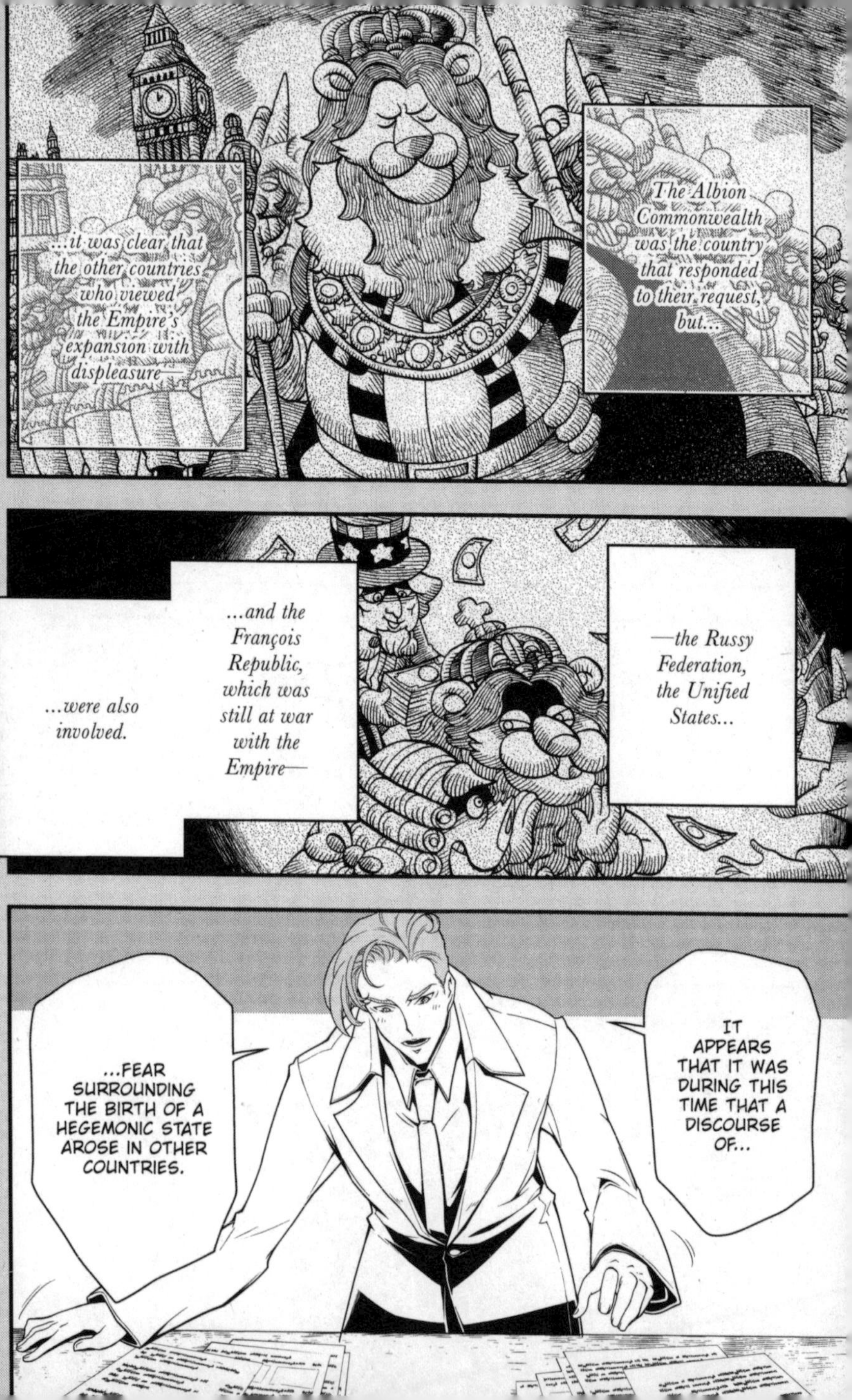
The Albion Commonwealth was the country that responded to their request, but...
...it was clear that the other countries who viewed the Empire's expansion with displeasure—
—the Russy Federation, the Unified States...
...and the François Republic, which was still at war with the Empire—
...were also involved.
IT APPEARS THAT IT WAS DURING THIS TIME THAT A DISCOURSE OF...
...FEAR SURROUNDING THE BIRTH OF A HEGEMONIC STATE AROSE IN OTHER COUNTRIES.

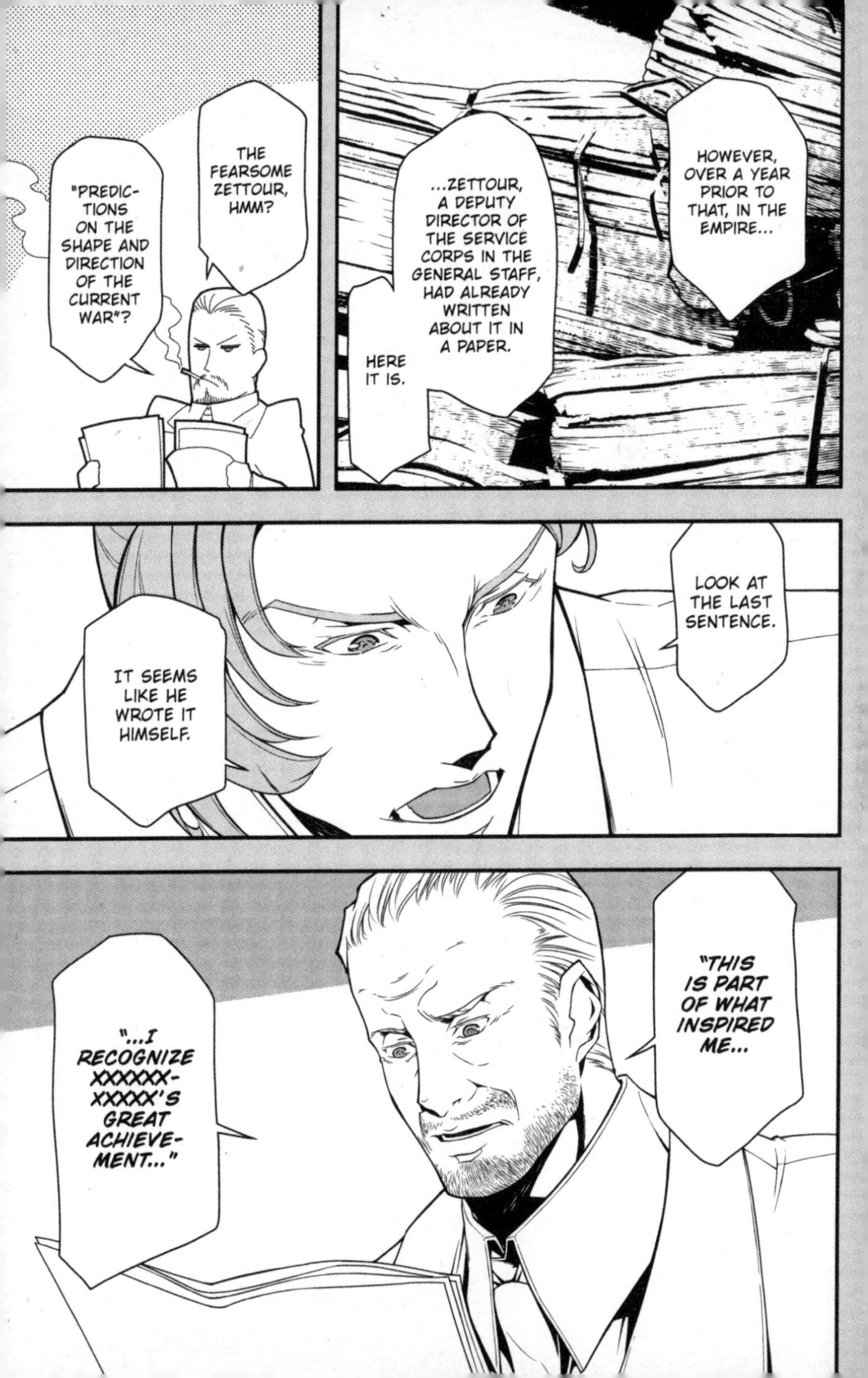
HOWEVER, OVER A YEAR PRIOR TO THAT, IN THE EMPIRE...
...ZETTOUR, A DEPUTY DIRECTOR OF THE SERVICE CORPS IN THE GENERAL STAFF, HAD ALREADY WRITTEN ABOUT IT IN A PAPER.
HERE IT IS.
THE FEARSOME ZETTOUR, HMM?
"PREDICTIONS ON THE SHAPE AND DIRECTION OF THE CURRENT WAR"?
LOOK AT THE LAST SENTENCE.
IT SEEMS LIKE HE WROTE IT HIMSELF.
"THIS IS PART OF WHAT INSPIRED ME...
"...I RECOGNIZE XXXXXX-XXXXX'S GREAT ACHIEVEMENT..."

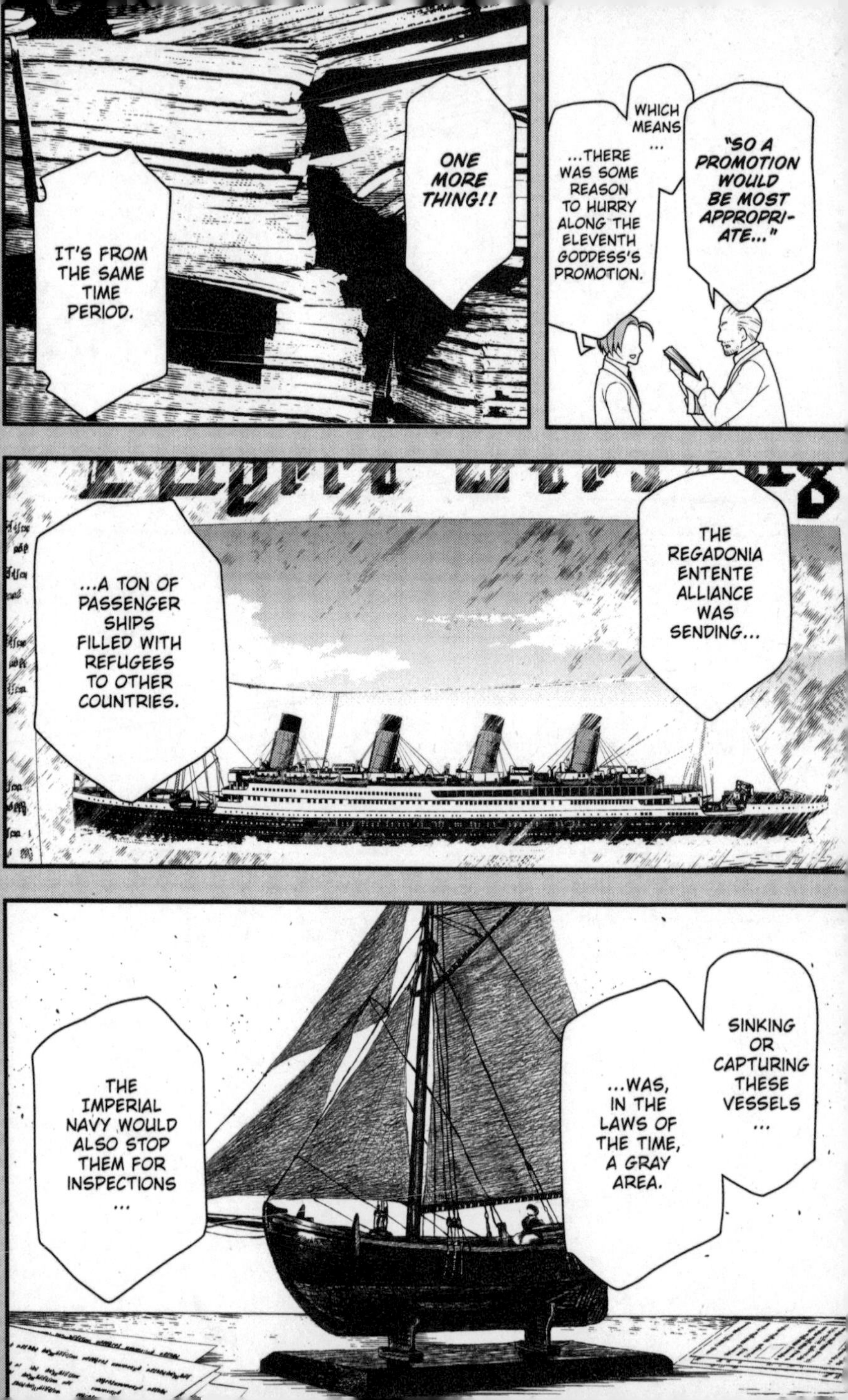
"SO A PROMOTION WOULD BE MOST APPROPRIATE..."
WHICH MEANS ...
...THERE WAS SOME REASON TO HURRY ALONG THE ELEVENTH GODDESS'S PROMOTION.
ONE MORE THING!!
IT'S FROM THE SAME TIME PERIOD.
THE REGADONIA ENTENTE ALLIANCE WAS SENDING...
...A TON OF PASSENGER SHIPS FILLED WITH REFUGEES TO OTHER COUNTRIES.
SINKING OR CAPTURING THESE VESSELS ...
...WAS, IN THE LAWS OF THE TIME, A GRAY AREA.
THE IMPERIAL NAVY WOULD ALSO STOP THEM FOR INSPECTIONS ...

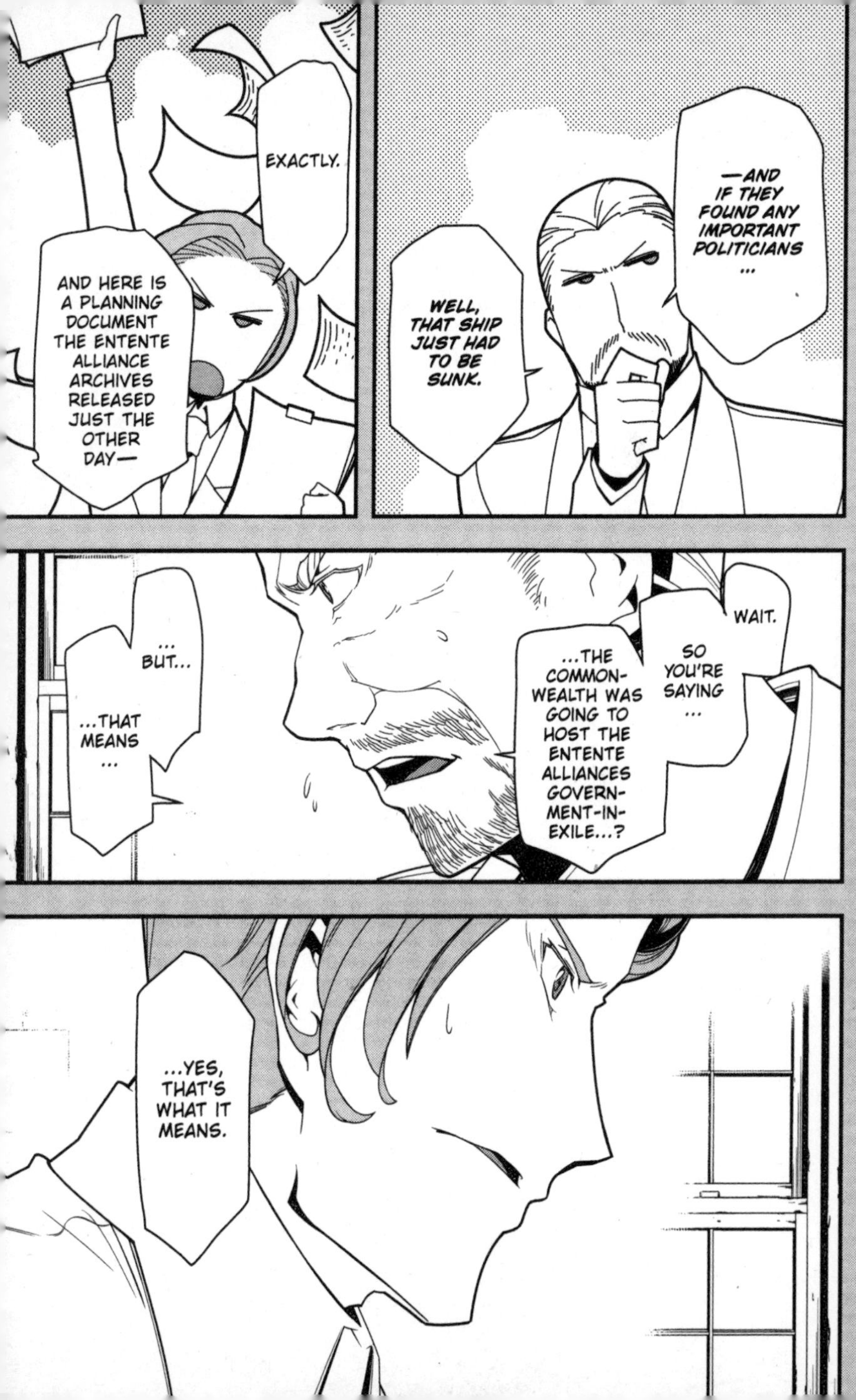
—AND IF THEY FOUND ANY IMPORTANT POLITICIANS ...
WELL, THAT SHIP JUST HAD TO BE SUNK.
EXACTLY.
AND HERE IS A PLANNING DOCUMENT THE ENTENTE ALLIANCE ARCHIVES RELEASED JUST THE OTHER DAY—
WAIT.
SO YOU'RE SAYING ...
...THE COMMONWEALTH WAS GOING TO HOST THE ENTENTE ALLIANCES GOVERNMENT-IN-EXILE...?
... BUT...
...THAT MEANS ...
...YES, THAT'S WHAT IT MEANS.

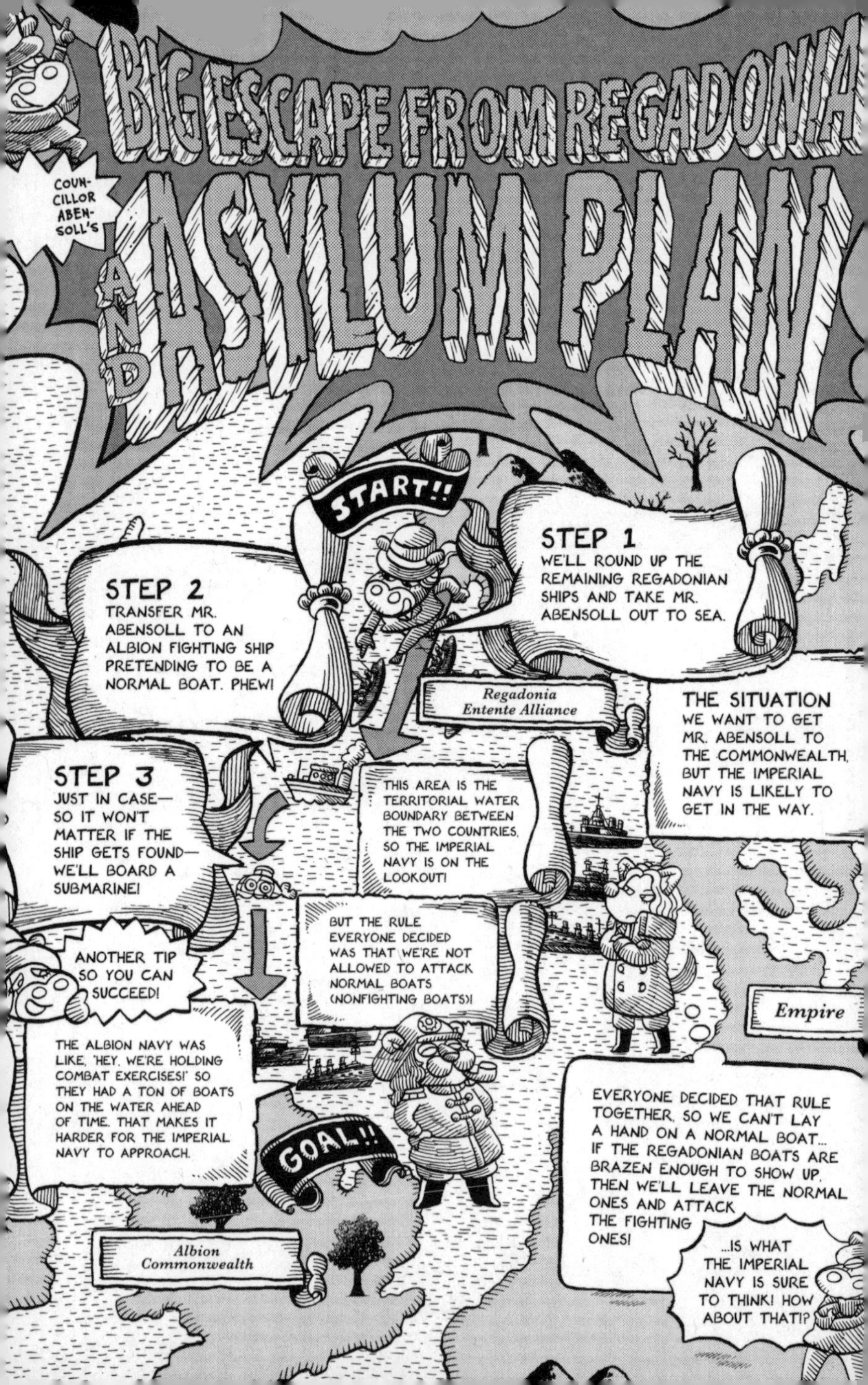

COUNCILLOR ABENSOLL'S
BIG ESCAPE FROM REGADONIA AND ASYLUM PLAN!
START!!
STEP 1
WE'LL ROUND UP THE REMAINING REGADONIAN SHIPS AND TAKE MR. ABENSOLL OUT TO SEA.
STEP 2
TRANSFER MR. ABENSOLL TO AN ALBION FIGHTING SHIP PRETENDING TO BE A NORMAL BOAT. PHEW!
Regadonia Entente Alliance
THE SITUATION
WE WANT TO GET MR. ABENSOLL TO THE COMMONWEALTH, BUT THE IMPERIAL NAVY IS LIKELY TO GET IN THE WAY.
THIS AREA IS THE TERRITORIAL WATER BOUNDARY BETWEEN THE TWO COUNTRIES, SO THE IMPERIAL NAVY IS ON THE LOOKOUT!
STEP 3
JUST IN CASE—SO IT WON'T MATTER IF THE SHIP GETS FOUND—WE'LL BOARD A SUBMARINE!
Empire
BUT THE RULE EVERYONE DECIDED WAS THAT WE'RE NOT ALLOWED TO ATTACK NORMAL BOATS (NONFIGHTING BOATS)!
ANOTHER TIP SO YOU CAN SUCCEED!
THE ALBION NAVY WAS LIKE, 'HEY, WE'RE HOLDING COMBAT EXERCISES!' SO THEY HAD A TON OF BOATS ON THE WATER AHEAD OF TIME. THAT MAKES IT HARDER FOR THE IMPERIAL NAVY TO APPROACH.
EVERYONE DECIDED THAT RULE TOGETHER, SO WE CAN'T LAY A HAND ON A NORMAL BOAT... IF THE REGADONIAN BOATS ARE BRAZEN ENOUGH TO SHOW UP, THEN WE'LL LEAVE THE NORMAL ONES AND ATTACK THE FIGHTING ONES!
...IS WHAT THE IMPERIAL NAVY IS SURE TO THINK! HOW ABOUT THAT!?
GOAL!!
Albion Commonwealth

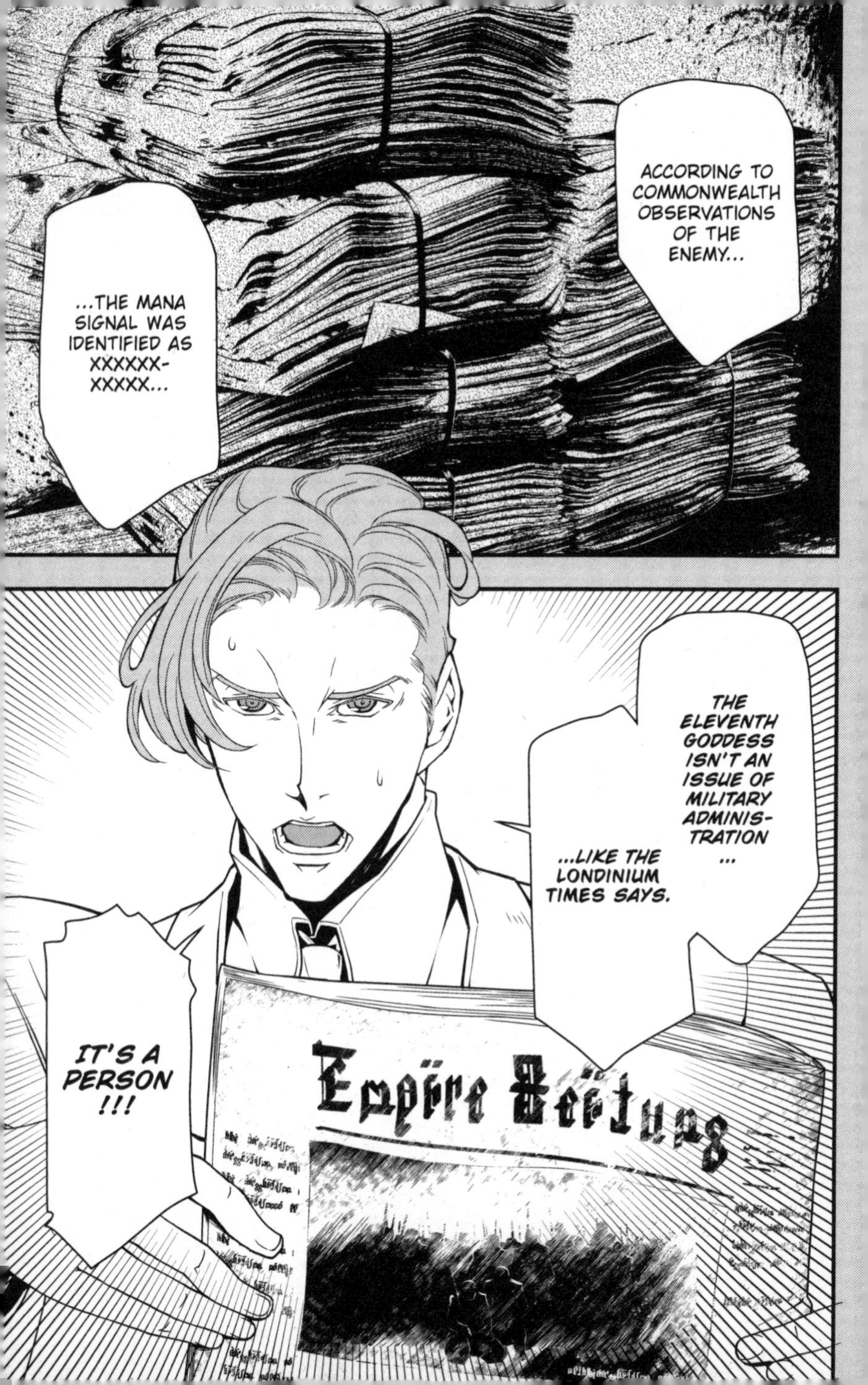

ACCORDING TO COMMONWEALTH OBSERVATIONS OF THE ENEMY...
...THE MANA SIGNAL WAS IDENTIFIED AS XXXXXX-XXXXX...
THE ELEVENTH GODDESS ISN'T AN ISSUE OF MILITARY ADMINIS-TRATION...
...LIKE THE LONDINIUM TIMES SAYS.
IT'S A PERSON!!!

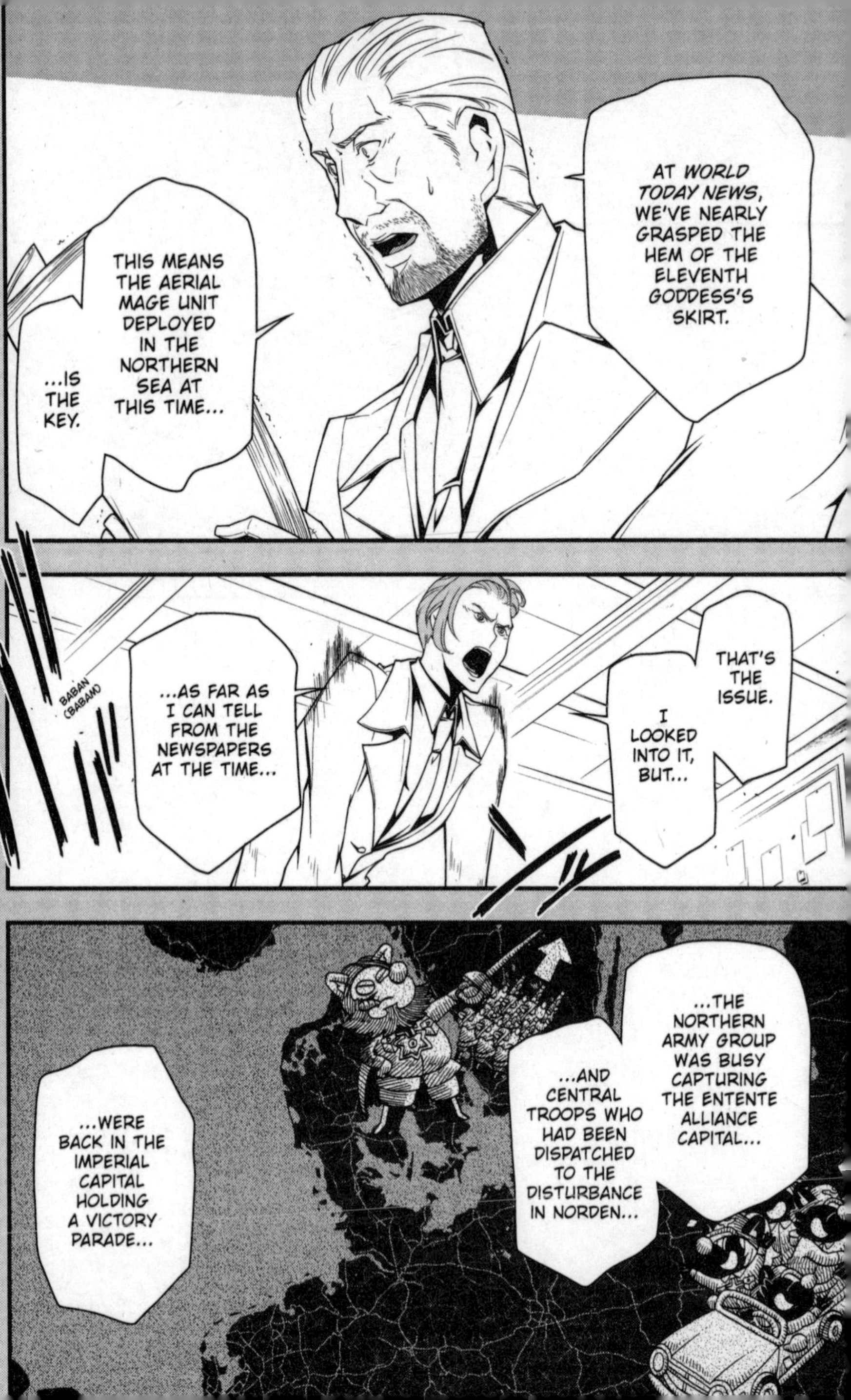
AT *WORLD TODAY NEWS*, WE'VE NEARLY GRASPED THE HEM OF THE ELEVENTH GODDESS'S SKIRT.
THIS MEANS THE AERIAL MAGE UNIT DEPLOYED IN THE NORTHERN SEA AT THIS TIME...
...IS THE KEY.
THAT'S THE ISSUE.
I LOOKED INTO IT, BUT...
...AS FAR AS I CAN TELL FROM THE NEWSPAPERS AT THE TIME...
BABAN (BABAM)
...THE NORTHERN ARMY GROUP WAS BUSY CAPTURING THE ENTENTE ALLIANCE CAPITAL...
...AND CENTRAL TROOPS WHO HAD BEEN DISPATCHED TO THE DISTURBANCE IN NORDEN...
...WERE BACK IN THE IMPERIAL CAPITAL HOLDING A VICTORY PARADE...

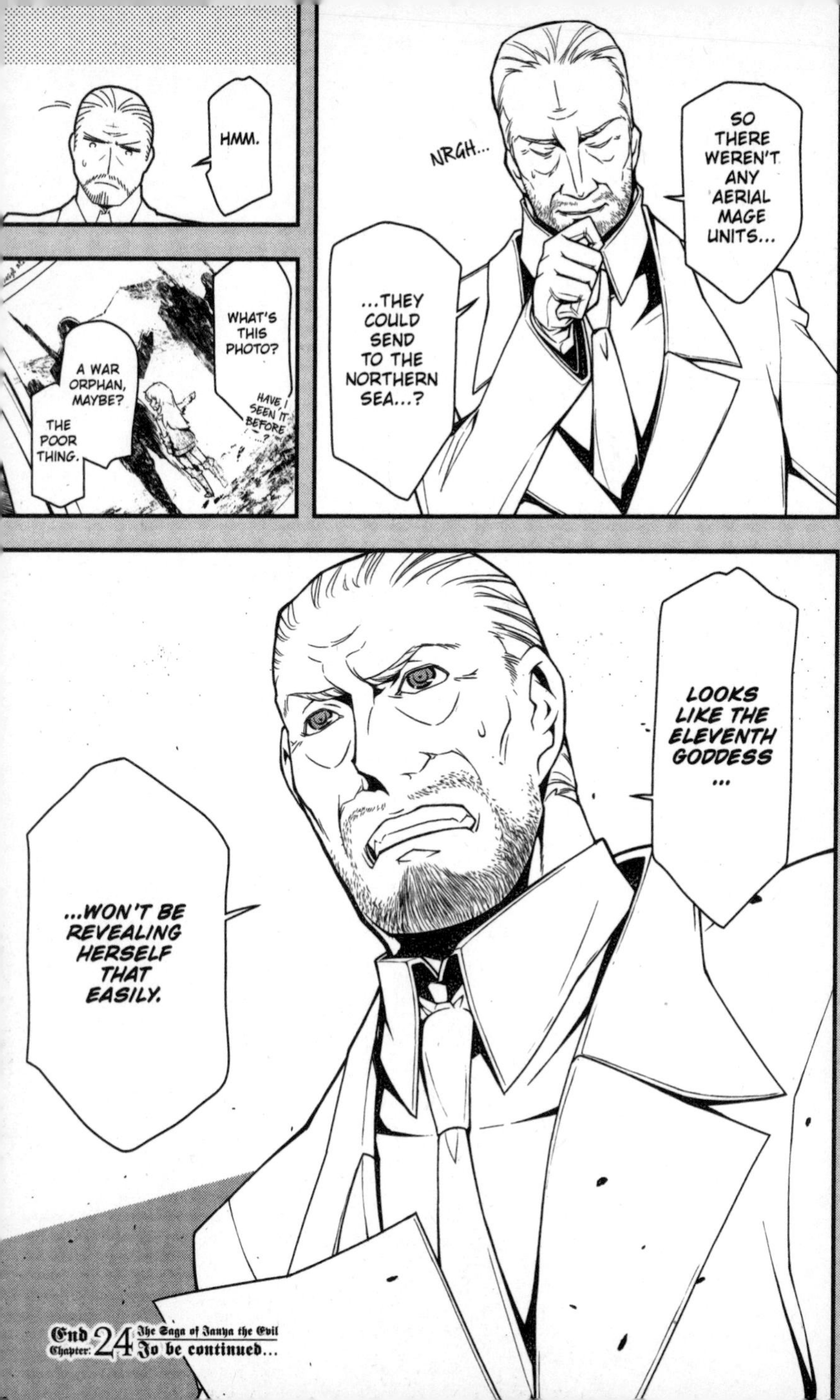
SO THERE WEREN'T ANY AERIAL MAGE UNITS...
NRGH...
...THEY COULD SEND TO THE NORTHERN SEA...?
HMM.
WHAT'S THIS PHOTO?
HAVE I SEEN IT BEFORE ...?
A WAR ORPHAN, MAYBE?
THE POOR THING.
LOOKS LIKE THE ELEVENTH GODDESS ...
...WON'T BE REVEALING HERSELF THAT EASILY.
End Chapter: 24 The Saga of Tanya the Evil
To be continued...

The Saga of Tanya the Evil

08

Original Story: Carlo Zen   Art: Chika Tojo
Character Design: Shinobu Shinotsuki

Special Thanks

Carlo Zen

Shinobu Shinotsuki

Takamaru

KURI

Miira

Yamatatsu

Agatha

Kuuko

Shinno Himegami

THE SAGA OF TANYA THE EVIL 08

ORIGINAL STORY: Carlo Zen

ART: Chika Tojo ❧ CHARACTER DESIGN: Shinobu Shinotsuki

Translation: Emily Balistrieri ❧ Lettering: Rochelle Gancio

YOUJO SENKI Vol. 8
©Chika TOJO 2018
©2013 Carlo ZEN
First published in Japan in 2018 by KADOKAWA CORPORATION, Tokyo.
English translation rights arranged with KADOKAWA CORPORATION, Tokyo
through TUTTLE-MORI AGENCY, INC., Tokyo.

English translation © 2019 by Yen Press, LLC

Yen Press
150 West 30th Street, 19th Floor
New York, NY 10001

Visit us at yenpress.com
facebook.com/yenpress
twitter.com/yenpress
yenpress.tumblr.com
instagram.com/yenpress

First Yen Press Edition: October 2019

Yen Press is an imprint of Yen Press, LLC.
The Yen Press name and logo are trademarks of Yen Press, LLC.

Library of Congress Control Number: 2017954161

ISBNs: 978-1-9753-5781-8 (paperback)
978-1-9753-5782-5 (ebook)

10 9 8 7 6 5 4 3 2 1

WOR

Printed in the United States of America